D1014178

The American History Series

SERIES EDITORS

John Hope Franklin, *Duke University*

A. S. Eisenstadt, *Brooklyn College*

Alan M. Kraut
AMERICAN UNIVERSITY

The Huddled Masses

The Immigrant in American Society, 1880–1921

SECOND EDITION

HARLAN DAVIDSON, INC.
WHEELING, ILLINOIS 60090-6000

Copyright © 1982, 2001
Harlan Davidson, Inc.
All Rights Reserved

Except as permitted under United States copyright law, no part of this
publication may be reproduced or distributed in any form or by any
means, or stored in a database or any retrieval system, without prior
written permission of the publisher. Address inquiries to Harlan
Davidson, Inc., 773 Glenn Avenue, Wheeling, Illinois 60090-6000.

Library of Congress Cataloging-in-Publication Data

Kraut, Alan M.
    The huddled masses, the immigrant in American society, 1880–
    1921 / Alan M. Kraut—2nd ed.
        p. cm. — (The American history series)
    Includes bibliographical references and index.
    ISBN 0-88295-934-4 (alk. paper)
    1. United States—Emigration and immigration—History.
    2. Immigrants—United States—History. 3. Americanization—
    History. I. Title. II. Title: American history series (Wheeling,
    Ill.)

    JV6450.K7 2001
    304.8'73'009034—dc21   00-047505

Cover photo: Immigrants on an Atlantic liner. *Library of Congress, LCUS262 11202.*

Manufactured in the United States of America
04   2 3 4 5 MG

In loving memory of my parents,
Jeanette and Harry Kraut

FOREWORD

Every generation writes its own history for the reason that it sees the past in the foreshortened perspective of its own experience. This has surely been true of the writing of American history. The practical aim of our historiography is to give us a more informed sense of where we are going by helping us understand the road we took in getting where we are. As the nature and dimensions of American life are changing, so too are the themes of our historical writing. Today's scholars are hard at work reconsidering every major aspect of the nation's past: its politics, diplomacy, economy, society, recreation, mores and values, as well as status, ethnic, race, sexual, and family relations. The lists of series titles that appear on the inside covers of this book will show at once that our historians are ever broadening the range of their studies.

The aim of this series is to offer our readers a survey of what today's historians are saying about the central themes and aspects of the American past. To do this, we have invited to write for the series only scholars who have made notable contributions to the respective fields in which they are working. Drawing on primary and secondary materials, each volume presents a factual and narrative account of its particular subject, one that affords readers a basis for perceiving its larger dimensions and importance. Conscious that readers respond to the closeness and immediacy of a subject, each of our authors seeks to restore the past as an actual present, to revive it as a living reality. The individuals and groups who figure in the pages of our books appear as real people who once were looking for survival and fulfillment. Aware that historical subjects are often matters of controversy, our authors present their own findings and conclusions. Each volume closes with an extensive critical essay on the writings of the major authorities on its particular theme.

The books in this series are primarily designed for use in both basic and advanced courses in American history, on the undergraduate and graduate levels. Such a series has a particular value these days, when the format of American history courses is being altered to accommodate a greater diversity of reading materials. The series offers a number of distinct advantages. It extends the dimensions of regular course work. It makes clear that the study of our past is, more than the student might otherwise understand, at once complex, profound, and absorbing. It presents that past as a subject of continuing interest and fresh investigation.

For these reasons the series strongly invites an interest that far exceeds the walls of academe. The work of experts in their respective fields, it puts at the disposal of all readers the rich findings of historical inquiry, an invitation to join, in major fields of research, those who are pondering anew the central themes and aspects of our past.

And, going beyond the confines of the classroom, it reminds the general reader no less than the university student that in each successive generation of the ever-changing American adventure, from its very start until our own day, men and women and children were facing their daily problems and attempting, as we are now, to live their lives and to make their way.

John Hope Franklin
A. S. Eisenstadt

CONTENTS

ACKNOWLEDGMENTS

The first edition of *The Huddled Masses* was published almost twenty years ago, and the list of scholars whose knowledge and expertise has recast my thinking about immigration and ethnic history has lengthened. Their considerable contributions to my understanding are reflected in the text of this new edition. Their names are mentioned in the bibliographical essay. However, not unlike a Broadway play in revival, the second edition of a publication is a production that often reflects changes in cast as well as interpretation. This book was originally signed to a contract by the late Harlan Davidson, a grand gentleman whose kindness and good humor were legendary. He became a dear friend. His son, Andrew, has capably taken over the leadership of the press that bears his father's name. In an era when publishing houses are the subsidiaries of large, impersonal corporations, I am grateful for the warm friendship and generosity that has characterized my association with Andrew and his family over the years. Series editors John Hope Franklin and Abraham Eisenstadt were patient with the young historian who wrote the first edition and have remained his loyal supporters and warm friends ever since. Many thanks to production editor Lucy Herz who skillfully and attentively shepherded the manuscript from submission to press.

I am deeply grateful to those scholars who took valuable time from their own busy schedules of research and writing to read and criticize the second edition. Two specialists in immigration and ethnicity, David Reimers, recently retired after a distinguished career at New York University, and David Gerber, who teaches at SUNY, Buffalo, deserve special thanks. My office mate and colleague, James W. Mooney, a superb teacher and knowledgeable American intellectual historian, also read the manuscript with the care and sensitivity that is his hallmark. Our conversations and comraderie enrich me daily. Dr. Suzanne Michael, a sociologist by training and humanist by inclination, teaches about immigration and directs the community interpreter project at Hunter College's Center for the Study of Family Policy. Her insight into the immigrant family and perceptive comments are consistently valuable and refreshing. Since the early 1980s, it has been my honor to serve as a member of the History Committee of the Statue of Liberty–Ellis Island Foundation. My fellow committee members, especially Rudolph J. Vecoli, Kathleen Neils Conzen, Roger Daniels, Victor Greene, Moses Rischin, Virginia Yans- McLaughlin, and Dwight Pitcaithely all contributed to my work through countless conversations before, after, and during meetings as we did our best to make certain that the interpretation of these crucial historic sites reflected state-of-the-art historical thinking. Advising on the Ellis Island monument and museum, bringing immigration history to a broader public outside the academy, has truly been one of the formative influences on my intellectual development as reflected in this volume. With so much expertise and good advice at my disposal, I justly bear the responsibility for whatever errors of content or style still intrude upon the text.

My students, especially my present and former graduate students, have assisted me considerably to rethink the content and sharpen the prose of *The Huddled Masses*. Dr. Sarah Larson has admonished me repeatedly not to neglect the experiences of immigrants in rural America. Even as she has carved out a fine career as a public historian, founding a community museum in Reston, Virginia, she has generously and with exceptional skill continued to edit my chapters (in inks of many colors, but never red), always challenging my ideas and arguments. Her co-editorship of the photographic essay proved to be just the first occasion of a warm

collaboration and friendship that I value greatly. Dr. Melissa
Kirkpatrick created the index for the first edition and took time
from her work as a church educator to help her friend and former
teacher yet again. Shelby Shapiro, a doctoral candidate at the University of Maryland, came across town to take my seminar at
American University two years ago. Lucky day for me. His interest and enthusiasm in immigration and ethnic history, his knowledge of Yiddish language sources, and his voracious reading habits
make him a splendid intellectual sparring partner and an attentive
reader who alerted me to errors of both omission and commission
in my draft manuscript.

Finally, there is the family. Some things have changed and others
have not. After twenty-seven years of marriage, Deborah Aviva
Kraut remains my life-long companion, staunchest supporter, and
dearest friend. She continues to goad me to the writing desk every
morning and never fails to be outraged at the results, usually tem-
pering her severe criticism with encouraging words and strongly
suggested alternative phrases. In the first edition's acknowledg-
ments, I mentioned that Deborah nourished us with Chinese take-
out while she was scalding my prose. For the second edition she
switched to Indian. Julia Rose Kraut was a perky infant, "perched
atop my desk," as I decribed her in the first edition's acknowledg-
ments. Now she is a pretty young lady of nineteen, a university
sophomore. In the intervening years she learned to challenge her
father's views on the past and just about everything else. She became a good writer with an enthusiasm for the Constitution, even
keeping a small copy of it in her handbag. Upon my inquiry, she
told me that she used it during class discussions to "settle arguments." This year Julia will declare her major. A wise father
knows when not to offer an opinion. One dear member of the
household is no longer with us as the second edition goes to press.
Our cat, Mooskala, sat curled up on a chair not far from my writing desk ever since he joined our family. Muses come in many
shapes and sizes. His furry presence and soft purr cheered me and
reminded me that I was not alone even as I engaged in what is necessarily a lonely endeavor.

Alan M. Kraut

INTRODUCTION

The land flourished because it was fed from so many sources—because it was nourished by so many cultures and traditions and peoples.

Lyndon Baines Johnson
October 3, 1965

On the chilly, foggy afternoon of October 28, 1886, the Statue of Liberty was unveiled by its sculptor, August Bartholdi. The 151-foot copper statue had been a gift from France to the United States in celebration of the American centennial in 1876. Now, a decade later, it was complete, mounted atop a 150-foot concrete pedestal on Bedloe's Island in New York Harbor. The ceremony was given over to speeches, most of them praising Franco-American relations and the principles of democracy. President Grover Cleveland and other speakers remarked on international goodwill and peace and the beneficial influence that American political ideals could have on nations throughout the world.

At the tip of Manhattan, within view of Bedloe's Island, crowds of foreigners scrambled off boats, anxious to partake of

American ideals and opportunities. That Liberty might be raising her giant torch in welcome to these immigrants did not occur to most of those addressing the crowd in 1886. Only Emma Lazarus had envisioned the statue as a beacon to those arriving from foreign shores. In a poem written in 1883, "The New Colossus," she imagined the monument issuing a dramatic invitation to the world's nations:

> Give me your tired, your poor,
> Your huddled masses yearning to breathe free,
> The wretched refuse of your teeming shore,
> Send these, the nameless, tempest-tost to me,
> I lift my lamp beside the golden door!

Lazarus's verse, written to help raise money for the statue's pedestal, received merely polite applause at the dedication ceremony. Not until many years later would the general public come to share her understanding of the statue's symbolic importance.

"Huddled masses" by the millions had already been landing in the United States since the 1840s. Prior to the Civil War, most arrivals were emigrating from northern and western Europe. Immigration ceased only temporarily during the war's turmoil and resumed in the prewar pattern soon after the South's surrender. However, by the early 1880s the main sources of migration gradually shifted to southern and eastern Europe; nations such as Italy, Greece, Russia, Lithuania, Latvia, and the smaller Balkan states sent large numbers of emigrants. By 1907, over 80 percent of the 1,285,000 immigrants reaching the United States were from these countries, as compared to only 13 percent in 1882. There was growth in the migration from Asia, as well. Approximately 125,000 Chinese arrived by the 1880s. Despite legal restrictions imposed after 1882, they were joined by another 55,562 arriving between 1890 and 1920. The Japanese did not confront restrictions on immigration until 1907. In the forty years between 1880 and 1920, 240,714 Japanese arrived. Meanwhile, within this hemisphere hundreds of thousands of French Canadians from the north and Mexicans from the south crossed America's borders, often without even formally registering their presence. Between 1880 and 1921, over 23,500,000 people from other lands took advantage of America's lenient immigration policies and came to the United States.

Emma Lazarus's vivid imagery of those newcomers as "huddled," "wretched," "tempest-tost," travelers awash on the shores of America is compelling, if exaggerated. It has stirred the souls of many authors and has inspired the titles of countless books, including this one. Readers are perennially moved by the image of the Statue of Liberty and Lazarus's verse because together they suggest that the story of immigration is somehow a particularly relevant symbol of the United States.

Yet ours is only one chapter in a much larger tale. Throughout human history, people have been on the move, propelled variously by unease or yearning or optimism or fear. However, if migration is a universal dimension of the human condition, the particulars of the migration experience are distinct to individual peoples. It is the job of the historian to listen to the voices of these individuals and to distill from them a common story.

Using diaries, ships' logs, port records, newspapers, health reports, and all the other clues that migrants leave in their wake, historians follow behind asking questions. Where did you come from? Why did you leave? How did you travel? What was your destination? How were you received there? In what ways were you changed by your journey? What happened to the place you left behind? In what ways did you change the new land you chose to call home?

Many societies have been peopled by migrants. Travelers from north central Asia wandering across the land bridge that is today the Bering Straits settled in many regions of the Americas, not just the part of North America that would eventually become the United States. Nor was this country the only nation that welcomed people moving across its borders in search of better lives. What, then, caused the United States to claim the unique title of "nation of nations" or a "nation of immigrants"? Historian Donna R. Gabaccia ("Is Everywhere Nowhere? Nomads, Nations and the Immigrant Paradigm of United States History," *Journal of American History,* 86, December 1999) has suggested that while recently, some countries, such as France and Argentina, quickly incorporated newcomers into the nation, making them "invisible as distinctive social or cultural groups," the United States, as well as Canada and Australia, rejected the notion of a "melting pot" in favor of a model in which "ethnic identity coexists peacefully with . . . civic nationalism." Of course, even these nations historically circumscribed their multiethnicity by race to ensure "peaceful coexistence" among caucasian groups. Until the second half of the twentieth century Canada and Australia imposed severe racial restrictions on nonwhite immigration, while the United States imposed restrictions on the entrance of Asian groups and had a history that included slavery and discrimination against African Americans well before the more general restrictive legislation of the 1920s.

This book explores one of the busiest eras in United States immigration history, 1880–1921. It is designed to sift out the many different experiences of individuals and groups migrating to the country in this period to discover the contours of the many nations within the nation. These experiences are then synthesized into the story of immigration in a particular era of American history when vast human migration transformed the nation culturally and economically.

This volume is a second edition, and there have been dramatic historiographical changes since I first borrowed Lazarus's words in the early 1980s. Then I numbered myself among the growing chorus of scholars taking issue with the moving, poetic image of immigrants headed for the United States so hauntingly portrayed in Oscar Handlin's *The Uprooted* (1951). While I reveled in the imagery, I hoped to substitute a more nuanced perspective for Handlin's faceless European peasantry, headed so hopefully to America's shores after being pushed by poverty or persecution from their homelands.

Once in America, so the story went, plucky immigrants ascended from rags to riches through perseverance and will, or were broken—harassed by American immigration officials, trapped within the poverty and squalor of urban industrial life, exploited in mines, factories, and sweatshops. According to this interpretation, America's unparalleled economic growth provided the newcomers with incredible opportunities, provided they submerged themselves in American society and abandoned the cultural legacies of their homelands.

When I published the first edition of this book in 1982, historians were beginning to take issue with this simplistic, monolithic concept of race and ethnicity. No longer did scholars treat all immigrants collectively as history's dissatisfied masses who hoped to escape their downtrodden conditions by flight. Nor did they insist that members of each racial or religious group all shared like motives for emigration. There were fewer casual references to "the Italians," "the Poles," or "the Jews" as if these subgroups were homogeneous in values, beliefs, and behavior. There was greater attention to the agency of individual immigrants in deciding where they would go and what they would do after they got there. This new focus on the individual shattered the previous interpretation of immigrants as passive souls, reactive and compliant before impersonal social forces, deserving of compassion and help.

Once historians began to listen to individual voices, they discovered the stories of people wise in the world's ways. Weak, beaten, men and women do not undertake transoceanic journeys to far-off lands unless they are herded aboard ships at gunpoint. Most immigrants knew that there was a price tag attached to every decision to migrate, even if the exact cost was for the moment indecipherable. And for many people, the price of emigration was too high compared with that of other options. For an east European Jew or Slavic peasant, emigrating to America was not the only means to a better life. One could learn new skills, move to a neighboring country or one in western Europe, change occupations, migrate to another region of one's own country, or pursue the struggle in place, hoping to earn enough to offer the next generation a better start in life's competition. The majority of the people in southern and eastern Europe—people who did *not* leave for America—are evidence that such an array of choices existed. Thus the story of the United States became, in part, a celebration of the

strength and ingenuity of those who grasped the chance to undertake the great and risky adventure of immigration.

During the past two decades, a rich scholarship undertaken by
historians, sociologists, economists, and cultural anthropologists
has altered the contours of American immigration historiography
and challenged scholars to rethink our perspectives. This second
edition of *Huddled Masses* echoes that fresh scholarship and my
own reflections upon it.

Today's scholarship is first and foremost characterized by a
transnational perspective. No longer do scholars think of immigrants as being drawn to a particular country as if they were under
the influence of a powerful magnet. The older model is viewed as
an artifact of an era in which history was narrowly bounded by the
experience of particular countries with little realization that the
human experience routinely spilled over national borders. This
"immigrant paradigm" has been replaced by a model that charac-
terizes immigration into countries and emigration from them as
part of the ebb and flow of population movement across the globe
being channeled and rechanneled by ever-shifting patterns of
world economics, war, famine, and disease. Eventually national
boundaries become irrelevant to the flow of commerce, information, and individuals. These global patterns challenge earlier con-
ceptions of national autonomy in which the unique needs of a particular nation's economy and the advantages (or disadvantages) of
its political and social systems were regarded by scholars as the
determinants of its immigration status, whether as a donor nation
from which migrants exited, or a host nation with newcomers at its
gates.

If scholars have challenged national autonomy in determining
migration patterns, they have also reconceptualized the agency of
those on the move. Instead of individuals deciding to depart and
choosing where to live after arrival in the United States, such decisions now appear to historians as the product of collective strategies. Families, ethnic groups, and classes develop strategies for
success. They move in chains and in subnational patterns, with
relatives and friends leaving a village in the Old World for a city or
town in the New World, directing others to follow. Often this chain

pattern included considerable redefinition of group identity after arrival. Sicilians and Neapolitans with distinctive historic pasts and cultural identities found themselves artificially aggregated and recast as "Italians" by their native-born hosts who had little appreciation for the significance of regional distinctions and identities. Moreover, historians' image of unfettered labor markets, free-wheeling marketplace competition, and equal opportunity encouraging immigrants to expend their best efforts, has been supplanted by the image of an economic sphere in which racial or religious discrimination and pre-existing differences of wealth and occupational skills give some newcomers advantages over others.

Identification of immigration's advocates and opponents in the United States has also undergone revision. Immigration was not always an arena of conflict between capitalists and their workers. Not infrequently, labor leaders hoping to keep up and drive higher the wage levels of union members, and capitalists opposed to the "mongrelization" of native American (caucasian) racial stock found themselves allied in opposing unrestricted immigration. At other times, recently arrived immigrant laborers hoping to bring relatives to the United States found ready pro-immigration allies in a business community starved for skilled, semiskilled, and low-wage unskilled workers capable of making quality products in workshops or factories, and then purchasing them as consumers in the American domestic marketplace.

Coming to America did not always mean remaining in America. The decision to emigrate, to cross oceans and continents, has long been regarded by scholars as a permanent choice selected from a menu of options. That scenario may be mythological. Recent studies suggest that after arrival in the United States, many migrants remained on the move. Options routinely exercised in a transnational pattern included repatriation, continuing the migration trail to another destination, or a dual residency such as the seasonal labor migration favored by southern Italians.

Shattering old mythologies requires the substitution of new wisdom for old. As immigration historian Virginia Yans-McLaughlin (*Immigration Reconsidered,* 1990) has observed, there is a fresh foundation upon which recent studies of immigration are constructed. That foundation is characterized, in part, by what she calls an "international ecology of migration; a questioning of the classical assimilation model, which proposes a linear progression of immigrant culture toward a dominant American national character; and, through references to other national experiences in Asia and Latin America, a denial of American exceptionalism."

Of course, in the efforts to link the structural requirements of local and regional economies with the larger patterns of movement included in the ecology of migration, it is possible to lose track of the individual migrant. Indeed, even families and ethnic groups may be rendered invisible by a welter of migration trends and labor statistics reflecting complex economic and social structures. However, as sociologist Ewa Morawska observes, individuals, families, and ethnic groups have a certain resilience that eludes the determinism of socioeconomic structures. They can adapt themselves to new conditions, or as she phrases it, they may "play within structures."

Not all individuals or groups "play" with equal success. Eastern European Jews were often the targets of persecution in their homelands and certainly felt the sting of discrimination in the United States after arrival. However, the fact that 66 percent of Jewish newcomers were skilled or semiskilled workers, often gave them an advantage in American capitalism's urban industrial labor markets. Recent scholarship has demonstrated that women immigrants had different patterns of social mobility from men and that the pattern of gender behavior, especially occupationally and within the family, differed from one ethnic group to another. Nor did male ethnic group members all enjoy equal success when "playing within structures." Irish and Italian laborers in the nineteenth century faced a capitalist system undergirded by middle-class values and perceptions they were required to share as the price of opportunity and respectability. Those who drank too much or failed to arrive at work on time found little understanding of their cultural customs or struggles to adjust to the American work ethic. The "cultural hegemony" of native-born Americans, as some scholars have termed it, set boundaries upon precisely how much "playing within structures" individual immigrants or ethnic groups were allowed in defining their values and behavior after arrival. Likewise, a domestic caste system grounded in race determined the segment of the American population and the social structures in which newcomers could expect to find their place. This pattern, dubbed *segmented assimilation,* profoundly affected people of color coming to the United States. From 1900 through the 1920s, many black arrivals from European colonial possessions in the West Indies settling in New York could find affordable housing only in Harlem. They were compelled to make their way in America as members of the African-American community, subject to the same patterns of discrimination and prejudice as American blacks. Their premigration education and class position did not matter at all to caucasian Americans, who perceived color first and prior social status a distant second, if at all.

While gender was becoming an increasingly popular lens though which to view the past in the early 1980s, many more scholars of migration and ethnicity are peering through it today. Studies of eastern European Jewish women and Italian women have been joined on library bookshelves by studies of Chinese, Japanese, and Latino women — their work experiences, their mobility patterns, and transformations in their family status during Americanization. More than merely the history of women migrants, a gendered history has allowed scholars to understand how male roles and female roles changed with respect to each other and across generational lines in the pressure cooker of American life.

While these changes and others have radically altered the way historians think about immigration, most Americans continue to see immigration as a romanticized struggle of Lazarus's "huddled masses" to find their place in America, the land of their dreams. Such a formulation makes all the more formidable the triumph of those who have succeeded. It is a version of history perpetuated by the victors and those who aspire to follow them. This anachronistic image of immigration as a one-way, irreversible process is problematic not only because of historical inaccuracy, but because public policy and popular thinking about immigration are all too often grounded in this misperception.

Beginning in the 1980s, the United States has hosted millions of newcomers, the majority of them from Southeast Asia, Mexico, Latin America, Africa, the Caribbean and, since the end of the Cold War, Russia and the other eastern European states. Similar to the arrivals at the turn of the last century, today's immigrants affect the lives of native-born Americans in some states more than others. New York, New Jersey, California, Texas, Illinois, and Florida have experienced dramatic population changes and the attendant social stresses triggered by high levels of immigration. Seventy-five percent of the newcomers are concentrated in these six states. However, the overall percentage of foreign-born in the American population has been growing, from 5 percent in 1970 to approximately 10 percent in 2000. While still less than the 14 percent of a century ago, the increasing percentage of newcomers and their visible impact upon American society and culture, as reported in newspapers and on television, has inspired panic in some quarters. Many Americans imbued with an outdated historical understanding of how earlier generations of immigrants behaved and affected American society fear immigration and are hostile to the newcomers. Proposed state referenda limiting health and educational benefits to newcomers, politicians' hysterical predictions that the newcomers will overrun the native-born and completely recast American culture, and sporadic acts of violence against immigrants all suggest that nativism, the fervent opposition to immigration, is alive and well among some Americans. Others continue to believe that newcomers benefit the economy and enrich the culture.

Bad history is the foundation of distorted assumptions that result in bad theory. Incorrect theoretical formulations and hypotheses can only lead to popular misconceptions and exaggerations of the challenges newcomers pose. Such flawed theory becomes the rationale for public policies that will serve neither the immigrant nor American society. At a moment in our nation's history when we are once again experiencing a peak in immigration, inaccuracies in our nation's immigration history is a price our country cannot afford. Nor can it afford to ignore that national patterns are an integral part of a broader global migration pattern.

This book is intended to shatter mythologies and correct misperceptions of the immigration to the United States that took place a century ago and continues to have implications for Americans today. *Huddled Masses* combines a general description of the migration from 1880 through the early 1920s with an analysis of the different aspects of newcomers' lives in America. Although the overwhelming number of migrants originated in southern or eastern Europe, no history of migration in this era would be complete without attention to the hundreds of thousands of Asians, especially Chinese and Japanese, who arrived, as well as Latinos, a group that includes Mexicans, Central Americans, and Caribbean migrants. Black migrants of African descent from the West Indies joined the flow as well. Such groups were as culturally different from one another as were southern and eastern European groups from the northern and western European voyagers of an earlier era. Patterns of prejudice were also equally varied. Asian immigrants were the first to be restricted by law. Those who settled on the Pacific Coast faced racial nativism greater than that suffered by their dusky European counterparts who entered the country through the bustling ports of the North Atlantic coast. Anti-Mexican prejudices were a fact of life throughout the Southwest, while black West Indians stirred the racism of native-born Caucasians and, at times, the class resentments of native-born African Americans.

Chapter One begins by placing the immigration to the United States between 1880 and 1921 into a broad perspective as just one phase of a larger westward migration taking place around the globe. Seen in this light, the migration to America represented a conscious choice made by individual immigrants in consultation with family members or neighbors. It was only one possibility among several practical alternatives, rather than the result of an almost mystical allure drawing immigrants through America's "golden door."

Chapter Two describes admission procedures at American immigration depots; for most, the first contact immigrants had with their new home. The immigrant is followed through a typical landing and inspection at Ellis Island, the nation's largest and busiest reception center. There, Americans' fears of disease from abroad and anxieties over admitting only those morally and physically fit converged, resulting in the most extensive set of federal bureaucratic procedures to examine immigrants ever enacted. The remainder of the chapter discusses how culture and economic opportunity set the boundaries of newcomers' crucial first decision: where to reside in this vast, unfamiliar country. Immigrant communities were not established by accident or fiat. Most immigrants chose to live in cities or large towns, but many opted for smaller towns in rural communities where relatives or friends were already in place or economic opportunity seemed greatest.

The decision of where to live was related to choice of occupation and attitude toward economic advancement in the burgeoning industrial capitalist economy of the United States. Chapter Three suggests that the various occupational choices were filtered through Old-World experiences and cultural values, the intention to settle permanently or return to their native land, uniquely individual talents and attitudes, and broad global market conditions. Different immigrant groups achieved material prosperity and social prestige at different rates, albeit over the same routes. These differences resulted from the divergent cultural priorities of particular groups. Not all immigrants shared with native-born Americans, or even other immigrants, a common definition of upward mobility and the good life. Nor were definitions of success necessarily the same for women as for men. Consequently, immigrant behavior in the marketplace was often misunderstood by those whose measure of success was gauged only by capital accumulation. Finally, this chapter explores how the presence of millions of immigrant laborers shaped America's growing economy even as individual newcomers tailored their work styles to suit society's labor requirements. Clearly, America was changed by the presence of newcomers even as the newcomers were changed by the opportunities and obstacles of American life.

Chapter Four treats in detail the pressure that every new arrival felt to Americanize and become incorporated into American society. Numerous economic and social incentives combined to exhort immigrants to abandon their culture and adopt the language and customs of their new home. Well aware of what was at stake, the members of each group tried to choose carefully which aspects of American life they would embrace and which they would resist. This chapter also discusses the role of public schools, political parties, and settlement houses as institutional vehicles for the transformation of aliens into proper Americans.

Chapter Five examines immigrant responses to nativism. Newcomers were confronted with both *ad hoc* and highly organized crusades directed against them by native-born Americans bewildered and threatened by the strange customs and sheer numbers of newcomers. This chapter traces the gradual spread of anti-immigrant sentiment, which culminated in national laws restricting immigration, latching shut the golden door.

Finally, a brief conclusion looks to the impact of the immigration experience on both the travelers themselves and the society they entered. What were the benefits to the society as well as the newcomer of introducing 23.5 million strangers into the United States? And how did the experience of the 1880–1921 period begin an era in which immigration policy became a matter of perennial national debate and transnational concern?

Insights derived from recent scholarship enrich this second edition of *Huddled Masses* and have prompted changes in emphasis and interpretation. However, at least two fundamental positions remain at the volume's foundation. Specifically, this volume seeks to understand the collective or group dimension of the immigrant experience while tenaciously insisting upon a certain self-determinism, or agency, for the individual immigrant. Second, *Huddled Masses* persists in emphasizing that culture and premigration experience (as much or more than capitalist market-conditions) shaped the choices that newcomers made about where and how to live in their new American home.

The "huddled masses" exist only until the morning mist blows clear to reveal individuals and families standing separately and resolutely. On closer examination, the faces of this "wretched refuse" take on a determined, rather pugnacious expression. The immigrant experience was neither romantic nor glamorous; many people starved, many retreated into taverns or insanity. But the great number of arrivals made a success of their lives, mapping out goals according to their own specifications, making those compromises with American society which they considered necessary. And in the end, the *contadini* of the *Mezzogiorno,* the Jews of the *shtetlakh,* the peasants of the Steppes, the *campesinos* of Mexico, and the French-Canadian farm workers of Quebec changed America even as they were changed by it.

CHAPTER ONE

Emigration:
A Matter of Change
and Choice

Migrants to the United States and to other countries in the nineteenth century were set in motion by pushes and pulls. Sometimes
the pushes were as simple as the desire to improve one's economic
lot in life. Ignazio Ottone from Cicarro Monferrato, Italy, worked
on his father's farm, earning only 10 to 15 cents per day. He explained, "That's why I left and come to this country. . . . Because I
don't like to work on the farm. It was too hard over there.
. . . I liked it but it was too much, too many hours for nothing."
Nicolas Gerros, from a small village in Macedonia, followed his
father to Cincinnati, Ohio, after Nicholas's mother died when he
was only nine years old. He recalled the transnational labor migration in which his father participated, "The way life in the village
was the men always had to go out of their homes into other lands
to make a living, come back, stay with the family a length of time
till the money was gone. They used to have little farms around that
didn't produce enough to live on, so naturally they had to go to
other countries." After her father died, Sadie Frowne came with
her mother from Poland to America because "we heard it was

much easier to make money. Mother wrote to Aunt Fanny, who lived in New York and told her how hard it was to live in Poland. ... She [Aunt Fanny] said we should both come at once, and she went around among our relatives in New York and took up a subscription for our passage."

Economics was hardly the only push. Racial and religious minorities fled to other countries. David Toback wrote, "I was born in 1875. . . . Don't think it is an easy thing to be born a Jew. Under Czar Nicholas there had been a reign of terror. Edict after edict was issued against us. We were not supposed to do this, or travel here, or do business in that—the faster we thought of ways to keep a crust of bread in our mouths, the czar and his court thought of some way of snatching it away. We, the Jews were the chosen and the despised people." For Mexicans, the unrest occasioned by the Revolution of 1910 pushed over 700,000 peasants across the border to the north. In his autobiography, *Barrio Boy,* Ernesto Galarza recalled how his family felt, caught in the crossfire between the federal troops allied with Porfirio Díaz and the rebels led by Francisco Madero. Some headed to Tucson, others to Sacramento. "The farmhands of the haciendas were running away and gathering in bands in the mountains. . . .Young men were leaving the *milpas* [cornfields] to join the guerillas, which they called *'bolas.'* A bola could start in any pueblo and take off for the hills, to join other bolas and form a command under a *jefe revolucionario* [revolutionary leader]."

The pulls were equally well documented in the personal testimony of migrants. Economic pulls often consisted of job availability and high wages. Italians in Barre, Vermont, found jobs as stone cutters in the quarries. Joseph Cerasoli recalls "I was fifteen years old in April and I went to work for Joe Martell grindin' tools. This was August. Come Christmas my boss, Frenchman, Martell, said to me, 'My boy, how'd ya like to cut stone[?]' . . . my father said, 'What else you gonna do 'round here?' . . . I cut stone till 1960." One eastern European Jew who settled in Pittsburgh told an interviewer, "A neighbor came back [from America] with 600 Russian rubles. I had a great desire to go." The political climate in the United States was unquestionably a pull for those who had experienced tyranny. Another Pittsburgher who once lived in Russia recalled that he had heard, "America was heaven for Jews. A free country where a Jew could even become president."

These individual decisions to emigrate were made by men and women calculating their opportunities at home and abroad. A single individual or family's choice to go or stay was conditioned by larger social and economic forces, some local, and others global in scope and magnitude. Collectively these decisions not only affected the fate of those who migrated and those who stayed behind, but often they shaped the fate of nations for decades to come.

Patterns of migration to the United States in the late nineteenth century cannot be divorced from larger global schemes, nor did they immediately break with earlier flows. Immigrants continued to arrive from Ireland, Germany, and Scandinavia in the last two decades of the nineteenth century, but increasing numbers now arrived from southern and eastern Europe and parts of Asia. This shift in the pattern of immigration to the United States between 1880 and 1921 was but one event in a much larger process. During this period, millions of individuals in various regions of the globe decided to leave their homes, some permanently, many others only temporarily.

While migration has always been part of human history, at no other time did people go so far, so quickly, and so cheaply. The telegraph, the railroad, and the steamship allowed emigrants to learn of conditions abroad, travel less expensively, arrive more quickly and safely than previously, and, if they chose, go home again. Between 1887 and 1888 alone, it is estimated that a million people left the continent of Europe for destinations in the United States, Canada, Australia, New Zealand, Argentina, Uruguay, and Brazil. Countless others remained in Europe but migrated from their towns or villages to larger towns and cities, frequently to those in western Europe. In their wake, these restless people shattered not only their own economic and social patterns, but those of communities they left and joined.

The mighty wave of immigration was breaking upon many beaches. Moreover, neither the United States nor the other nations receiving immigrants at this time were disinterested observers of the moving millions. Economic competition born of industrial capitalism stimulated a spirited race among industrializing nations to lure vast quantities of cheap, unskilled labor within their borders.

I

It is platitudinous to characterize a particular historical era as "a time of change." Every period in human history includes transformation—great or small. The economic and social alterations of nineteenth-century Europe were not unprecedented intrusions into stagnant societal waters. What created a crisis of vast proportions were the changes in how people lived. The family, the church, the social hierarchy, the political establishment—the cement of community in traditional European societies—proved unable to absorb the shock waves of change. A rapidly increasing population, the decline of an aging agrarian system, and the emergence of the industrial revolution fractured traditional political, economic, and social relationships. And when people lost confidence that long-respected political institutions and social customs could stabilize their lives, they sought to cope with their anxieties not collectively, but as individuals or as families, making decisions they perceived to be in their own best interests.

Migration had always been an option for populations plagued by the ravages of starvation, disease, or conquest. Whatever the circumstances of particular individuals or families that encouraged migration, the local conditions in particular countries or regions influenced choices, often pushing migrants abroad. What were the push factors for some of the world's populations that put people in motion in the late nineteenth and early twentieth centuries?

One push factor was population growth in migrants' home countries. Southern Italians found a sharp upsurge in population especially unsettling. As early as the 1870s, the natural increase per year was slightly over six per thousand, as compared with three per thousand several decades earlier. By the 1880s, the figure had risen to 11 per thousand. Meanwhile, Italian mortality figures fell from 30 persons per thousand annually to under 20 per thousand in the years from 1870 to 1910. Only halfway through the forty-year period did birthrates show a marked decline. Despite the major Italian emigration that proceeded throughout the period, the total population of the country actually rose by more than 6 million between 1880 and 1910. In 1895 alone, births exceeded deaths by some 350,000. Similar figures available for Poland and other parts of eastern Europe, while not quite as dramatic, confirm an increase in population for the continent.

The greater the number of people, the greater the competition for the resources of life, especially economic resources. Agriculture was the foundation of the economy in southern and eastern Europe. While rural populations of countries in the west were decreasing in size by 1850, the rural population of eastern Europe did not level off until well into the twentieth century. As the general population increased, the size of family farms decreased.

Landlords took advantage of inheritance laws to displace newly emancipated peasants and divide estates into small plots of land for rental at high prices. In Bulgaria, fewer than 4 percent of all holdings exceeded 50 acres, while over 100,000 farms appear to have been less than $2^1/_2$ acres in size. Often plots composing a farmer's holdings were scattered geographically. In Galicia, in 1900, only about 1,500 holdings exceeded 50 acres, 500,000 were $7^1/_2$ to 50 acres, while 600,000 were between $2^1/_2$ to $7^1/_2$ acres. More than 200,000 holdings were even smaller.

Some European peasants manufactured small articles in their homes during the long winters. The products of such cottage industries were marketed locally and regionally. In Poland and the Slovak countries, women kept looms and flax in their homes to make hats, linens, lace, and rugs, while their husbands and sons carved objects from wood to be sold at market. Individuals owning a mule often performed local services, hauling wood or stones for neighbors or engaging in long-distance transport of goods over the plains of Galicia or the western provinces of Russia, as had their fathers and grandfathers before them.

Industrial capitalism disrupted the traditional economic structure of southern and eastern European nations, transforming habits of work and altering avenues of commerce. Mechanization in agricultural areas, such as the wheat fields of Hungary, reduced the need for migrant labor. The railroads, which had once provided construction work for laborers throughout the eastern half of the continent, were now completed, making obsolete the services of those whose hands had built it. No longer would goods be hauled overland by mule, nor would there be as many ships involved in the coastal trade. Railroads were faster and cheaper but, inevitably, provided fewer jobs for those at the bottom of the socioeconomic scale. Railroads linked areas of manufacturing, bringing goods to even remote regions more cheaply than those same items could be produced by cottage industries.

As economic opportunities shriveled in rural provinces, they increased in cities. Urbanization, the helpmate of industrialization, upset traditional lifestyles that had remained unchanged for centuries. Farmers, artisans, and unskilled laborers in rural communities experienced economic uncertainty and many migrated to cities to work in the factories, machine shops, mills, and distilleries. Austria's urban population trebled between 1843 and 1900. From 1850 to 1900, Vienna's population sprang from 431,000 to almost 2,000,000. Warsaw quadrupled in population during the same half century. While the populations of eastern European countries remained essentially rural, the trend was clear, and migration quickened. Large towns burgeoned; large cities grew into metropolises.

Entrenched governments of countries in southern and eastern Europe brought little relief to their people and pushed many to emigrate. These nations had long been characterized by wide discrepancies between the very rich and the very poor. Wealthy landowners and merchants exercised control over the state and saw little reason to initiate any social or economic reforms. Industrialization frequently shifted power from landowners to a new middle class, but social change was limited. Labor strikes, such as those in Italy and Hungary in the 1890s, precipitated only minor reforms, and the Romanian peasant revolt of 1907 failed to accomplish any major improvement. The autocratic governments of southern and eastern Europe, aware that economic and technological influences beyond their control were transfiguring their countries, sought to resist, for as long as possible, any adjustments that would shift the balance of power. Taxes were kept high, and bulging urban areas made it easier than ever to impose compulsory military service. Young male urban dwellers could not elude conscription as could those in forested areas or remote villages. The political climate became increasingly repressive.

For millions of politically hamstrung southern and eastern Europeans, then, emigration appeared to be a path to relief from the pressures of overpopulation, agricultural change, and industrialization.

Modernization cast its confusing mantle over all regions, lending a thread of similarity to the stories of widely diverse ethnic groups. Case studies of the two largest groups to arrive in the United States during the late nineteenth and early twentieth centuries, southern Italians and east European Jews, can illuminate the specific pressures that caused substantial numbers of these groups to emigrate. Separate geographically, and disparate culturally, these groups are, nevertheless, worthy of comparison because both were threatened by overwhelming transformations in lifestyle. Those who chose emigration generally preferred the risks that leaving entailed to the uncertainties in store for those remaining behind.

All of the provinces of the newly unified Italian nation were affected in some way by the country's expanding population, changing agrarian order, and increasing industrial production during the last two decades of the nineteenth century and the first two of the twentieth. However, the drastic effect of this upheaval on the country's southern provinces coupled with a long history of poverty in that part of Italy made many southern Italian townsmen, or contadini, especially willing to risk a long journey and separation from their beloved *paese* ("village") if only temporarily.

Those who have studied the Italian-American experience, such as historians Virginia Yans-McLaughlin (*Family and Community, Italian Immigrants in Buffalo, 1880–1930,* 1977), Gary R. Mormino (*Immigrants on the Hill: Italian Americans in St. Louis, 1882–1982,* 1986), and sociologist Richard Gambino (*Blood of My Blood,* 1974), have emphasized the reputation of Il Mezzogiorno, the southern provinces of Italy, as a "land that time forgot." Governments came and went, but the Mezzogiorno remained the same. For the contadini, *la famiglia* ("the family") and *l'ordine della famiglia* ("the rules of family behavior and responsibility"), not the government, determined how one lived. The contadini had long and bitter experience with government officials as well as the large landholders, whom the corrupt officials protected. Exploitation left contadini with cynical attitudes toward all forms of authority other than the family. The cynicism summed up by the adage *la legge va contrai cristiani* (the law works against people) was not dispelled by the unification. The lot of the contadini deteriorated; reform never filtered south.

The northern Italians who controlled the post-unification government were largely unconcerned about the south. Those who thought of the region at all considered it populated by lazy, impoverished, irresponsible, crude, and often violent primitives, rather than by shrewd, hard-working, independence-loving, family-oriented contadini. The results of this attitude were legal and economic impositions that strangled the Mezzogiorno. The tax burden on the south was increased considerably, and the region was trapped in a maze of increasing debt. In Sicily alone, the tax rate increased 30 percent over that imposed by Bourbon monarchs before unification. The large landowners, the *latifondisti,* quickly established an understanding with the government, maintaining their status quo and successfully evading the new tax burdens. While cows and horses, most often the property of the wealthier latifondisti, were exempted from taxation, mules and donkeys, the mainstays of the contadini, were taxed heavily. Likewise most of the church land the new government confiscated was transferred to the latifondisti; almost none of it went to the contadini.

In Italy, the majority of those who worked the land were tenants rather than its actual owners. Some southern Italians were sharecroppers, with the landlord providing the capital and renewing the tenancy from generation to generation, thus perpetuating an almost peasant-like attachment to the land among tenants. Other tenants had to provide their own working capital and renew their tenancy at frequent periods. There were also combinations of different arrangements. Some peasant farmers owned part of the land they cultivated, but rented other plots. Landlords, too, played varied agricultural roles. The same landowner could be an active manager on one of his estates and an absentee landlord, dependent on a hired manager, on another. There were also large estates resembling antebellum plantations in the American South. These were cultivated by large gangs of poorly paid laborers, people who hoped one day to own even the smallest plot of land.

Heavy tax burdens imposed upon contadini who owned small plots of land forced them to secure mortgages, often from the agents of larger absentee landowners, at exorbitant rates ranging from 400 to 1000 percent. Inexorably, larger landlords captured land through defaults; a report to the Italian Parliament in 1910 stated that several hundred latifondisti owned or controlled over 50 percent of the land in the Mezzogiorno. According to Leonard Covello (*The Social Background of the Italian-American School Child,* 1944), in Calabria there were 121 landowners per thousand inhabitants in 1882, but only 91 per thousand by 1901. In Sicily, the reduction was from 114 to 94 per thousand, between 1882 and 1901.

Not all southern Italians farmed. Some were artisans who worked in factories manufacturing textiles such as silk. To protect northern industry, high tariffs were passed by the central government. These crippled the unprotected industries of the Mezzogiorno, where unemployment rose markedly. The agony of the Mezzogiorno was intensified in the last third of the nineteenth century by a series of natural disasters. The vineyards, the nucleus of the southern Italian economy, were devastated by a grape blight, phylloxera, that had originated in southern France. The disease, coupled with heavy French tariffs on Italian wines and competition in the world market from American citrus products from Florida and California, crushed the economies of certain provinces. Calabria, Apulia, and Sicily, known for their wines, were hardest hit. The competition of oranges and lemons from the United States also stifled the citrus industry in Basilicata, Calabria, and Sicily.

In 1905, a series of earthquakes jarred Basilicata and Calabria. In 1906, another natural disaster occurred when Vesuvius erupted, burying a whole town near Naples in the province of Campania. Another volcano, Etna, erupted in 1910. However, the worst disaster, by far, was the earthquake and tidal wave that struck the Strait of Messina between Sicily and the Italian mainland in 1908. The city of Messina was leveled and over 100,000 of its inhabitants killed. Over 300 smaller towns were destroyed in this disaster. In the city of Reggio di Calabria alone, another 20,000 people died. Natural disasters such as these were rarely the root causes of emigration, but they often acted as catalysts.

The Jews of eastern Europe had historically been an oppressed minority. The people of the diaspora first began to migrate eastward in the thirteenth century when Boleslav the Pious, King of Poland, opened his kingdom to settlement by European Jews. The monarch hoped the Jews would function as money lenders, tax collectors, merchants, innkeepers, and artisans, fostering prosperity in his backward agrarian nation. Because of their crucial role in Poland's economy, Jews were protected by law and a growing number of western European Jews settled there.

Despite periodic episodes of persecution such as the Chmielnicki massacres between 1648 and 1655, Jewish civilization survived and at times even prospered in Poland until the nation was conquered and divided in the eighteenth century. The majority of Poland's Jews fell under Russian rule, while the rest lived in areas controlled by Austria and Prussia. The tsarist government viewed the Jews through a prism of superstitious apprehension, despising them with medieval fervor as Jesus's betrayers and fearing the enlightened minds and affluence of the Jewish middle class. To undermine Jewish influence, the government sought to divert Jews from commerce into agriculture and confined most of them to the Pale of Settlement. The Pale was an area of about 386,000 square miles from the Baltic Sea to the Black Sea. It included Congress Poland (the nation that had been created at the Congress of Vienna, lasting as an independent entity for only fifteen years; most of it became part of Russia), Lithuania, Byelorussia, and the Ukraine (excluding Kiev). A few Jewish merchants managed to survive and even prosper in Russia's larger cities, but most Jews found themselves in the Pale, attempting either to farm the desolate steppes or scratch out a living as artisans and craftsmen in small towns.

Life in the Pale fluctuated between periods of repression and toleration. The reign of Tsar Nicholas I, 1825–1855, proved to be a time of Jewish suffering. In addition to the periodic expulsions of Jews from villages, the monarchy deliberately upset the cultural and religious life of the Jewish community. Books printed in Yiddish and Hebrew were heavily censored, and the curriculum of Jewish schools was "adjusted" by government officials. Worst of all, perhaps, were the conscription laws that commandeered boys—especially those of the poorer classes—between the ages of twelve and eighteen for stints of military service of up to twenty-five years. Because of the economic restrictions against them, Jews were especially vulnerable to conscription. Jewish parents, too poor to bribe officials, often either hid their sons or assisted them to flee the region.

Nicholas's successor, Tsar Alexander II, was politically moderate, and under his rule the Jews fared much better. By 1874, compulsory military service was reduced to six years. A small number of Jews were permitted to enter the universities, and Jewish businessmen were allowed to travel to parts of Russia from which they had been excluded. Even so, most Jews continued to live in rural poverty.

Many of the traditional roles played by Jews in the Russian economy were altered when Tsar Alexander II freed the serfs in 1863. Prior to that event, Jews had worked as middlemen, selling the produce raised on feudal estates by the peasants or functioning as nobles' agents in distant cities. With emancipation, the nobles took more direct control of their affairs and eliminated the expense of middlemen. Jewish merchants in small towns and cities became economically expendable. Only a few fortunate merchants rose to economic prominence in Moscow, St. Petersburg, or Kiev.

By the 1880s Russian tyranny hardened. Laws were passed prohibiting Jews from owning or renting land outside towns or cities and discouraging them from living in villages. Jewish students, subjected to harsh quota systems, were frequently excluded from secondary schools and universities. Jewish merchants who had remained in the cities were now expelled without warning. By 1897, over 4¹/₂ million Jews lived in the Pale, 94 percent of Russia's total Jewish population.

Most Jews in the Pale lived marginal existences in villages or shtetlakh. One observer described a *shtetl* as a small town with cobbled streets and "a jumble of wooden houses clustered higgledy-piggledy about a market place . . . as crowded as a slum. . . ." (Maurice Samuel, *The World of Sholom Aleichem,* 1943). The streets were winding, turning into alleys and lanes, and reemerging, all in no particular pattern or design. The center of the town was always a marketplace, "with its shops, booths, tables, stands, butcher's blocks." Every day, except during the winter, peasants from the surrounding area brought their livestock, produce, fish, hides, and grains to market. In exchange, they purchased from Jewish merchants a selection of hats, shoes, dry goods, boots, lamps, oil, and other manufactured products. Jews bought and sold, and bargained with customers, conducting business only yards from their homes. Legal restrictions placed on their residences and occupations by the Russians hobbled the Jewish community economically. According to renowned Jewish historian Salo Baron,

In many communities, fully 50 percent of the Jewish population depended on charity. . . . In Russia, as in other countries going through the early stages of modern capitalism, the rich grew richer, while the poor became more and more indigent. . . . It has been estimated that in many communities up to 40 percent of the entire Jewish population consisted of families of so-called luftmenschen, that is, persons without any particular skills, capital, or specific occupations.

Skilled or not, Jews suffocated under a blanket of Russian restrictions. It is little wonder, then, that even before the political turmoil and pogroms at the end of the nineteenth century, some of the poorest Jews had begun to migrate westward. Many traveled only as far as Germany or England before their funds ran out. Of this group, some found jobs and settled in western Europe, while others stayed there only long enough to earn the fare for the next leg of the journey to America.

Unable to own land and displaced from their homes and villages as a matter of government policy, the Jews, unlike the southern Italians, had little affiliation to the land on which they lived or to the larger community that oppressed them. The Jews' heritage was based on a history and religion that defined and codified appropriate behavior. Their religion and its traditions shaped the pattern of the east European Jews' existence and sustained them. As Irving Howe (*The World of Our Fathers,* 1976), described it, "The world of the east European Jews was a world in which God was a living force, a Presence more than a name or a desire. . . ." Jews had an intimate relationship with their God, praying to Him in Hebrew but speaking to Him in Yiddish, the mixture of Middle High German, Hebrew, and Russian that was the colloquial language of the Pale. To survive culturally, as well as physically, Jews disciplined their life with religious ritual. There were ritual commandments to cover almost every aspect of life, from the marriage ceremony to how shoes should be put on each day. Life in the shtetl was strengthened by religious observance, but it was a narrow, rigid life.

In the early nineteenth century, these demanding religious ideas were challenged by liberal thought from the countries of western Europe. Just as the Enlightenment ideas of Voltaire, modified by two centuries and filtered through western Europe, were affecting the thoughts of Russian intellectuals, this *Haskala* or Jewish Enlightenment captured the hearts and minds of many Russian Jews, especially the young. Fresh ideas—individualism, liberty, socialism, Zionism—and a craving for social and economic change challenged the credibility of the rabbinate and fragmented Jewish communities.

The assassination of the relatively liberal Tsar Alexander II in 1881 by a group of nihilists living in the home of a Jewish woman had severe repercussions for the Jews. The subsequent harsher program of Tsar Alexander III, and the brush fire of violence that swept through Jewish communities in the aftermath of the assassination caused many Jews to flee. Some left Russia entirely, journeying to western Europe and the United States. Others began the move to large cities within the Pale in their struggle for survival.

Those individuals and families who moved once were the most likely to move again.

Younger Jews often moved from the shtetls to the slums of Minsk, Vilna, Warsaw, and Bialystok in search of work. They were at the mercy of employers and often worked fourteen to sixteen hours a day for wages as low as two or three rubles per week. They organized to improve conditions and, in the last two decades of the nineteenth century, a socialist labor party, the Jewish Labor Bund, led strikes that improved conditions, if only temporarily.

The economic turmoil was compounded by new violence. The escalation of the pogroms, especially the bloody Kishinev massacre of 1903 in which forty-nine people were killed and more than 500 injured, persuaded many remaining Jews to finally leave Russia. Those already gone now sent for wives, children, and parents.

There were thus two phases to Jewish emigration from Russia. Between 1880 and 1900, Jewish immigrants tended to be those displaced merchants and impoverished artisans of the Pale pushed by their search for economic opportunity. After the turn of the century, however, the increasing intensity of pogroms and other forms of religious persecution encouraged rabbis, secular intellectuals, the wealthy, and middle-class businessmen to depart as well. Young Jewish socialists disheartened by an abortive revolution in 1905 also packed up their dreams and headed westward. As historian Gerald Sorin explains, the east European Jewish immigration swelled only as other options were exhausted (*A Time for Building, The Third Migration, 1880–1920*, 1992).

Neither the southern Italians nor the east European Jews were strangers to hard times. In earlier periods people had coped with crises by turning to the values and institutional structures of their group. Southern Italians found in their families sanctuary from the oppression of landowners and government officials. East European Jews drew sustenance from ancient traditions to ward off the indignities of discrimination and the pain of persecution. Few members of either group ever migrated far from family and community, though individuals occasionally left the country for the town to find work. However, the unprecedented pressures of modernization in the late nineteenth century combined with advances in transportation and communication to make long distance migration a viable option. Individuals could emigrate across borders on railroads and across oceans on steamships at a cost affordable to nearly all. News of conditions abroad could be more accurately and quickly transmitted. More information and faster, cheaper modes of travel turned emigration into an escape hatch for large numbers of people, rather than only the isolated, adventurous individual.

The experiences of the southern Italians and Russian Jews exemplify those of other groups that felt pushed to choose a solution to their discomfort and selected migration. For all immigrants to the United States, emigration from their homelands was only one of many options and usually not the first considered. Most people preferred to remain in their native countries and familiar communities as long as possible: those barred from certain occupations learned others; those removed from the land moved to the cities; others moved to different regions in their country or crossed the border into an adjoining country. In short, most resigned themselves to staying put, expecting to earn enough money to survive and hoping that circumstances might change so that their children might one day enjoy the prosperity that had eluded them. But those who refused to wait deliberately chose emigration. Even among the emigrants, however, there were those who regarded their departures as temporary. Home governments reconciled themselves to migratory patterns beyond their control. A Hungarian law in 1881 provided that emigrants would be permitted to leave the country only on authorized shipping lines. For nearly a quarter of a century, no such line was so authorized. However, when this and other measures failed to stop the exodus, the Hungarian government consoled itself with the license fees collected from transportation companies permitted to carry emigrants abroad by the Ministry of the Interior. Similar legal impediments to emigration were imposed by other countries but also foundered and were removed.

II

Even if particular groups felt pushed to emigrate, not all members of the group were equally likely to make the journey. Who actually migrated abroad in the years between 1880 and 1921? And what pulled them to one country rather than another? Until the turn of the century, most migrants were young males in their teens or early twenties who had left behind their parents or young wives and children to pursue opportunity abroad. The Irish from the southern provinces were an exception. Prior to the 1846 famine, migration from Ireland had been a primarily male undertaking. But during the "great hunger" whole families departed the Emerald Isle. From 1880 to 1910, there was a greater proportion of females to males. Women comprised 53.8 percent of all Irish immigrants to the U.S. in 1900, as compared to 35 percent in the 1830s. Historian Hasia Diner has demonstrated that many young Irish women shunned early marriage and emigrated. Initially they found opportunities as cooks and domestics. Those who acquired education could aspire to posts as teachers, nurses, or librarians (*Erin's Daughters in America,* 1983). However, the Irish model was the exception. Immigration officials estimated that 78 percent of the Italian and 95 percent of the Greek immigrants to the U.S. were men. Asian emigrants in the period also tended to be young males. However, after 1900, the character of migration changed among some groups. By 1920, 48 percent of southern Italian arrivals in the U.S. were female. Among Poles, the proportion of men to women was almost evenly divided. And among Slovaks, female immigrants outnumbered males 65 percent to 35 percent. In other groups, however, the newcomers to the United States continued to be mostly male. Almost 80 percent of the Greek arrivals were men and boys in 1920.

The percentage of female migrants among some groups was often increased by the "picture brides" ordered by lonely male workers from their homelands. Selected by their photographs, young women desperate to escape poverty and parental authority sought new lives by marrying men they had never met. The 1907 Gentlemen's Agreement that imposed immigration restrictions on the Japanese made picture bride marriages quite popular. Japanese men fearful of not being readmitted to the United States if they went home to find a mate were married by proxy to their picture brides in Japan. These young wives were then sent to join their new husbands in America. Some Caucasian Californians regarded the custom as a plot to flood the state with additional Japanese immigrants, but it saved many Japanese men from lives of loneliness.

Many young migrants seeking opportunity abroad did not regard their emigration as permanent. Indeed, they traveled back and forth across the ocean routinely. American immigration officers often referred to seasonal labor migrants as "birds of passage" because they followed a regular pattern of migration to and from the United States, following the ebb and flow of labor markets. Others, disenchanted with the United States, returned home permanently. How many migrants to the United States remigrated? Data are sketchy. However, between 1908 and 1923, the United States government tried to count both immigrants and emigrants. The federal data indicate that during this fifteen-year period, 9,949,740 migrants entered the United States and 3,498,185 departed, meaning 35 percent of the newcomers returned home. Eighty-eight percent of the returnees were Europeans. (This data cannot account for the Europeans who entered the United States via Canada or Mexico.) And the rate of return varied from group to group. According to historian Mark Wyman, 46 percent of Greek emigrants returned between 1908 and 1923, while 34 percent of Italians did so in the 1901–1906 period, and 38 percent in the period 1907–1914, with an overall rate of 50 percent between the 1880s and the 1920s. Jewish return rates are especially difficult to calculate because they are spread over several nationalities, but Wyman estimates the rate at between 15 percent and 20 percent. This relatively low rate of return makes sense during periods of tsarist pogroms and revolutionary upheaval, with few Jews sufficiently homesick to risk the dangers of a return home (*Roundtrip to America,* 1993).

Italian, Greek, and Slavic men in particular ventured forth in the spring and remained abroad until late fall, returning home for the winter months. Seasonal patterns of migration were especially common for outdoor laborers in agriculture, mining, or construction and were affected as well by the availability of jobs. Those who could not find work or had been unable to save sufficient earnings to return paid the penalty, remaining in the United States during the bleak winter months. Canadian workers took advantage of the open border to migrate back and forth at will. In the Southwest, Mexican laborers with visas, and often those without, arrived for planting and harvesting seasons, returning to Mexico when jobs were scarce.

Annual variations in migration patterns were the products of capitalism's cycles, changing conditions in home countries, and domestic American policies. An Immigration Commission report on migration patterns for 1907–1908 explained: "The fiscal year 1906–07 being one of unusual industrial activity, was marked by the largest immigration in the history of the country, but following the beginning of the industrial depression in October of the fiscal year 1907–08 there was a sudden reversal of tide, and during the remainder of that year there was a greater exodus. . . ." As World War I loomed over Europe, record numbers of people seeking to avoid hostilities fled to America, bringing 2,400,000 newcomers in 1913–1914. Others, fearing separation from family by wartime restrictions, streamed home, the volume of repatriation rising from approximately 200,000 in 1910 to 300,000 the following year and remaining high for the next three years. After the war, labor strikes and economic depression in the United States, and a general distrust of foreigners and supposed radicals combined to enlarge the number of returnees to 660,000 between 1919 and 1921.

But many planning to return home at war's end never did so. Constantine Panunzio (*The Soul of an Immigrant,* 1921), an Italian newcomer, described in his recollections how too little money and a series of small, personal crises delayed his return to Italy by twelve years. By that time he had become a naturalized American and no longer wished to return to the old country for more than a visit.

Members of ethnic minorities, especially, did not feel as bound to the lands of their birth as Panunzio, and had little incentive to return to them. Newly arrived Germans from Slavic countries, Greeks from Romania, Croats and Serbs from Hungary, Turks from Bulgaria, and the French from Canada, among others, had often felt the sting of discrimination and sometimes had been the target of official and unofficial acts of repression in "homelands" they no longer missed. East European Jews felt little nostalgia for the Old World after having survived the wave of early twentieth-century persecution. In 1908, the peak year of Jewish immigration to the United States, only 2 percent of immigrants returned to Europe. Those making the journey to America usually brought their families, suggesting that most came to settle rather than to earn money quickly and return. Jews, often fleeing religious persecution as well as pursuing economic advantages, hoped to find in the United States a haven from oppression. They displayed little hesitation about leaving Europe and seeking a permanent residence elsewhere.

Whatever their pattern of migration or their plans for the future, most immigrants arriving in the United States were leaving from southern and eastern Europe, not northern and western Europe as in earlier years. The chart on pages 34–35 demonstrates the shift in migration from northern Europe to Austria-Hungary, the Russian Empire, Italy, and the smaller countries of Romania, Turkey, and Greece. By 1896, migrants from these new donor nations accounted for almost 80 percent of all new arrivals.

Approximately 4,500,000 Italians entered the United States between 1880 and 1921. Over 80 percent of them came from Il Mezzogiorno. The total migration from Italy changed course and intensity several times during this period. Until the late 1880s, most of Italy's annual migrants, approximately 100,000, left for the western European countries to the north. As more Italians chose to emigrate—300,000 after 1895 and 500,000 in most years after 1900—more chose to go farther than Europe, and crossed the Atlantic. Before the turn of the century, the most popular destination was Latin America, especially Brazil. In 1897, 104,510 Italians emigrated to Brazil, while only 59,431 came to the United States. However, just a year later the trend began to reverse, and two years later, in 1900, fewer than 20,000 Italians landed in Brazil, while over 100,000 disembarked in the United States. Argentina also surpassed Brazil and moved into second place in the competition for cheap Italian labor. Though some Italians still would not migrate beyond western Europe, an ever-increasing number chose a country in the Americas. Economic opportunities

Decennial Immigration to the United States, 1880–1919

	1880–89	Percentage	1890–99	Percentage	1900–1909	Percentage	1910–1919	Percentage
TOTAL	5,248,568		3,694,294		8,202,388		6,347,380	
Northwestern Europe								
United Kingdom[1]	810,900	15.5	328,759	8.9	469,578	5.7	371,878	5.8
Ireland	674,061	12.8	405,710	11.0	344,940	4.2	166,445	2.6
Scandinavia[2]	671,783	12.7	390,729	10.5	488,208	5.9	238,275	3.8
France	48,193	0.9	35,616	1.0	67,735	0.4	60,335	1.0
German Empire	1,445,181	27.5	579,072	15.7	328,722	4.0	174,227	2.7
Other[3]	152,604	2.9	86,011	2.3	112,433	1.4	101,478	1.6
Central Europe								
Poland	42,910	0.8	107,793	2.9	not returned separately		not returned separately	
Austria-Hungary	314,787	6.0	534,059	14.5	2,001,376	24.4	1,154,727	18.2
Other[4]	—	—	52	[6]	34,651	0.4	27,180	0.4
Eastern Europe								
Russia[5]	182,698	3.5	450,101	12.7	1,501,301	18.3	1,106,998	17.4
Romania	5,842	0.1	6,808	0.2	57,322	0.7	13,566	0.2
Turkey in Europe	1,380	[6]	3,547	0.1	61,856	0.8	71,149	1.1
Southern Europe								
Greece	1,807	[6]	12,732	0.3	145,402	1.8	198,108	3.1
Italy	267,660	5.1	603,761	16.3	1,930,475	23.5	1,229,916	19.4
Spain	3,995	0.1	9,189	0.2	24,818	0.3	53,262	0.8
Portugal	15,186	0.3	25,874	0.7	65,154	0.8	82,489	1.3

Other Europe	1,070	(6)	145	(6)	454	(6)	6,527	0.1
Asia								
Turkey in Asia	1,098	(6)	23,963	0.6	66,143	0.8	89,568	1.4
Other	68,673	1.3	33,775	0.9	171,837	2.1	109,019	1.7
America								
British North America[8]	492,865[7]	9.4	3,098[7]	0.1	123,650	1.5	708,715	11.2
Mexico	2,405[7]	(6)	734[7]	(6)	31,188	0.4	185,334	2.9
West Indies[9]	27,323	0.5	31,480	0.9	100,960	1.2	120,860	1.9
Central and South America	2,233	(6)	2,038	0.1	22,011	0.3	55,630	0.9
Other Countries								
Australia[10]	7,271	0.1	3,225	0.1	11,191	0.1	11,280	0.2
Other	6,643	0.1	16,023	0.4	40,943	0.5	10,414	0.2
		100.0[11]		100.0		100.0		100.0

[1] England, Scotland, Wales
[2] Norway, Sweden, Denmark
[3] Netherlands, Belgium, Switzerland
[4] Bulgaria, Serbia, Montenegro
[5] Includes Finland and boundaries prior to 1919
[6] less than one-tenth of one percent
[7] Immigrants from British North America and Mexico not reported from 1886 to 1893
[8] including Canada
[9] including Jamaica
[10] including Tasmania and New Zealand
[11] Totals are rounded to nearest percent as in Census report.

From N. Carpenter, "Immigrants and Their Children," *U.S. Bureau of the Census Monograph*, No. 7 (Washington, D.C., 1927) pp. 324–25.

were more plentiful across the Atlantic, and improved transportation brought America closer to Italy for "birds of passage" who preferred to spend the winter with family and friends.

Some countries, such as Russia, experienced losses, primarily among minority elements of the population. In 1907, Russia lost 250,000 people to other countries. Of these, 115,000 were Jews and 73,000 were Poles (approximately 4 percent and 6 percent of the Russian population, respectively). Most of the others were Lithuanians, Finns, and Germans. Though 66.8 percent of the country's population were of Russian ethnic stock, only a tiny fraction of that group emigrated.

It is impossible to know precisely to what degree non-Russian emigrants left Russia for economic rather than political reasons. However, for one group—the Jews—the pull of western Europe and the Americas was freedom from the complex pattern of discrimination and persecution they experienced as a religioethnic minority. Three waves of pogroms occurred in Russia, each more destructive than the last: 1881–1884, 1903–1906, and 1917–1921. Although violent persecution had all but disappeared in western Europe by the end of the nineteenth century, pogroms persisted in Russia and elsewhere in eastern Europe. The absence of such violence pulled Jews westward toward western European nations, Latin America, Canada, and the United States

The United States already had a reputation for religious freedom, though many Jews feared that a liberal, secular democracy inspired by the Reformation and the Enlightenment would prove a difficult climate in which to sustain Orthodoxy. Therefore, the Orthodox, the better educated, and the relatively prosperous tended to remain behind. Between 1880 and 1900, most of the 1,000,000 Jews arriving in the United States were young, relatively uneducated, and anxious to improve their lot. However, after 1900, a gradually increasing number of intellectuals and prominent businessmen were lured to America from Russia as well as Romania and other eastern European countries by the prospect of escape from escalating persecution, byproducts both of famine and political discord. Two hundred and sixty-nine Jewish teachers came to America in 1907 as compared with only ninety-one who had arrived in 1895; 197 "other professionals" landed in 1891 and 1,045 in 1907. After 1905 many members of the Jewish socialist movement, or Bund, came, some to avoid jail, others frustrated with the minimal possibilities for change in eastern Europe.

Even as migrants from southern and eastern Europe crowded America's ports, newcomers were raining down upon the United States from the north. Since the mid-nineteenth century, French Canadians had crossed the open border with the United States to work in mines, mills, quarries, and lumberyards. Most were farmers from Quebec forced to find work elsewhere because of the depressed state of agriculture in French Canada. Outmoded agrarian methods had depleted the soil there, and the little land available for new farms was often inaccessible to markets because of inadequate roads and bridges. In addition, the old French inheritance system prevailed. Land holdings already too small were further subdivided among the many offspring of French Canada's large families, reducing farms to strips too narrow to yield an adequate living.

When upper and lower Canada were joined in 1840, Canada's government made every effort to encourage immigration from Europe because French Canadians refused to settle the extensive lands of western Canada. Instead, the French Canadians became itinerant workers in America, intending to return to Canada with the money they saved to rebuild family farms and pay off debts. While some laborers found work in northern New York, western Pennsylvania, and Ohio, the majority headed for nearby New England, where they competed with Irish laborers who had replaced the Yankee farm girls in textile factories. Over 40,000 French Canadians fought for the Union army during the Civil War, many just to collect the bounties.

In the late nineteenth century, Canadian emigration to the United States increased and many of those who came remained to take advantage of opportunities in New England's burgeoning industrial economy. French Canadian immigrants were a ready source of cheap, industrious, and uncomplaining labor. New England Yankees dubbed them "the Chinese of the Eastern States," regarding them as poor, ignorant, degraded, and resistant to Americanization. The immigrants' Catholicism fueled Protestant Yankee antagonisms. Nevertheless, railroads continued to transport French Canadians across the border, while Canadian officials tried in vain to stop the emigration with legislative investigations, ecclesiastical admonitions, and propagandistic literature that imputed to the emigrants such base motives as extravagance, love of luxury, and adventurism.

In the period from 1890 to 1900, the number of Canadian-born French immigrants in the U.S. increased by over 90,000. In 1896, a wave of Canadian prosperity and the election of the first French Canadian Prime Minister deterred many French Canadians from leaving and brought others home. Yet, by 1900 there were more than 500,000 French Canadians in New England. Between 1900 and 1910, French Canadian immigration to America began to decline. Only 10 percent of those who arrived in this period ever returned permanently to Canada.

As French Canadians filtered into the industrial economy in the northeastern states, Mexican immigrants penetrated the Southwest's agrarian economy. When the treaty of Guadalupe Hidalgo ended the War with Mexico in 1848, approximately 75,000 Mexicans lived in the Southwest, with the largest concentrations in the areas that became California and New Mexico. However, economic development in the entire region at the turn of the century pulled Mexican laborers across the border in droves. Whether legally or illegally, permanently or temporarily, for the day or until the planting and harvesting cycle was completed, Mexican laborers were plentiful and worked cheaply. They helped complete and repair southwestern railroad lines; made southern California, Texas, and Arizona into cotton country; and dug irrigation ditches that turned California's Imperial and San Joaquin Valleys into a fertile cornucopia. Mexicans mined in Arizona, harvested fruit in Texas and California, and staffed packing plants all over the Pacific coast.

Impoverished Mexican migrant laborers crossed the border easily and often, taking jobs once held by Asian laborers. Crowded by a sharply increasing population and propelled by economic and political turmoil, Mexican workers migrated northward, often risking the penalties of illegal entry. But during World War I, all contract labor laws were suspended for the war's duration and thousands of Mexicans who could not previously obtain visas were admitted to cultivate the crops needed for the war effort. As part of the ongoing pattern, Mexican immigrants were welcome whenever there was a labor shortage, but they were not welcome as permanent residents striving for citizenship.

Economic dislocation brought thousands of Asian immigrants to the United States between 1880 and 1921. Most of the Chinese who emigrated to the United States were impoverished agricultural laborers from Toishan, a district of Kwangtung in southern China. Unable to survive as farmers, some Toishanese turned to commerce and left for the U.S. from the port of Hong Kong. By 1880, the number of Chinese in the United States was still only about 100,000, concentrated mostly on the West Coast. Nativists and West Coast laborers who feared economic competition from this cheap labor supply fought for the passage of the Chinese Exclusion Act in 1882. This act virtually halted emigration from China to the United States until after World War II and prohibited Chinese aliens from acquiring citizenship. (See chart on page 40.)

The largest Asian group to arrive in the United States during the late nineteenth century was the Japanese. However, early emigrants did not go to the United States but to Hawaii, then a sovereign nation. In 1868, 148 Japanese contract laborers went to Hawaii. Many were unhappy with their decision and were returned by the Japanese government to their homeland. During the next seventeen years, Japan did not permit any contract laborers to leave the country.

Even as the worldwide demand for inexpensive labor increased, the Hawaiian economy became progressively dependent on a single crop, sugar cane. Cheap plantation labor became crucial, and the Japanese were a ready supply of willing laborers. Economic turmoil in Japan, including severe inflation, unemployment, and subsequent social unrest left the Japanese government searching for a safety valve. Hawaii was the answer. In 1885, an agreement between Hawaii and Japan brought twenty-six ships carrying 28,691 Japanese to Hawaii between 1886 and 1894. The Japanese who answered the call for contract labor came primarily from Hiroshima and Yamaguchi prefectures. Over 300 people in

Decennial Immigration to the United States From China and Japan, 1880–1929

	1880–89	Percent	1890–99	Percent	1900–09	Percent	1910–19	Percent	1920–29	Percent
Total	5,248,568		3,694,294		8,202,388		6,347,380		4,295,510	
China	65,797	1.0	15,268	0.4	19,884	0.2	20,916	0.3	30,648	0.7
Japan	1,583	0.03	13,998	0.4	139,262	1.7	77,125	1.2	42,057	1.0

From: *The Statistical History of the United States From Colonial Times to the Present* (New York, 1976), pp.105, 107–108.

the first group of 600 to depart for Hawaii came from one spot on one small island, Oshima District on Yamaguchi.

Because farming and fishing alone could not support Oshima's dense population, islanders often took second jobs as carpenters, stone cutters, or in other trades for supplemental income. Their wives engaged in home industries such as weaving cotton. Then, in 1884, economic pressures were worsened by a typhoon and landslide. Two years later, the emigration began. Not everyone applying to leave Oshima was accepted. Married couples were given preference. However, by far the greatest number of applicants were single men, 40 percent of whom returned to their villages in Japan after their contracts expired. They usually returned with sufficient funds to pay their debts, buy small plots of land, or build homes.

Emigrants from Hiroshima Bay followed a slightly different pattern. Seven hundred and seventy-seven people left this area over a fifteen year period—624 to Hawaii, 151 to the United States, and small groups to Canada, the French West Indies, Peru, and Australia. All but 10 of the 194 females in the group were married. Emigration from this area affected the moderately well-off as well as the needy, but many of those who left returned to Japan. One village later became known as "American Village": of its 1,687 inhabitants, one-sixth had been born in Canada or the United States during the period of migration, and seven of the village's ten families still had relatives abroad. Still, most emigrants never returned, even to that village. Fifty-one families had emigrated permanently in the earlier period, taking almost everyone in the village along.

In general, most Japanese emigrants to Hawaii were young agricultural laborers or small peasant-farmers. Males left more frequently than did females by a ratio of four to one. The poorest left first, followed by those who were better off but still in search of improved economic opportunities. Those who went to Hawaii were unskilled laborers, while those traveling to America generally came from more prosperous districts and higher social classes than those who contracted to work on Hawaii's sugar plantations. Of those who sailed for America most were merchants, students, and skilled laborers.

Migrants did not pour forth equally from every corner of the globe or from every rank of society. Dramatic shifts in world migration patterns between 1880 and 1921 pulled an increasing number of southern and eastern Europeans westward, Chinese and Japanese eastward, Canadians southward, and Mexicans northward. The trans-Atlantic migration increased sharply, first to Latin America and to Canada, and later primarily to the United States. If large-scale social and economic forces were pushing and pulling those able to move, the migrants found themselves actively courted by countries and companies who needed them. Only then did their own countries realize the potential economic loss resulting from their departure.

III

As their labor supply gradually drained westward, unwilling donor nations launched counteroffensives in the propaganda war to stop the flow. In 1887, local officials in Austria were instructed by the Ministry of the Interior to oppose foreign efforts to recruit their country's labor force. That same year, in Greece the Minister of the Interior ordered local officials to publicize the hardships of trans-Atlantic voyages. In 1905, the provincial government of Croatia-Slavonia published dire warnings about the gravity of economic conditions in the Americas. Aside from persuasion, most countries did not interfere with emigration, hoping only that it would be temporary. Migratory laborers often relieved the pressures of poverty and unemployment in their home country, as they found jobs elsewhere and sent money back to their families. Emigration was thus a kind of safety valve relieving the threat of domestic unrest in countries under economic stress. Greece, Italy, Hungary, Japan, and Mexico, among others, welcomed home their seasonal workers returning from abroad with their earnings. It is estimated that between 1897 and 1902, 500 million lire (almost $100 million) entered Italy in the pockets of returning emigrants, who quickly circulated their capital into their country's economy by purchasing real estate, building homes, or opening small businesses. Emigration, then, was often as beneficial to the capitalist economies of donor nations as it was to those of the receiving nations. However willing donor nations might or might not be, they were rarely able to counter the recruitment efforts of host nations anxious to receive the migrants and benefit from their labor.

By 1900, the Canadian government was spending over $1 million annually to lure foreign labor. Most of these funds were used to maintain offices in sixteen cities in the United States, in which agents were given a commission of $300 a head to persuade the recently landed emigrants—if they were "white"—to continue their journey the relatively short distance to the Canadian border. Offices in London distributed the *Canadian Settlers Handbook,* which provided glamorous descriptions of wages, job opportunities, prices, and immigrant living conditions. Ironically, even as the Canadians advertised for European workers, French Canadians flowed south across the border in pursuit of higher wages in America's mills and factories.

The Brazilian government, badly in need of labor after the abolition of slavery in the 1880s, sought to establish agricultural colonies of immigrants. The Brazilians offered the immigrants trans-Atlantic and inland fares, duty-free entry of personal belongings, full civil rights to all new arrivals, and repatriation of widows, orphans, or disabled workers at minimal charge. Whether the newcomers were light- or dark-skinned, strong backs and occupational skills were Brazilian priorities.

Argentina was extremely aggressive in the recruitment process and was the United States' closest competitor for immigrants in the late nineteenth century. Though immigrants were required to pay their own ocean fares, they were guaranteed by the Argentinean government several days free lodging after arrival and free inland travel. Agents assisted the immigrants in purchasing land or finding agricultural employment. Books describing Argentina, often profusely illustrated, were distributed at European ports and, like the Brazilians, the Argentineans did not have a "white-only" policy.

The United States, in contrast to Argentina and Brazil, did not offer subsidized fares, immediate naturalization, or any other direct inducement for the enlistment of immigrants. While it offered the same open-door policy as did the other countries, except in the case of the Chinese, restricted by the Exclusion Law of 1882, and the Japanese, limited by the Gentlemen's Agreement of 1907, recruitment was conducted by agents of private companies such as railroads, or by steamship lines anxious to fill their vessels to capacity. State bureaus, too, sought to lure foreign workers to their factories and farms. The popularity of the United States as a destination for international migrants was the product of a fortuitous combination of economic opportunity, political liberty, and religious tolerance.

As it had from its earliest days, the United States offered newcomers an unusually high degree of economic opportunity. During the early and mid-nineteenth century, much of that opportunity involved land ownership. The United States possessed a vast domain and had a tradition of land distribution based on the fee-simple pattern rather than a feudal or semifeudal system. This meant land could be purchased, sold, or rented for money or its equivalent in goods without incurring further obligations beyond taxes. The federal government assumed a limited role in land distribution, its primary concern being the development of equitable procedures for distributing land to private citizens in order that they might settle on it and contribute their labor to its improvement.

In 1862, Congress passed the Homestead Act to induce settlers to migrate beyond the Mississippi. This act provided that the head of a household could acquire a quarter section of land (consisting of 160 acres) by agreeing to occupy and cultivate it for five years, after which time legal title to the land was granted. Only U.S. citizens, or those who had formally declared their intention to become U.S. citizens, were eligible. However, impoverished immigrants, such as those crossing the Mexican border, often lacked the capital to finance settlement even of public lands. In the meantime, speculators and railroad companies were quick to purchase huge tracts of land with the intention of reselling them later at inflated prices. Therefore, those immigrants lucky enough to have arrived with a little money were often gouged as they naively accepted mortgages at interest rates as high as 60 percent.

Still, there were opportunities for newcomers who insisted on working the soil. As Andrew Rolle discovered in his study of the

Italians in rural America (*The Immigrant Upraised,* 1968), the California vineyards required the labor of thousands. Opportunities also abounded for those involved in small-scale agriculture, or truck farming, the cultivation of garden vegetables and fruits for sale in nearby markets. New York's and New Jersey's rural counties and the New England countryside were perfect for truck farming, offering Italian newcomers a chance to earn modest livings tilling small plots of American soil that they owned. In the southern states there were other opportunities on the land. In a study of health, disease, and immigration, Alan M. Kraut described how in the Mississippi Delta, southern Italian laborers, many sharing the same immunity to malaria as black laborers of African origin, began as peons growing cotton for Leroy Percy and other large landowners. Some, such as Joseph Roncconi, were able to buy their own land and tried cotton farming, albeit with limited success (*Silent Travelers,* 1994). Historian Sucheng Chan (*This Bitter-Sweet Soil,* 1986) described the thousands of Chinese truck gardeners, tenant farmers, and agricultural commission merchants who helped transform California into the nation's premier agricultural state by the turn of the century. In its farming regions, such as the Sacramento–San Joaquin Delta, 80 to 90 percent of the Chinese in this part of the state earned their livelihoods planting and harvesting crops. However, Chinese in other parts of the state, 85 percent of California's Chinese population, turned to industry and gravitated to urban areas. There they joined other immigrants seeking higher wages and better opportunities.

By 1900, most immigrants found cities economically alluring. The United States had begun a period of rapid industrial expansion, necessitating a ready supply of cheap, unskilled, and semi-skilled labor for factories and mines. Thus, the industrial sector of the American economy generated jobs increasingly claimed by workers from abroad. In the New England states, the Irish and British immigrants of an earlier era competed with newer French Canadian arrivals. By 1910, a study of twenty-one industries reported that 52.9 percent of all employees were foreign-born, some two-thirds of them from southern and eastern Europe. In some industries such as textiles, clothing manufacturing, ore mining, meat-packing, slaughtering, and cigar manufacturing, the percentage was far higher. Like the Irish who landed in the 1840s, Slavs, Poles, and Italians frequently found jobs in railroad and construction work, two areas traditionally dominated by foreign-born labor.

The hours were long and the wages low, but compared to those in the immigrants' native countries, the labor opportunities held out by the United States seemed rich. Those who wanted work found jobs. And the apparent fluidity of the economy and social structure gave hope to those yearning to be self-employed. Some Irish and German immigrants of an earlier era had opened small businesses of their own, or had seen their children become entrepreneurs. Their modest successes encouraged newcomers in the belief that America was the portal to independence and security—perhaps even wealth.

By the end of the nineteenth century the United States already held a worldwide reputation as a haven for the victims of political oppression and religious persecution. Individual liberties were guaranteed by a written constitution and bill of rights. Because of the country's federal system and the vast size of the nation, the national government and its agents hardly touched the lives of most individual Americans during the nineteenth century. Rarely did federal laws place minorities at a legal or political disadvantage. There were exceptions. Because of a pervasive anti-Asian racism, Chinese, Japanese, Indians, and Koreans among others were excluded from citizenship. The Chinese did not become eligible for citizenship until 1943. In 1946 the Indians gained eligibility, and by 1952 all Asian immigrants could eventually become citizens. More often, though, state and municipal laws codified local prejudices. For instance, Sabbatarian laws barred Jews from doing business on Sundays, and Catholic parents were required to pay public school taxes to discourage them from paying additional tuition to parochial schools. A 1906 law in San Francisco segregated the mere handful of Japanese children into separate schools, and Japanese were forbidden from owning land.

State laws were relatively minor inconveniences compared with the legal restrictions on land ownership, university enrollment, and physical mobility suffered by some immigrants in their homelands. East European Jews, arriving in droves after the turn of the century, especially appreciated the absence of government sanctioned anti-Semitic policies. Religious liberties were protected by the Constitution, and east European Orthodox Jews discovered that if they lived in America they could worship publicly without fear of government reprisals or systematic persecution.

Favorable and attractive reports about the United States reached those contemplating emigration by three distinct routes: newspaper articles, printed publicity disseminated by private companies, and letters from those who had already made the journey. All three kinds of communications helped shape the chain migration pattern that led friends, neighbors, and relatives of earlier migrants to follow their loved ones.

Though literacy was not universal in the towns and villages of southern and eastern Europe, where most migrants originated, such communities often had some inhabitants who could read. Newspapers published in the larger cities were expensive, but often an educated individual—a doctor, a merchant, a teacher—subscribed to such a paper or several townsmen shared a subscription. Sixty years after his arrival, a Russian immigrant interviewed by the Smithsonian Institution in Washington, D.C., recalled sharing a Yiddish newspaper published in Moscow after it was delivered to his native village. When the weekly newspaper arrived at the post office, the recipient was expected to read the headlines aloud to all who gathered. This spate of news usually stimulated discussion and debate, so trips to the post office were never quick errands. In the case of joint subscriptions, each subscriber took a turn keeping the paper for a few days. Each subscriber might also invite neighbors for another reading and more discussion. The newspapers often had articles about the United States, and, thus, life in America became a matter of interest in the post offices and homes of these small Russian communities.

In each village which "lost" some members to the New World, letters arrived describing travails and triumphs. The names of far-off places—New York, Chicago, Brooklyn, Philadelphia—mentioned in newspaper articles took on new meaning when former neighbors and relatives lived there. In her memoir, Mary Antin

(*From Plotzk to Boston,* 1899) recalled that in Russia, "America was in everybody's mouth. Businessmen talked of it over their accounts; the market women made up their quarrels that they might discuss it from stall to stall; people who had relatives in the famous land went around reading their letters for the enlightenment of less fortunate folk. . . . children played at emigrating; old folks shook their sage heads over the evening fire and prophesied no good for those who braved the terrors of the sea and the foreign goal beyond it; all talked of it, but scarcely anyone knew one true fact about this magic land." Immigrant letters were often highly stylized. Frequently they were written for illiterate migrants by friends or professional letter writers. Whatever the anxieties and distresses of life in America, in their letters immigrants usually minimized the obstacles confronting them, preferring instead to report in extravagant detail all that was good in their new environment.

This image of the exaggerated bountifulness of America detailed in immigrant letters was skillfully reflected in pamphlets and posters published by private companies, railroads, and steamship lines. Material printed for mass distribution was designed to sell land, ocean passages, or seats on American trains. Agents, some from America, others hired on commission to represent American companies to their countrymen, dispersed these publications in foreign ports, towns, and villages. In the first half of the nineteenth century, such books and pamphlets about America were circulated throughout northern and western Europe, especially in England and the German states. Because many Americans considered northern and western Europeans as more desirable settlers than southern and eastern Europeans, advertising continued to be directed at the former area late into the nineteenth century, despite the apparent shift in migration patterns. In 1891, Thomas Cook and other British agencies still distributed folders describing the virtues of Chicago, Milwaukee, and St. Paul in northern and western European cities, even as the migrant flow to these cities was originating in other parts of Europe.

Although these pamphlets often contained outdated information, they continued to be widely circulated. Migrants from southern and eastern Europe departing for America from western European ports read about opportunities that no longer existed. For example, by the turn of the century, there was little land still being distributed by railroad companies in the American West at prices immigrants could afford. Yet, the Thomas Cook agent in Antwerp still distributed the company's pamphlet "Homesteads For All" with its assurances of abundant low cost land.

Trans-Atlantic steamship lines also advertised and competed vigorously for passengers. The port cities in Germany and England, from which many of the migrants departed, buzzed with agents seeking customers. In the southern provinces of Italy, 160 agents pursued the traveling trade, along with 4,000 subagents who were often village shopkeepers or tradesmen. Some of the guidebooks issued by steamship companies focused on the size and stability of the vessels or the comfort of the accommodations on board. Others stressed the speed of the journey or its low cost.

Steamship company pamphlets contributed to migrants' distorted image of America. Occasionally they included poems or American success stories to encourage those wavering at the pier. Colorful posters of America's scenic beauty covered the walls of Greek coffee houses and grocers' shops. No doubt, the same was true elsewhere in southern and eastern Europe. In most cases, these inspiring poems and posters portrayed a world that would prove elusive to newly arrived immigrants.

Among the Chinese, merchants had been coming to America in search of opportunities since the middle of the nineteenth century. However, once news of the gold discovery reached China, large shiploads of aspiring miners headed to the West Coast of the United States. Only after hopes of striking gold faded did these arrivals take the backbreaking, low-wage jobs offered Chinese in agriculture and railroad construction.

The counterbalance of fact and fantasy beckoning those who departed for the United States can never be calculated. The United States did offer unparalleled economic possibilities and guarantees of individual liberty. However, there can be little doubt that intolerable economic and social conditions at home were critical catalysts in precipitating migration. It may well be that glowing letters and ebullient propaganda were more influential in determining *where* the emigrants would go rather than *whether* they would go at all. Pamphlets may have prompted the choice of New York or Chicago over Rio de Janeiro or Toronto, but it is unlikely that even the most embellished description could budge a family basically content with its lot. The stereotype of a migrant dreaming of "streets paved with gold" is, nevertheless, a reminder of the persuasive power of fantasy. The colorful posters and exuberant letters, if not completely truthful, unquestionably pulled migrants by the cords of their imaginations. In short, this literature made the future seem ever sweeter and emigration to the United States especially tantalizing to those bent on moving.

Were there regrets among the immigrants over leaving their native cities, villages, regions, or counties? Some believed that whatever they found abroad would be an improvement over what they were certain to suffer at home. One former resident of County Komarom in Hungary wrote home from America:

Here a man is paid for his labors and I am certainly not sorry that I am here. I work from six in the morning until seven at night and get $10–11 a week. . . . There are 10,000 workers in this shop and my wife is working here too. She makes $9.50 a week. At home I made that much money in a whole month and people thought my job was very good. Here I am sewing dresses on a machine. In America there is no difference between one man and another. If you're a millionaire you are called a Mister just the same, and your wife is Missis.

Dr. George M. Price no doubt expressed the feelings of many east European Jews—and probably many non-Jews—when he considered whether or not he regretted emigrating from Russia. His diary reveals his conclusion:

Sympathy for Russia? How ironical it sounds! Am I not despised? Am I not urged to leave? Do I not hear the word *zhid* (Jew) constantly? Can I even think that some consider me a human being capable of thinking and feeling like others? Do I not rise daily with the fear lest the hungry mob attack me? . . . It is impossible . . . that a Jew should regret leaving Russia.

Constantine Panunzio, in contrast, retained warm memories of Italy and felt himself bound to it by "wonderful, inexplicable tendrils which so intertwine themselves around our human hearts in our infancy as to make the country of our birth, the very village, or hamlet in which we first saw the light of day, the one spot on earth around which cluster the sweetest of life's memories."

The "Ballad of the Immigrant," a popular Mexican *corrido,* or traditional epic ballad, included the lines,

> I'm going to the United States
> To earn my living;
> Good-bye my beloved country,
> I carry you in my heart.
> Don't condemn me
> For leaving my country
> Poverty and necessity
> Are at fault.

Whether they looked back with nostalgia or with rancor, most new immigrants who arrived in the United States elected to stay. Many wrote letters or made return visits in order to coax relatives and friends to join them and become part of a chain migration that led those who already knew each other in the Old World to follow one another to the new one. Apparently, their efforts were successful; 92 percent of the people arriving at the port of New York between 1908 and 1910 declared that they were joining friends or relatives who had sent for them. Still, even when encouraged to depart, the ultimate decision to pack up and go remained with the immigrants themselves. It was a gamble; no one could possibly foresee all the ramifications of setting off across continents and oceans. But it was a gamble waged deliberately by individuals or families, and often with hope and enthusiasm.

CHAPTER TWO

The Journey
and the Reception

Renowned immigration scholar Oscar Handlin is best understood metaphorically in *The Uprooted* when he described the emigrant leaving his community as a "man at the crossroads" who "moved alone." Although millions of young men and women traveled by themselves to the United States and other host countries, the act of migration was rarely a plan formulated by a single individual in isolation from family and friends. Nor was it always the first departure from home and family. Often, transoceanic migrants had already moved once or more before journeying abroad. Some had moved from country to city, region to region, or from village to village. Still, no matter how often one does it, moving can be emotionally as well as physically jarring, and knowing that others were making similar decisions could at best have been only moderately comforting to those departing.

The migrants' ordeal began almost as soon as the decision was made to pack. In addition to the emotional strain of leaving, they faced weeks of travel, hardship, and expense, with the distinct possibility that they might fail to reach their desired destination. Still, the migrants were never completely at the mercy of processes beyond their control. Individual migrants often exercised their cunning to determine whether craft or cash was the best lever for prying loose required certificates and passports from recalcitrant officials. Nor should it be forgotten that even the humblest travelers were consumers, their patronage prized by competing railroad and steamship lines. Those reaching America would be examined and questioned by immigration officers to judge whether they were sufficiently physically fit, mentally able, and morally sound to merit passage through the "golden door." Here the immigrants relied on their guile and hints gleaned from the letters of earlier arrivals to help them vault the final hurdle.

Clearing the threshold did not end the ordeal, however. In the weeks and months ahead, immigrants would face the task of finding the necessities of life—shelter, food, and a job—even as they adjusted to the strange ways of the New World. In the United States, resourcefulness and persistence proved the staunchest allies.

For most, the city was their decompression chamber. Job opportunities and scant knowledge of the country beyond the streetlights kept most newly arrived migrants huddled together in the growing urban centers of the Northeast and the Midwest. There newcomers would sink their roots through the cracked pavement and begin the final stage of their odyssey, the transformation from aliens to Americans. However, the city was hardly the only choice. Chinese migrants started life in America as agricultural workers in the southern valley of California, Mexicans harvested crops in the fields of the southwestern states, and some southern Italians grew cotton in the Mississippi Delta. Not all immigrants equated the American experience with pavement.

I

Once the decision to leave was made, emigrants began the process of uprooting themselves psychologically as well as physically. Fears and anxieties had to be overcome, friends and relatives bid painful farewell, and belongings sorted through for departure. The distance to America seemed vast and the journey so laced with danger that at times parents and children parted fearing they would never see each other again. Often they were correct.

In the tiny communities of southern and eastern Europe, where the fate of each affected all, the news of an emigration occasioned public reaction. In her memoir (*The Promised Land,* 1912), Mary Antin recalls the day she received the steamer ticket sent by her father in America: "Before sunset the news was all over Plotzk. . . . Then they began to come. Friends and foes, distant relatives and new acquaintances, young and old, wise and foolish, debtors and creditors, and mere neighbors—from every quarter of the city . . . a steady stream of them poured into our street, both day and night, till the hour of our departure." On the day of departure, a procession of townspeople escorted the family to the train station, Antin recalls:

The procession resembled both a funeral and a triumph. The women wept over us, reminding us eloquently of the perils of the sea, of the bewilderment of a foreign land, of the torments of homesickness that would await us. They bewailed my mother's lot, who had to tear herself away from blood relations to go among strangers; who had to face gendarmes, ticket agents, and sailors, unprotected by a masculine escort; who had to care for four young children in the confusion of travel, and very likely feed them trefah [non-kosher food] or see them starve on the way. Or they praised her for a brave pilgrim, and expressed confidence in her ability to cope with gendarmes and ticket agents, and blessed her with every other word, and all but carried her in their arms.

Leaving for America was a triumph, but one tinged with regret and the loss of a part of one's life and identity.

The emotional trauma of departure was compounded by the physical trials of the trip to the New World. Mexicans and Canadians often walked to America or, in the case of Mexicans, swam the Rio Grande. For those coming from across oceans, the trip often necessitated several means of transportation. First came the trek over land to the port of embarkation. For Italians and Slavs, the problem was largely logistical; how to cover the hundreds of miles separating one's village from the ocean. Many hiked for days and weeks, their belongings on their backs and in handcarts they pushed or pulled. Those who could afford it came in horse-drawn wagons they owned or rented. By the turn of the century, the European railway system was so complete that the journey to port was neither exhausting nor risky for most travelers. Special trains, often subsidized by the steamship companies, brought emigrants to the coast. German ports were used by approximately two-thirds of the emigrants from Austria-Hungary, though some did wander all across Europe to Liverpool, England, before leaving. After 1900, Austria and Hungary tried to secure profits from the lucrative business of shipping emigrants within their borders; their carriers competed with the English. In 1904, the Hungarian government signed an agreement with Liverpool's Cunard Line to begin sailing from its port of Fiume to New York under the name of the Cunard Hungarian American Line. The line held the monopoly on transporting America-bound immigrants and, in return, agreed to abide by Hungarian emigration laws, accept only Hungarian official documents, and place Cunard agents only at ports designated by the Budapest government. The agreement backfired when competing shipping lines lowered their rates drastically and immigrants proved willing to cross Hungarian borders illegally and sail from other ports for rates as low as eight dollars. The competition and Cunard's overcrowded ships resulted in not more than one-third and sometimes as little as one-fifth of Hungarian travelers departing from Fiume.

East European Jews had to cope with special hazards in addition to the high cost and inconvenience of travel suffered by all emigrants. In *World Of Our Fathers,* Irving Howe explains that Jews often traveled by indirect routes to port cities in western Europe to circumvent the anti-Semitic policies of some east European nations. Many Russian emigrants found ocean passage from Odessa longer and costlier than a railroad trip across Europe and a voyage from a north European port. However, most Jews took care to cross the Russian border into Austria-Hungary instead of Romania on their way west because "the Romanian authorities were feared as particularly savage anti-Semites, while the Austro-Hungarian empire seemed mildly benevolent." Because Russian port officials often used passport inspection as an occasion for harassing Jewish males old enough for military conscription, Jewish immigrants in the north refused to purchase the expensive Russian passport, and, instead risked an illegal border crossing into Germany. Many Russian Jews arrived in America bearing tales of their daring escapes across the border, aided by a paid agent and bribes. In his "Memoirs of a Russian Immigrant," (*American Jewish Historical Quarterly,* LXIII, September 1973), Max Vanger described his adventure:

... we went by wagon to a place not far from the Prussian border, where we stayed in a granary. We were forbidden to talk or smoke, and we would hear the Russian Cossacks riding on their horses. We stayed in that building until dark, and someone came to us and told us to come along. Whatever luggage we had was taken from us. We rode in a wagon until we reached a wooden section. In a short time there was a large group, perhaps fifty people and a leader. He told us not to talk to one another, not to smoke or light a match, and if we heard someone nearing us to lie down on the ground. It was dark and needless to say all of us were scared, but nothing happened. Finally we were told to stop walking. We did and the agent went ahead of us. He was gone awhile and came back and told us to walk in a single line which we did and after a short distance, two soldiers facing one another with rifles on their shoulders counted us. We were told that this was the border between Russia and Prussia, and the soldiers received one ruble a head for letting us through.

Once across the border, the emigrants rode by train to their port of departure in western Europe.

Following an especially virulent wave of anti-Semitic violence in Romania in 1899, small groups of Jews left the country on foot. These *fusgeyers* ("wayfarers") hiked hundreds of miles, living off the land and the charity of sympathetic peasants along the route to the sea. Fusgeyers often pledged to share with their fellows their last morsel of food. According to Irving Howe, fusgeyers tramped through the countryside singing songs in Yiddish and sometimes even offered amateur shows in villages along the way to raise funds. However, such romantic episodes were rare. More frequently, Jews sought to remain anonymous, hoping to cross the border into Austria or Germany without incident.

Jews were not alone in suffering inconvenience and exploitation. All emigrants were vulnerable. Hungarian emigrants departing Fiume were required to secure birth certificates and present them to government officials prior to departure. Male emigrants were checked for liability to military service before passports were issued. Since only those in possession of passports could buy tickets, bribery and the sale of falsified papers were quite common. All emigrants also had to undergo a medical examination before leaving, the result of increasingly stringent American health standards for immigrants. In 1907, nearly 40,000 people were rejected by physicians at European docks. At busy ports such as Liverpool, Havre, Trieste, Fiume, and Palermo, American physicians or those selected by American consuls worked with local doctors representing steamship companies or European governments. However, no procedure proved perfect, and medical certificates, like passports, were often available for the right price, even to the ineligible.

In *Crossings, The Great Transatlantic Migrations, 1870–1914* (1992), historian Walter Nugent masterfully explains how emigration became a global industry as steamship companies cooperated with railroad companies to transport migrants to coastal ports and built immigrant villages to house and process migrants prior to departure for Argentina, Brazil, and Canada, as well as the United States. Moving men and women across oceans and continents generated huge profits. Philip Taylor (*The Distant Magnet,* 1971), and Maldwyn Allen Jones (*Destination America, 1976*), offer descriptions of emigrant processing procedures. At Naples, the ship lines issued ration-tickets and travelers were sent to a licensed hotel and then to a restaurant for dinner, which often consisted of a thick soup or stew, melon, and wine. Vendors along the way peddled all kinds of food to those still hungry. On the day of departure, American consular officials saw each emigrant and provided vaccinations. After a final medical inspection by an American doctor and a last check of papers, the emigrants boarded and made last minute purchases of food, tobacco, and lucky charms from merchants in small boats bobbing around the anchored ship.

At Liverpool and western European ports, the steamship companies vied with each other to make the transfer from train to ship as smooth and comfortable as possible. Company employees met trains and transported emigrants to lodgings inspected and regulated by the companies. Such preparations shielded the travelers from thieves and confidence men. The Cunard Line built a complex of buildings that could house 2,000 people at a time in ten-bed dormitories with good sanitation and food. Kosher food was available for Jewish emigrants and staff members spoke a variety of east European languages. Perhaps the most elaborate facilities were built by the Hamburg-Amerika Line. The Line constructed an immigrant village for transients with its own railway station, churches, and a synagogue. Travelers could bathe while their clothes and luggage were disinfected. The emigrants were then examined by doctors and provided with inexpensive lodgings and food.

Though the facilities were an improvement over the neglect of the early nineteenth century, the inspection routine seemed dehumanizing. Emigrants resented being poked, jabbed, washed, and sprayed. However, shipping lines insisted on the procedure to curtail shipboard illness and avoid the expense of returning emigrants to Europe who had been refused admission to the United States by American inspectors.

After 1891, American immigration law required that the steamship companies vaccinate, disinfect, and examine their immigrant passengers prior to sailing; that they reimburse the United States government for the housing of detained passengers at American ports; and that they return rejected immigrants back to their ports of embarkation free of charge. In Rotterdam, during the cholera panic of 1893, the routine became even more elaborate. While their clothes were being disinfected, travelers were ordered to take an antiseptic bath. Males received close haircuts after a shampoo with a mixture of soft soap, carbolic acid, creolin, and petroleum applied with a stiff brush. Women and girls did not get haircuts, but did receive shampoos and were required to use fine tooth combs to remove lice from their hair. The process was undignified, but most immigrants preferred the inconvenience to being turned away.

By the 1890s, the trans-Atlantic journey took less time and was safer than it had been earlier in the century, before the age of steam. The threat of steerage epidemics was reduced by the shorter number of days spent at sea, an average voyage from Europe taking between eight and fourteen days. From Asia, the trip was several days longer. The potential dangers of such a trip, such as fires, shipwrecks, and collisions, were reduced by ship inspections conducted by governments, and the advent of iron ships. However, it was still an uncomfortable voyage for immigrants, most of whom traveled in steerage. "Steerage" referred to the one or more below-deck compartments of a ship located fore and aft, where the ship's steering equipment had been located in an earlier era. The steerage compartments of late nineteenth-century steamers were no more than cargo holds six to eight feet high: no portholes; only two ventilators per compartment; and crammed with two or more tiers of narrow metal bunks. Travelers had to bring their own straw mattresses, which were cast overboard on the last day of the voyage. Men and women were segregated, sometimes on separate decks but often by nothing more than a few blankets draped over a line in the center of the compartment. Children were permitted to stay with their mothers. Some of the larger ships sailing the Atlantic crammed as many as 2,000 men, women, and children into compartments unfit for any human habitation.

There were still occasional epidemics of typhus and smallpox on board ship. The air was always fetid because of the poor ventilation. On the ships departing from Europe, emigrants had to bring their own cups, plates, and utensils. They cooked their own meals in one of several small galleys shared by everyone in steerage. The galleys had ranges, boilers, and a few vegetable cookers. Many immigrants brought food with them. However, most had to buy at least some of their provisions on board. They paid high prices, and the fare provided was almost always the same—herring. Herring was inexpensive, nourishing, and helped to combat sea-sickness. Toilet facilities varied from vessel to vessel. Some earlier ships had in steerage as few as forty toilets per 2,000 emigrants.

The details of the journey's hardships suggest that even before reaching America, the migrants began a readjustment in their lives. They learned to live in close proximity to those from different countries practicing different customs and worshipping God in ways unlike themselves. Many began the slow and painful process of compromising some of their own values and customs to the demands of the environment. And finally, most newcomers in steerage mastered the art of survival under the severe stresses and strains of daily life in a strange environment, far from the support of family and friends. Immigrants were weaning themselves from the Old World even before they landed in the New World.

However, not all the compromises were made by the travelers. As consumers, immigrants patronized certain steamship lines, which competed for their lucrative trade by improving shipboard conditions. A popular innovation was the elimination of steerage travel. After the turn of the century, ship companies built third-class accommodations in new ships. Third-class facilities were considerably less sumptuous than the first two classes but far more comfortable than steerage. All emigrants were in two-, four-, and six- berth cabins. There were more toilets and washrooms, a small covered promenade, and even lounges and smoking rooms. Meals were served in small dining areas and kosher food was provided. Bars sold beer, soft drinks, and tobacco. Ship lines provided an increased number of nurses and physicians, and after a Papal statement in 1906 complained that the spiritual needs of migrants were being neglected, Italian ships provided Catholic chaplains to serve passengers.

The news of land in sight triggered enormous excitement among the weary travelers. Despite the orders of the captain and the crew's efforts, newcomers pushed close to the rails on deck. Children were lifted high above the crowd. Nighttime dockings postponed the thrill until morning. Europeans and those from the Caribbean arriving at the port of New York gazed in awe at the tall buildings on shore. Filled with anticipation, and some apprehension, everyone scrambled to wash and dress in their best clothing. There was often much anxious speculation about what questions American customs officials and immigration inspectors might ask. Immigrants who had made the journey before coached novices at the last moment on what to say and what not to say.

The dock was chaotic. Passengers were separated by class to collect their baggage. Orders were shouted in various languages, officials raising their voices over the shouts of vendors selling fruit and other refreshments to the bewildered travelers. The immigrants had arrived in America, but the journey was not over yet. A ferry boat waited to transfer all passengers to a depot where they would be inspected, examined, questioned, processed, and either admitted or rejected. Approximately 98 percent of the newcomers would be admitted and permitted to embark upon the next stage of their journey.

Migrants fortunate enough to get close to the ship's rail might have tried to catch glimpses of their future, even as they prepared to discuss their past with immigration officers. As they stumbled down the gangplank, their legs may have been shaky and their heads light from the physical rigors of the voyage. Stepping on dry land, they may have crossed themselves or murmured a prayer. Perhaps they thought about all they had left behind even as they rushed to board the ferry for what lay ahead.

II

In the years prior to 1850, admission of newly arrived immigrants into the United States was casual, and records were kept haphazardly by local port officials, when they were kept at all. However, the deluge of 4,500,000 immigrants from northern and western Europe by midcentury persuaded state officials at major ports to adopt more systematic procedures and provide specific facilities for receiving the newcomers.

Between 1855 and 1892, after docking in New York, the busiest port of entry, the immigrants would have been taken by ferry boat to Castle Garden at the tip of Manhattan Island. The Garden was built as a fortress shortly before the War of 1812, only to be converted into an amusement center and concert hall. In 1850, Jenny Lind, the Swedish Nightingale, made her American debut there. Five years later, the chaos created by hundreds of thousands of immigrants forced the State of New York to begin operation of the Garden as America's first Emigrant Landing Port. Other states with major ports such as Massachusetts, Maryland, and Pennsylvania also haphazardly tried to cope with the problem.

The migration from southern and eastern Europe placed an increasing strain on what few American immigration facilities there were. Responding to reports of abuses and inefficiency, Congress appointed the Ford Committee to investigate state immigration procedures. The Committee's report in 1889 was highly critical of the states' ability to cope with the magnitude and character of the new immigration. And the report reflected an important change in the attitude of American officials toward the immigrant. Earlier in the nineteenth century, state officials were primarily concerned with protecting the immigrant against the hardships of America. Now state concern shifted to protecting America from potentially dangerous elements in the immigrant population. One witness testified that because of an inability to weed out undesirables among the large numbers of seemingly impoverished arrivals, New York State spent $20 million annually caring for paupers and the insane. A federal law in 1891 established a Bureau of Immigration to curb such inefficiency and regularize immigration procedures. The Bureau assumed the responsibility of protecting America from those it defined as unfit to care for themselves and, therefore, likely to become public charges. Inspection of all newcomers was designed to effectively bar "idiots, insane persons, paupers or persons likely to become public charges, persons suffering from a loathsome or dangerous contagious disease, persons who have been convicted of a felony or other infamous crime or misdemeanor involving moral turpitude, polygamists, and also [those] assisted by others to come, unless it is affirmatively and satisfactorily shown on special inquiry that such person does not belong to one of the foregoing excluded classes, or to the class of contract laborers. . . ."

Later legislation sharpened the criteria for exclusion. A 1903 law made specific mention of beggars, the insane, prostitutes, and anarchists as unfit for admission. Four years later, Congress again expanded the categories of unacceptable aliens to include the feebleminded, imbeciles, persons with physical or mental defects that might affect their ability to support themselves, those afflicted with tuberculosis, children under sixteen unaccompanied by their parents or legal guardians, and persons who admitted having committed a crime of moral turpitude or having engaged in prostitution. It also raised the penalty against shipping companies carrying immigrants found to be unfit by U.S. officials. A comprehensive law enacted in 1917 included all the categories of the earlier laws and added some new classes for exclusion. One new provision required that all immigrants be able to read and write a language. The literacy requirement was especially aimed at the peasants of southern and eastern Europe; this was a thinly veiled attempt to discriminate against the largest group of newcomers.

Long-established quarantine procedures required that state health officers talk to ship physicians to ensure that there had been no incidence of such feared infectious diseases as cholera, smallpox, typhoid, or typhus. After 1890, new federal guidelines called for extensive and careful examination of each immigrant seeking admission, a process that included mental and physical tests. The federal government ordered procedures in all American ports standardized under the supervision of the United States Marine Hospital Service (later renamed the U.S. Public Health Service) and provided new facilities where necessary, to handle the task. However, most ports continued to process immigrants in a casual fashion. All passengers traveling first or second class were inspected in the privacy of their cabins and in a perfunctory manner. In Boston, Philadelphia, and Baltimore, doctors and inspectors rushed through procedures on board ship or in a small shed on shore. In San Francisco, Asian passengers were detained in a two-story shed at the Pacific Mail Steamship Company wharf until immigration inspectors processed them. Often, as many as 500 people were crammed into the facility at one time. When Chinese community leaders in San Francisco complained about the conditions, processing was relocated to a station constructed on Angel Island in 1910. Most of those inspected on Angel Island were Asian arrivals. American officials believed that the island location would prevent the newcomers from conspiring to get themselves admitted with Chinese already in the United States, while protecting Americans from germs that might be borne on the bodies of the new arrivals. In contrast, Mexicans crossing the border were not even systematically counted until 1907, and the absence of a border patrol until 1924 meant that Mexicans came and went virtually unencumbered. Because New York was by far the most popular port for the millions of Europeans headed westward, Congress abandoned New York State's old Castle Garden depot for a new and larger immigration depot on Ellis Island, which opened in 1892.

A low-lying islet, close to the New Jersey shore, Ellis Island was doubled in size with landfill. Armaments stored there since the Civil War were removed. An initial wooden structure was built to receive immigrants, but it burned in 1897. The following year the federal government ordered the construction of an enormous complex of red-brick buildings to house the immigrant processing depot. It was completed in 1901. The first floor of the main building held baggage-handling facilities, railroad ticket offices, food-sales counters, and a waiting room for those traveling beyond New York. A mezzanine floor held observation areas and, later, administrative offices. The registry room or Great Hall on the second floor was the largest room, 200 feet long, 100 feet wide, and 56 feet high. The floor space was divided into narrow alleys by iron railings. The second floor also included detention areas, offices, waiting areas, and special inspection offices.

More than any other physical characteristic of Ellis Island, the iron railings intimidated many immigrants. The bars were only erected to create aisles to facilitate orderly movement, but newcomers saw them as the iron bars of a prison or cattle pen. Persistent immigrant complaints about the railings resulted in their eventual removal from the Great Hall. However, other intimidating structures, detention areas, separated from the rest of the floor by wires, were perceived as cages and continued to frighten immigrants.

Ellis Island became the model for all inspection depots. The facility could easily handle 5,000 immigrants per day, and often many more were rushed through inspection. Nearby, another building housed a restaurant, laundry, and shower facilities capable of bathing 8,000 people per day. There was a powerhouse and, across the ferry slip, the island was extended to accommodate a new hospital. Eventually Ellis Island would be enlarged with yet more landfill and a second hospital built to treat contagious diseases. The new hospital, constructed in pavilion style, consisted of separate wards in which all those with the same contagious disease were confined. Physicians re-gowned and re-gloved as they moved through the breezeways separating the ward buildings.

The eating facilities and food especially are remembered by those who entered the United States through Ellis Island. Long after her journey to America, one woman remembered her amazement upon seeing the dining room. "There were long tables and benches, and everything was on the table, fish, vegetables, whatever, water, water pitchers. These people, they really looked pathetic, most of them, but they seemed to enjoy their food. . . ." The food itself was alternately described by newcomers as tasty or terrible, as interesting or as institutional rot. Often the fare aroused curiosity and awe: "I never saw a banana in my life," recalled one Slavic woman, "and they served a banana. I was just looking at it." Others who ate their first banana with the skin on it soon learned that it was better peeled. At other immigration depots, food became the subject of protests. Chinese immigrants detained on Angel Island so detested the unfamiliar food they were served that they staged disturbances. Subsequently, signs were posted in Chinese ordering diners not to make trouble or dump food trays on the floor. In 1919, one such food riot prompted immigration officers to summon federal troops to quell the disturbance.

Although the time spent at both the Ellis Island and Angel Island depots was usually only a few hours, the experience was, for many immigrants, the most traumatic part of their voyage to America. Contemporary American journalists such as Broughton Brandenburg, who investigated the system on Ellis Island, were impressed with its thoroughness and "the kindly, efficient manner in which the law was enforced." Some writers conceded, however, that the immigrants had to contend with language problems, fears, and insecurities that no investigative reporter could fully appreciate. Professor Edward Steiner, who had himself emigrated to the United States, cautioned, "Let no one believe that landing on the shores of 'The land of the free and the home of the brave' is a pleasant experience; it is a hard, harsh fact surrounded by the grinding machinery of the law, which sifts, picks, and chooses, admitting the fit and excluding the weak and helpless." Thomas Pitkin, in *Keepers of The Gate* (1975), suggests that immigration officials were defensive about the austere appearance and coldly efficient operation of Ellis Island, denying its reputation as "a cross between Devil's Island and Alcatraz." On Angel Island, Chinese immigrants scrawled poems on the walls in pencil or ink, recording their complaints and anxieties. Some were carved into the wooden posts and could not be completely obscured with paint. In the 1980s many of the poems were found and translated by students. One such poem reads:

Everyone says travelling to North America is a pleasure
I suffered misery on the ship and sadness in the wooden building.
After several interrogations, still I am not done.
I sigh because my compatriots are being forcebly detained.

The experience that led some immigrants to refer to Ellis Island as the "Isle of Tears" or "Heartbreak Island" can best be appreciated by following a small group of immigrants through the grueling inspection procedure. After arrival on Ellis Island, immigrants were approached by a uniformed officer who pinned an identity tag on their clothing. The tag was inscribed with an identification number, corresponding to that in the ship's manifest. As they climbed the stairs to the main hall, carrying all their luggage, the immigrants were quite unaware that the first test had begun. "Line inspection" took place at the top of the stairs and was designed to permit federal physicians, these doctors at the gate, to scrutinize the immigrants under conditions of physical stress such as that produced by carrying heavy luggage up a flight of stairs. Hands, eyes, and throats were closely examined. The heart of an immigrant who had carried luggage up the stairs could be easily judged strong or weak, and the exertion would reveal deformities and defective posture.

As historian Alan M. Kraut observes in *Silent Travelers: Germs, Genes, and the "Immigrant Menace"* (1994), germ theory, which evolved from the research of Germany's Robert Koch and France's Louis Pasteur, was increasingly accepted by American physicians, including those of the U.S. Marine Hospital Service. Those federal doctors assigned to Ellis Island understood their mission as protecting the nation's health from these "silent travelers," harmful microorganisms that might arrive in the United States on the bodies of immigrants. A second concern was excluding those newcomers whose physical or mental disabilities might prevent them from being productive workers and likely in need of charitable support. As part of the line inspection, immigrants were given stamped identification cards. As the immigrants examined the card, physicians checked for defective eyesight. Eyelids might then be checked for trachoma. This painful examination involved the use of a glove buttonhook to turn the immigrants' eyelids inside out. Scalps were probed for lice. Immigrants were also required to turn their heads so that their facial expression could be examined. Certain expressions were believed by the examiners to be indicative of mental disorders.

As they proceeded to the Great Hall, immigrants might have noticed that others leaving the examination area had chalk marks on the right shoulders of their garments. Letters marked in chalk stood for the particular disability that might well cause that immigrant's detention, or even rejection: L for lameness, K for hernia, G for goiter, H for possible heart problems, E for eye problems, X for mental illness, and so on. All who failed to pass the medical exam were detained for a more thorough inspection. Sometimes a few days of rest and some nourishing food was sufficient to prepare an immigrant for reexamination.

An immigrant fortunate enough to pass this first series of tests was now herded into one of the pipe-railed alleyways that led to the immigration inspectors. With the help of interpreters, the inspectors would ask each immigrant a series of questions. What is your name? Nationality? Marital status? Occupation? Who paid the passage? Is that person in the United States? How much money do you have with you? Have you ever been in a prison or an almshouse? After 1917, all immigrants over the age of sixteen were required to demonstrate literacy in a language, with exemption for elderly relatives of legally admitted aliens or citizens. Often the inspector, who did not speak a foreign language, gave the immigrant a card with an instruction written in the immigrant's native tongue, such as "Scratch your right ear." Immigrants who did so were presumed to have read the card and to be literate.

Names were a source of puzzlement for the immigration inspectors. Not all immigrants could spell their names in English, and perplexed inspectors often recorded names as they sounded or occasionally took the liberty of shortening or "Americanizing" a name. There is no evidence that Immigration Bureau officers systematically changed newcomers' names, but some immigrants left Ellis Island with names their relatives would never recognize. Millions of Americans still bear these "Ellis Island" names. The story of Sean Ferguson, apocryphal perhaps, nevertheless illustrates the process by which an immigrant might acquire a new identity. A Russian Jew became so flustered by the impatient questioning of an inspector that when asked his name he sputtered, *"Shoyn fargesn"* (I forget already). The inspector, not understanding Yiddish, but hearing the words, welcomed "Sean Ferguson" to America. Members of the same family often emerged from Ellis Island with different surnames. The similar sound of the Ukrainian "G" and English "H" and an inspector's poor penmanship, left half of one Ukrainian family named Heskes, and the other half named Gesker.

Immigration officers also had to listen closely and use their imaginations to determine the newcomer's destination in America. Frequently, the only information that an immigrant woman or man might have was a crumpled scrap of paper upon which was scrawled an illegible address. Those headed for "Nugers" were fortunate if their inspector bothered to help them clarify where they hoped to go in New Jersey. Sometimes, a convenient substitute was provided by a frustrated inspector, merely complicating the newcomer's search for family or friends.

Of the 300 to 400 people per day who passed before immigration officers during peak years, 80 percent were admitted without difficulty. These fortunate ones returned to the first floor of the main building where they might be met by friends or relatives who accompanied them on the ferryboat to New York. Others went to the railroad ticket office located on Ellis Island, where they could purchase train tickets and await barges that would transport them to New Jersey railroad terminals for the last leg of their journey.

What of the unlucky 20 percent? Those not immediately admitted were detained on Ellis Island for various lengths of time, often in compartments created with wire, clearly visible to all other newcomers. Conditions were cramped, often unsanitary, and poorly ventilated. People slept in three-tiered steel bunks, set in long rows with narrow aisles between them. The space between tiers was about two feet and the air was muggy, especially on hot summer nights. Often the bunks became lice infested. Most of the people stopped by the inspectors were held for medical reasons. Some of the physically ill were hospitalized. About 1 percent of the detainees, who had readily detectable physical and mental abnormalities, were reexamined. A Board of Inquiry was presented with the medical report of these detainees, and this board made the final decision on each immigrant's admissibility. After 1903, boards of inquiry automatically excluded those immigrants diagnosed as unfit by medical personnel. However, medical personnel refused to sit on these boards. Physicians believed that their duty was medical diagnosis, not interpreting federal laws and regulations concerning eligibility for admission.

Families were often separated when one or more members were rejected. In such cases, private charitable organizations often intervened to help. If a child under eleven years old was rejected, the child's mother was encouraged by such organizations to return also. One worker for the Hebrew Immigrant Aid Society (HIAS) recalled how sad she and her colleagues were when "a little immigrant" had to go back and be treated "on the other side." Return passage was free, the same HIAS representative noted, because the shipping company was held responsible for delivering a sick immigrant, "But they (the companies) were not responsible to bring them back here to this country, so the poor father had to again struggle and save and put penny to penny."

Immigrants who were penniless but claimed to have relatives or friends who would defray their expenses until they found jobs were not immediately admitted. These immigrants, often as many as 10 percent of annual arrivals, were held briefly until funds from their sponsors were actually received by letter or telegram. Often a financially well-off relative or friend would be notified and come to Ellis Island to assist the newcomer. Women and children were those most frequently detained for inadequate funds. They were given a place to sleep in the detention dormitory and urged to contact by letter those responsible for them. If no one arrived within a week, the detainees could apply to one of the many immigrant aid organizations for assistance, or accept deportation.

Known criminals, those suspected of being contract laborers, or those considered likely to become public charges received immediate hearings. By the 1890s, a federal law had been passed to protect the jobs and wage rates of American workers from the competition of foreign workers recruited in Europe and imported by American businessmen. A tricky question asked of each immigrant concerned employment status. The person who confessed to a lack of job prospects risked deportation. Immigrants learned from the sad experiences of others to say only that they had "good prospects" or "a relative's promise" of a job. If declared unfit for admission, such immigrants were returned to their port of departure within two weeks.

While the statistics on detentions are fragmentary, the existing records suggest that a very modest percentage of immigrants were turned back at Ellis Island, despite rumors and anxieties generated by the inspection process. The total number of detentions in all categories was often as high as 20 percent on an annual basis, but over half of those detained were held only temporarily for minor health problems or until funds arrived. Only about 1 percent of the annual total were hospitalized and rarely did Board-of-Inquiry detentions exceed 10 percent. In 1907, a peak immigration year, there were 195,540 detentions as compared to a total of 1,004,756 admissions. Of those stopped, 121,737 were temporarily detained, 64,510 were held for specific inquiry, and 9,203 were hospitalized. Board-of-Inquiry exclusions constituted approximately 15 percent of the total cases heard. The average individual immigrant arriving at Ellis Island need not have feared. Throughout the peak period of immigration, exclusion averaged 2 percent to 3 percent annually. Admission was the rule and rejection the exception.

Occasionally, corrupt immigration officials engaged in exploitation. In the summer of 1901, a scandal erupted involving the issuance of fraudulent naturalization papers that permitted those who could afford a $5 fee to land directly from their ships and bypass Ellis Island. This and other outrages caused President Theodore Roosevelt to appoint William Williams, a tough young

Wall Street lawyer and former government employee, Commissioner of Immigration at Ellis Island. Williams dressed his own agents—many of them friends from Wall Street invited for the occasion—as immigrants, and allowed them to undergo the full inspection procedure to smoke out the dishonest or inefficient. As a result, many of the concessionaires bilking the newcomers were ousted. A lucrative contract to exchange foreign currency was taken from a firm of swindlers and later given to the highly reputable American Express Company, which exchanged currency and sold railroad tickets.

Immigrants were as often cheated by those purporting to be their friends as they were by immigration officials. Shyster lawyers often took advantage of the formal examination procedures, the boards of inquiry, and the increasingly strict criteria for admission to gouge immigrants of their savings, even victimizing those of their own ethnic group. The Immigration Bureau ruled that lawyers could charge no more than $10 to represent a detained client at a hearing, but abuses were frequent. Dishonest merchants and con men also hoped to dupe the new arrivals before they left Ellis Island. Criminals dressed as police officers or immigration inspectors sold newcomers phony licenses and official papers, which they insisted the immigrant could not do without.

In response, social reformers and religious missionaries maintained a constant presence on Ellis Island to protect bewildered foreigners from scoundrels. Most missionaries represented a particular Protestant denomination or a nondenominational benevolent society. The Salvation Army, the Women's Home Missionary Society, and the New York Bible Society were among those represented. In 1907, the Industrial Committee of the Y.M.C.A. established a comprehensive immigration program and placed agents in major foreign ports and on board many ships as well as on Ellis Island. All societies were investigated by the federal government before being permitted to station representatives at the immigration depot. Only upon the recommendation of the Commissioner of Immigration did aid societies receive permission to visit detention rooms and interview detained immigrants. Representatives of these organizations were prohibited from securing the admittance

of an alien through misrepresentation to inspectors at boards of inquiry and were forbidden to accept remuneration from immigrants
for their services.

Many of the denominational societies were also warned not to
attempt to convert beleaguered travelers. The American Tract
Society was cautioned by immigration officials not to force Christian tracts, written in Hebrew or in Yiddish, on east European Jews
landing at Ellis Island. One Commissioner of Immigration explained the rationale for the warning: "A great many of our immigrants are Hebrews, who are on their way from persecution by one
style of Christians, and when they have Christian tracts—printed
in Hebrew—put in their hands, apparently with the approval of the
United States government, they wonder what is going to happen to
them there."

The ethnic organizations made certain that the insults suffered
by the members of their respective groups were brought to the attention of immigration officials for appropriate action. Such organizations as St. Raphael's Society, the Society for the Protection of
Italian Immigrants, the Polish Catholic Union, and the Hebrew
Immigrant Aid Society (HIAS) were highly respected by immigration officials, not only for their vigilance but for their active assistance.

The activities of HIAS workers suggest how such ethnic societies served their own. Men and women wearing blue caps em-
broidered with the letters HIAS in Yiddish met the ferryboats landing at Ellis Island. They distributed information sheets printed in
Yiddish to Jewish immigrants which explained the inspection procedures. They eased the fears of the anxious with warm smiles and
advice on how to answer questions. And the immigrants asked
them many questions: Should one lie or tell the truth? Should one
claim poverty or show one's money? Would the immigration inspectors expect bribes such as those Russian officials had demanded? Society agents urged the immigrants to be honest and in-
terceded with immigration officials so that the nervous, confused
immigrant might have adequate opportunity to provide the correct
information.

HIAS prosecuted swindlers who tried to exploit the naive and ran an employment bureau that remained open "every night except Friday." Newspapers would be brought by HIAS workers to Ellis Island on the ferry and all-night staff members would work to match each immigrant to a job advertisement. By World War I, HIAS had grown from a small, welfare society financed by a handful of benefactors, into a large organization with a nation-wide membership, worldwide affiliates, and offices in Washington, D.C., and all major port cities. Still, until the tide of east European Jewish immigration ebbed in the 1920s, Ellis Island remained a major focus of HIAS activities.

If most immigrants were admitted to the United States, why were the hours on Ellis Island so often remembered, even by those who passed unhindered, as the worst experience of their lives? The testimony of those who endured the "Island of Tears" and are now Americans suggests that they were not timorous but had good reason for being unsure of themselves upon arrival. First, this was the initial official contact between the newcomers and America. The immigrants, already exhausted by their journey, were often confused by the procedures and intimidated by the cold, unfamiliar manner of immigration officials who did not speak their language or share their past. Second, many immigrants associated this new set of uniformed men with those whom they had feared in their home countries. This antipathy toward government officials was part of the emotional baggage borne by many new arrivals. They wondered whether these American gatekeepers expected bribes as had those in their native lands; they had no idea what limits were set on the agents' authority. Third, the detention of some immigrants and the separation of other families moved even those not affected. And finally, many experienced a wrenching moment of panic that life was the same everywhere, that the hazards of their homeland were present in America; perhaps they had journeyed halfway around the globe for nothing.

Viewing their treatment on Ellis Island through a veil of past abuses and immediate anxieties, most immigrants perceived themselves to have been treated more harshly than they actually were.

One might also speculate that immigrants who recalled Ellis Island fifty years or more after being there remembered it as more brutal than it seemed even at the time because to do so enhanced their own achievement in surmounting the final obstacle between themselves and America.

Millions of men and women who had made the conscious decision to depart for America arrived on Ellis Island anxious to enter, but unprepared for the final hurdle. Even here, however, shrewd and resourceful migrants, though unfamiliar with the language, culture, and law of the United States, seized the initiative. They asked questions of those who had been through the process before; sought the advice of those who represented immigrant aid societies; and, in general, refused to capitulate to their own fears of America and the strange greeting it tendered. As they left Ellis Island the immigrants could congratulate themselves. They had survived their first encounter with American officialdom and gained valuable experience in coping with their new home.

III

The confusion of Ellis Island behind them, migrants faced a myriad of fresh decisions that would shape their lives in the United States. A first choice concerned where they would live and work in this strange, new country. Many newcomers congregated in cities, some never leaving the port city in which they landed. Unlike earlier immigrants, the latest migrants from Europe soon found that their own skills and preferences, as well as the burgeoning state of American industrial capitalism, combined to make cities attractive. However, many newcomers from Latin America, Asia, and Canada still found their way to America's rich farming soil.

Historian Walter Nugent has observed that the United States held two advantages over its rivals for attracting newcomers: its vast size and the "large area of cheap, accessible land governed by land laws that encouraged smallholding." The migrants from northwestern Europe arriving in mid-nineteenth-century America came to a rural society of farms and small towns. German and

Scandinavian immigrants often came with the minimum capital necessary to buy inexpensive tracts of prime farmland in Iowa, Wisconsin, Minnesota, and other states of the north-central United States. For those unable or unwilling to farm, new towns and cities of the West had provided abundant markets for peddlers, small merchants, or artisans. The Irish, most of whom had arrived with little money, capitalized on their brawn. They labored for low wages, building the canals and railroads linking the farms of the hinterland with the markets and ports in the East. By the end of the century, however, American society had taken a new turn. America's workbenches were no longer mostly in Europe, where Thomas Jefferson had preferred them to remain, but in its own cities.

The metamorphosis of a rural, agrarian society into an urban, industrial one had begun before the Civil War, but the pace of change had quickened considerably by the end of the nineteenth century. The inexpensive land that had attracted earlier immigrants was no longer available in abundance. Still, there were Chinese, Japanese, and Mexican agricultural laborers who labored under the hot sun of the American West while dreaming of one day owning some of the land on which they worked or saving sufficiently to buy land in their home countries upon returning. Nor was there a need for vast quantities of laborers, whether skilled or unskilled, in the towns of rural America. However, such labor was needed in the growing industrial centers of the East and Middle West and in the mine fields that yielded the natural resources which nourished the city's factories.

The first to heed the siren call of the city were rural Americans unsettled by an agricultural depression in the 1870s and attracted by the sheen of urban life. The depopulation of the countryside was especially noticeable in the Middle West and the North Atlantic states. Between 1880 and 1890, more than half the towns in Iowa and Illinois declined in population, yet both states gained substantially in their overall number of inhabitants. In New England, 932 out of 1,502 towns, including two-thirds of those in Maine and New Hampshire and three-fourths of those in Vermont, declined in population during the 1880s. However, the region actually gained 20 percent in total population through urban growth.

Thousands of farms were abandoned and houses left to decay. Farmers who left the country for the city were met there by the new immigrants, who also hoped to find a niche in urban America. By the 1890s, young African Americans, the daughters and sons of sharecroppers and tenant farmers, joined the internal migration from country to city. In flight from the mounting debt that tied their parents to another person's land and patterns of racial segregation and disenfranchisement, the children and grandchildren of former slaves headed to the cities of the North and Midwest.

Some newcomers hoped to take advantage of the abundance of cheap and available land in the United States. However, many European immigrant groups, including the Italians, Slavs, and Greeks, rejected agrarianism and consciously chose to settle in cities after arrival. Oscar Handlin claimed that immigrants missed working the land, over which they "once bent in piety." But later research disputes Handlin's contention. Joseph Lopreato, a student of Italian settlement patterns, suggests that their Old-World experience left most Italian immigrants feeling that farming was a punishment, for both stomach and soul. In southern Italy, the contadino's (villager's) dependence on agriculture had, according to Lopreato, "reduced him nearly to the status of the donkey and goat." Many newcomers considered themselves finally liberated from the soil and vowed never to return to it.

Efforts to divert the flow of Italian immigrants from congested urban areas proved largely unsuccessful. The United States government, the Italian government, and a variety of state governments and private agencies encouraged the development of agricultural settlements for Italian immigrants in Texas, Arkansas, Alabama, Mississippi, and Louisiana. However, with few notable exceptions, these experiments failed. The gentry in Italy had not farmed and neither would the transplanted Italian farm worker. Even those Italian agrarians such as the Italian cotton farmers of the Mississippi Delta, who grew cotton for the powerful Leroy Percy and his family, tended not to remain in farming. Wealth, power, prestige, and all worldly comforts were associated with a nonagrarian lifestyle. John W. Briggs (*An Italian Passage,* 1978) found that those Italians with the will and resources to emigrate came largely from "the upper levels of the working classes in the town and from the middle range of agriculturists." Though his data are limited to the emigrants of only three communities—Termini, Serradifalco, and Villa Vallelonga—they are nevertheless suggestive. Italians already removed from the soil may well have viewed farming in America as a step backward socially. Although some such as the Gallo family became prosperous winegrowers, most Italians sought urban jobs and dreamed of returning home with copious savings. Italian immigrants enjoyed the safety and support of residence in an Italian urban enclave, and many regarded a move west or south as impractical because they intended their stay in America to be temporary.

Polish immigrants scattered across three dozen states and thousands of American communities. Most Poles were concentrated in the industrial cities of the Great Lakes Basin—from New York to Illinois—but at least one-third of Polish immigrants lived in small, rural towns and villages. The American Polonia, as the immigrants referred to their presence in the United States, was not a tightly knit geographical entity. Wherever they lived, most Poles planned only to remain long enough to earn high wages and return to Poland. As John Bukowczyk (*And My Children Did Not Know Me, A History of Polish America,* 1987) observes, "The temporary migrants among them chose to forego risky business ventures or low-paid white collar jobs even though they may have offered greater mobility potential. Instead they elected steady, well-paid blue-collar work." Therefore, most preferred the higher salaries offered in the coal mines of Scranton, Pennsylvania; the stockyards of Chicago, Illinois; or the steelworks of Buffalo, New York. Only after many Poles settled permanently in their American homes, did some seek to buy land for cultivation. With little capital and rising prices of land, those who preferred agriculture often became truck farmers serving local markets.

The character of Polish urbanism was often derived from noneconomic priorities, especially Catholicism. According to Bukowczyk, "Catholic to the core, they valued humility, prayer, and other-worldly rewards." Since the vast majority of Polish immigrants were Roman Catholics, they tried to organize a parish as soon as possible after arrival and live in close proximity to it. Poles themselves often called their communities by parish names.

In Polish, adding the suffix *owo* to a parish name formed a community name. Thus, in Chicago the Polish community near St. Stanislaus Kosta Church became the *Stanislawowo* or "St. Stanislaus District."

As did the majority of Italians and Poles, most Greeks settled in urban areas, either in New England mill towns or large northern cities such as New York and Chicago, where they worked in factories or found jobs as busboys, dishwashers, bootblacks, and peddlers. A somewhat less popular alternative was to go west. By 1907, there were already between thirty and forty thousand Greeks west of the Mississippi. In the Rocky Mountain region, Greek workers became the miners and smelters of Colorado and Utah. In California especially, but in other states as well, they worked on railroad gangs. Fewer Greeks settled in the South; only one in fifteen settled in one of the old Confederacy's eleven states. The South offered little industrial employment or commercial opportunity, so Greeks going there frequently carried with them sufficient capital for a restaurant, fruit store, or shoe-shine parlor. Greeks created economic opportunity for their fellow immigrants, such as in Tarpon Springs, Florida, where John Cocoris and his brothers organized a sponge business. They brought 500 Greeks from the Aegean and Dodecanese Islands to dive, hook, clean, sort, string, clip, and pack. Tarpon Springs remained America's sponge center and a Greek mecca until after World War II. However, most Greek immigrants cared little for sponges and even less for lives of rural isolation, choosing a city as their American address, while they saved for the day when they could return to Greece.

Most European immigrants, then, rejected agriculture and rural life in America, at least initially. These immigrants consciously chose to remain in the port city where they disembarked or to journey inland to another urban area, often becoming links in a chain migration that reunited family or friends from abroad in an ethnic enclave, where they could create a new world on their own terms.

Mexican immigrants often began as agricultural laborers before migrating to cities. Many thousands crossed the border initially to engage in agricultural labor, often migrant labor. By the late 1920s, one-third of the labor force of the Imperial Valley was of Mexican origin, and the trend spread northward in the state to the San Joaquin Valley. In this era Mexicans formed the largest single ethnic group among California farm workers. Historian George J. Sanchez (*Becoming Mexican American, 1993*) observes that many of those emigrating had already moved several times in pursuit of higher wages and were living in towns near the border such as Ciudad Juarez, Nogales, or Nuevo Laredo prior to migrating across it. However, working in the countryside did not always mean living in the countryside. According to Sanchez, "Many farmworkers in the 1910s and 1920s could live in the city [Los Angeles] and take Red Line train cars to work in the fields." At times, Mexican workers left their families in San Antonio or El Paso while working part of the year in the "steel mills of Indiana, the auto plants of Michigan, or the agricultural fields of Kansas or Colorado." Anxious to cease the migratory life, increasing numbers of Mexicans sought permanent urban employment in Los Angeles. Those who had worked on railroad lines found Los Angeles to be a major depot with ample facilities for railroad repair. Mexican immigrants, too, often found urban life appealing.

Many of the urban hardships immigrants suffered initially were also shared by those native-born Americans who came to the city during the late nineteenth and early twentieth centuries. Most American cities were ill-equipped to sustain the vast multitudes of new residents—foreign and native born—arriving annually. Transportation, housing, sanitation, and health facilities constructed in a preindustrial age for smaller populations were inadequate to meet the needs of burgeoning urban populations. In New York City, the foreign-born population skyrocketed from 567,812 in 1870 to 902,643 in 1890, yet declined from 38 percent of the total population to 36 percent. By 1910, the figure was almost 2 million (still only 41 percent of the total). Quite obviously, the city was being filled just as quickly from the hinterland as from the docks.

The strain placed on city services and facilities by these new urban dwellers was unanticipated. When the new immigration began in the 1880s, residents of major American port cities depended

on facilities that had been planned and built before the Civil War
and were already outdated. In *Boss Tweed's New York* (1965),
Seymour Mandelbaum's description of city streets rendered im-
passable by the sheer volume of traffic suggests that even the
nation's largest city proved antiquated in design:

No one moved above the streets, no one below them. Vehicles of every
description and function crowded together in the same narrow thorough-
fares. There were no limited-access highways, no special truck routes. No
Manhattan rail connections served the docks. Cargo and passengers were
forced into the same struggling line of movement. Wooden planks split
under the pressure of a business traffic for which they were never intended. Cobblestones were torn loose faster than they could be replaced.

As the immigrants, fresh from the docks themselves, found
their way uptown, they needed only to glance at their shoes or take
deep breaths to realize that America had yet to master the problems of densely populated industrial cities. Year round filth and, in
winter, ice and snow accumulated on city streets. Not all streets
were paved, and those that were surfaced were cleaned by private
companies under contract to the city; when funds were in short
supply, streets were neglected for weeks at a time. Sewage presented an even greater problem. Prior to 1865, city sewers were a
patchwork of pipelines set down by private property owners without any central coordination. By the end of the century, these pipes
were too narrow to handle the increasing load. Those improperly
laid often burst. Mains opened into the rivers at many points,
rather than at a few central spots. In the older parts of cities, where
immigrants usually found their first homes, clogged mains frequently caused sewers to overflow, flooding the streets with waste.
After a heavy rainstorm, city streets with improper drainage became little lakes of brown mud and slime.

Tired of wading through mud or of being jostled on congested
streets, the newly arrived immigrants might board streetcars. In
the late nineteenth century, horse-drawn vehicles were rapidly being replaced by electric trolley cars, while in New York a vast elevated and underground light-rail system was under construction.
Prior to consolidation and public financing in many cities, streetcars were owned and operated by private companies. Competitive

lines crowded close to one another along high-demand routes that promised high profits. Without the planning of municipal government whole areas of the city were left isolated from one another by a chaotic distribution of lines. Traveling at four to six miles per hour, streetcars hardly provided rapid transit, even if a rider was lucky enough to catch one going in just the right direction.

Whether they walked or rode about the city, the new immigrants' first priority was to find food and shelter. Those settling in New York, Chicago, or any other large city would not necessarily have found their first American home in one of the towering tenements that have come to symbolize the immigrant experience. Despite an acute shortage of housing for the urban poor reaching back decades, tenements were not built in large numbers until the early 1880s. Initially, single-family wooden houses were converted into apartment buildings. Some of the larger houses became the first urban tenements.

New immigrants, such as the Slavs and the Greeks, who often labored in mines or on construction sites, lived in nearby shacks that soon became part of scattered shanty towns. According to Victor R. Greene in *The Slavic Community on Strike* (1968), permanent residents in the anthracite coal country of Pennsylvania referred to the group of shacks where the Polish and Lithuanian miners lived as the Slavic mining "patch." Shacks in many ways resembled the peasant cottages the immigrant had left behind in Poland. Crowded within were the owner, the family, and frequently several male boarders, who wanted the least expensive lodgings. Lucky was the immigrant who found such lodging and did not have to sleep outdoors, as did many unable to find affordable shelter.

The less fortunate were frequently exploited by non-Slavic landlords, frequently Irish or English, who crammed as many as eleven people into one-room cellars, eleven feet square; or twenty-one into a two-storied stable, sixteen by fourteen; or six men into a room without ventilation measuring only fourteen by nine feet. Improvement came when the family could buy or rent land for their own one-room shanty. Shanties were built with whatever material was available, such as railroad ties, timber, driftwood, and empty tin cans. An addition or a second story might later be built for boarders.

The tenement was born of a desire to squeeze greater profits from limited space. As historian Moses Rischin (*The Promised City, New York's Jews, 1870–1914,* 1962) noted, "New York's division of city lots into standard rectangular plots, 25 feet by 100 feet deep made decent human accommodation impossible." Builders found themselves unable to allow for proper light and ventilation and still provide profitable housing to meet the great demand created by the new immigration. The result was the construction of blocks and blocks of dumbbell-style tenements.

At first glance, the tall tenements appeared to loom romantically against the sky. Novelist and social critic William Dean Howells (*Impressions and Experiences,* 1896) admired the structures from afar but changed his mind after entering one:

> But to be in it, and not have the distance, is to inhale the stenches of the neglected street, and to catch the yet fouler and dreadfuller poverty smell which breathes from the open doorways. . . . It is to see the work-worn look of mothers, the squalor of the babies, the haggish ugliness of the old women, and the slovenly frowsiness of the young girls.

Even those who, like Howells, saw romance in tenement silhouettes, soon agreed with the author who said that, "had the foul fiend designed these great barricades they could not have been more villainously arranged to avoid any chance of ventilation. . . ."

Each end of the six- or seven-story, dumbbell-shaped structure was composed of four apartments to a floor, two on either side of a separating corridor. The front apartments generally contained four rooms, while the back apartments had three each. Only a single room in each apartment received direct light and air from the street or from the required ten feet of yard space at the back of every tenement. Often there were two stores on the ground floor with a small apartment behind each. These rooms received little light but adequate air from windows facing air shafts. The air shafts, five feet wide and sixty feet deep, separated the tenement buildings. Toilets were communal, four per floor, located off the air shafts. The lack of sufficient toilets forced residents away from home to use vacant lots or, in the evening, the sides of wagons. Unsurprisingly, the streets stank, and summers were especially unbearable. Tenement dwellers sought to escape the heat of their apartments and the smells of the street below by moving mattresses onto roofs and fire escapes.

When fire did occur, the closely packed tenements became death-traps. Of the 250 recorded fatalities in Manhattan fires between 1902 and 1909, one-third were Lower East Side victims of tenement fires. Often families cramped for space had cut off their own paths of escape by piling furniture and belongings onto fire escapes.

Most families could not afford the privacy of their own three- or four-room apartment, but took in lodgers or boarders who required little space and made the monthly rent of $10 to $20 more affordable. Still, the precariousness of the immigrants' economic conditions often ended in an eviction. Some years, over 10,000 eviction notices were issued to residents of Manhattan's Lower East Side.

Regardless of the squalid and dangerous conditions they afforded residents, tenements of the dumbbell variety provided landlords with handsome annual profits. Immigrants, leery of contact with authorities, permitted landlords to blatantly ignore health and housing laws. Not until municipal governments, pressured by urban reformers, outlawed dumbbell tenements were some abuses corrected. In New York, the Tenement House Law of 1901 established new guidelines for builders. All new buildings had to have windows opening a minimum of twelve feet from the building opposite. Each unit had to have its own toilet and running water, clear access to fire escapes, and sturdy staircases. Older buildings had to undergo alterations, at least to the extent of installing modern toilet facilities. A Tenement House Department was organized in New York to enforce the new legislation, but inefficiency and corruption plagued its operation. At best, this legislation was an acknowledgment of the threat tenements posed to the health and safety of occupants, most of whom were immigrants.

Urban immigrants, staring through smudged windows to the air shaft wall, rarely had a balanced diet, often scarcely any food at all. The newly landed immigrants found American food much too expensive. Their diet was frequently heavy with starches and fats, and low on protein. Italians ate bread, potatoes, some eggs, fish, and pasta. Slavs and east European Jews subsisted for days on herring, bread, and tea, with potatoes, and cheap meats such as lung among other staples. Greeks ate sausage with rice, potatoes, eggs, lentils, or greens during the week. Only on occasional Sundays did they enjoy the luxury of soups or a roast. In *The Bitter Cry of the Children* (1906), reformer John Spargo observed that, among some immigrants, long periods without nutritious food caused children to develop stomachs "too weak by reason of chronic hunger and malnutrition to stand good and nutritious food."

The clamoring demand for inexpensive food tempted some businessmen to cut costs by ignoring health standards. Upton Sinclair's novel, *The Jungle* (1905), chronicles the exposure of Jurgis Rudkis, a Lithuanian immigrant, to the exploitation and depravity of Chicago's meat-packing industry. However, the food industry also offered honest prosperity to those catering to their own ethnic groups' preferences or ritual necessities. Food stores often broadened their stock to include items geared toward attracting the patronage of specific immigrants.

Migrants adjusted their diets even as they accommodated themselves to the rigors of life in the American communities in which they settled. They had already chosen to leave their homes and families in search of greater prosperity. They had survived the trauma of departure and the trials of the journey, using the ruses and resources at their command to surmount natural and man-made obstacles. Whether they had embarked from European ports or the West Indies, the sea and Ellis Island's inspectors were behind them, but much remained to test their fortitude and perseverance. The same was true of those who crossed the border on foot from Mexico or Canada.

Many newcomers returned to the land in the United States because that was how they had always made their living. But, with the United States in the midst of rapid industrialization and increasing urbanization, newcomers as well as natives found in cities the most plentiful opportunities for economic advancement— but there was a price. For immigrants the cost was often physical deprivation and psychological strain as they pitted their sagacity against the jarring reality of a strange, sometimes hostile environment. Appetizing food and affordable housing were scarce in congested cities designed for the smaller populations of a preindustrial order. It was the economic magnet of employment and good wages that had drawn them to American cities, or to the towns near mills and mines. Occupational choices were not always in slavish synchronization with the labor market's cycle of supply and demand, alone. It was often the particular ethnic backgrounds and Old-World experiences of individual immigrants that would shape their choice of jobs and the character of their neighborhoods within the broader context set by industrial capitalism's ups and downs.

CHAPTER THREE

Smokestacks and Pushcarts: Work and Mobility in Industrial America

In the last decades of the nineteenth century and the first decades of the twentieth, millions of immigrants came to the shores of the United States searching for economic prosperity. They risked the journey's perils and an alien environment to reap material abundance and opportunity that were beyond expectation in their countries of origin. Some hoped to stay only long enough to collect what they needed to prosper upon their return home. Others would not even consider repatriation, hoping to climb high on the ladder of success and suspecting that their best chance for enjoying what they earned and making still more was in the United States.

When the American economy was growing and times were prosperous, native-born Americans welcomed, if not embraced, immigrant workers and their families. Even when times turned temporarily bad, faith in the economy's future caused those who understood American dependence on immigrant labor to proclaim their country the land of opportunity for the foreign born. But during an economic down-turn that stretched from the autumn of 1907 through the following year, 717,814 aliens returned to their homelands, almost as many as had arrived during the same period, 724,112. Acknowledging the disappointment that led to the exodus, a *New York Times* editorialist blamed inflated expectations, willingly admitting that American labor agents in their zeal to recruit newcomers may have stoked those expectations, exaggerating the benefits and rewards of the American workplace. Nevertheless, the *Times'* scribe concluded, "We need immigrants as much as ever and this is still a land of wide opportunities."

Not all agreed. Some critics of immigrant labor complained that newcomers took jobs away from American workers or reduced wage scales by accepting lower salaries than native-born workers. Others argued that immigrant labor was inefficient because newcomers seemed careless about their equipment and even their own bodies. In a 1913 article entitled "Our Expensive Cheap Labor," social critic Arno Dosch wrote that the Slavic workers he had observed, "lacked the intelligence and initiative either to avoid the ordinary dangers of rough labor or to keep in efficient health; and their employers have to pay the bills for teaching them." Dosch deplored industrial exploitation of immigrants, but concluded, "If they [the immigrants] come through their experience and develop into American citizens it is through no effort of their own, but through the enlightened self-interest of their employers. Comparatively few of these people ever get more than a glimmering of American ideals."

If some Americans were troubled by the foreignness of the immigrant labor force upon whom the country was increasingly dependent, their disappointment was no greater than that of the newcomers themselves. While few immigrants expected America's streets to be paved with gold, neither had they expected to pave those streets with their own back-breaking labor. Few experienced rapid upward socioeconomic mobility. Frustration abounded. For most immigrants the American saga was not one of instantaneous rags to riches. Instead each immigrant confronted the demands of industrial capitalism by drawing on his or her group's experience and their own individual ambitions and capabilities. Even for those without capital or skills, there were opportunities. Discriminatory barriers fabricated by nativist prejudices were never completely absent. Still, newcomers improved their own lot or paved the way for their children's prosperity with the individual economic choices they made, decisions nonetheless bounded by capitalism's law of supply and demand.

Upward occupational mobility, acquiring increasingly higher skilled jobs that generally pay higher wages, is a yardstick historians have frequently used to measure the economic success of newcomers. Scholarly studies suggest there was little occupational mobility among newcomers at the end of the nineteenth or beginning of the twentieth century. Josef Barton's analysis of data on Italians, Romanians, and Slovaks in Cleveland between 1870 and 1890 indicates that a mere 14 of every 100 unskilled Italian blue-collar workers moved to a higher occupational level during their working lives. Even in opportunity-rich New York City, only 14 percent of Italians who were unskilled laborers rose to white-collar status, while another 10 percent acquired sufficient expertise to qualify as skilled labor. For Mexicans in the same era, the data indicate even less mobility. A study in Santa Barbara suggests that less than 5 percent were upwardly mobile. However, had they not at least believed in the possibility of improvement, immigrants would have hardly continued coming to the United States.

Historian John Bodnar observes that "While significant occupational mobility was not normally part of the immigrant experience in industrial America, some individuals and groups did better than others. . . ." Why? Premigration skills and where newcomers settled could make a difference. Especially crucial was whether or not newcomers shared their new neighbors' definition of economic improvement. Economic behavior accepted as appropriate by natives of agricultural societies with seasonal, family-oriented patterns of work was often perceived as laziness by Americans. Upward mobility, then, cannot be divorced from its cultural context among immigrant peoples.

Economically ambitious immigrants sought out others in their ethnic group who shared this emphasis on upward mobility. They often created mutual benevolent societies to generate economic assistance among themselves. Regional organizations of Japanese and Chinese immigrants, respectively, were often the means whereby Asian immigrants progressed economically, drawing upon the advice, encouragement, and even capital of other group members. These voluntary societies were often the mechanism for reconciling New-World needs and Old-World economic patterns. As immigrants devised strategies for scaling the peaks of economic success, their struggle to succeed became an important chapter in the larger narrative of American capitalism.

I

European and Canadian immigrants generally entered the American economy through the factories and mines of the northeastern United States, the hub of America's industry. Eighty percent of these immigrants remained in the Northeast. Their settlement patterns formed a triangle: New England at the apex, with the southeastern point at Washington, D.C., and the southwestern point at St. Louis. Two-thirds of all European and Canadian immigrants could be found in New York, the New England states, Pennsylvania, and New Jersey, while substantial numbers also went west to Illinois and Ohio. While Asian and Latino immigrants migrated to the same eastern states, the majority of these newcomers settled in California and other western states. Few immigrants ventured into the southern states, since industry was still scarce there, and job competition against low-paid white and African-American labor in field and mill was substantial. Fear of discrimination dissuaded dark-complexioned immigrants from settling in the South, except for the more cosmopolitan port cities such as New Orleans and Charleston.

The major cities of the North—New York, Philadelphia, Baltimore, Boston, and Chicago—were attractive to newcomers. Jobs for the unskilled were plentiful in these industrial centers. The presence of relatives and friends because of chain migration patterns often helped newcomers adjust quickly to the daily rhythms of urban industrial life.

Caroline Golab, in *Immigrant Destinations* (1978), pointed out that these older cities remained centers of commerce into the late nineteenth and early twentieth centuries, and "continued to support what had once been the nation's handicrafts and household industries—the making of clothes, shoes, silverware, wooden toys and the like." Thus, there were opportunities for skilled artisans and craftsmen as well as unskilled laborers. In turn, the high concentrations of population in these cities provided a market for small merchants.

Some older cities actually became cities of immigrants. According to the census records of 1910, 75 percent of the populations of New York, Chicago, Detroit, Cleveland, and Boston consisted of immigrants or their children. Many of these were the offspring of earlier settlers such as the Irish and Germans, but most were newcomers from southern and eastern Europe or Canada. Foreign enclaves of sizable proportion were also located in Philadelphia and Providence—cities linked to the nation's expanding industrial network by rail. In the West, the port city of San Francisco was particularly popular with immigrants, especially those from China and Japan. By 1916, over 72 percent of the population in that city regarded a foreign language as their primary tongue. Meanwhile in the West, labor from Mexico was transforming Los Angeles. Historian Ricardo Romo (*East Los Angeles, History of a Barrio*, 1983) describes that city in the early twentieth century as having become "an exporter of manufactured goods, processor of agricultural products, importer of machinery and technology, supplier of labor, and distributor of financial capital." This economic transformation demanded skilled and unskilled labor that Mexico supplied, much as it had been supplying agricultural and railroad workers for decades.

Newly arriving immigrant groups concentrated in regions with the opportunities that matched the capabilities and cultural preferences of their members. One scholar, Monika Glettler (*Pittsburgh-Wien-Budapest*, 1980), estimated that 25 percent of the world's 3 million Slovaks came to America before 1913, four-fifths of them seeking work in Pennsylvania's mines or mills. Various other Slavic groups settled in the mining and industrial regions of Ohio, Illinois, Michigan, New York, as well as large areas of western Pennsylvania. They were predominant in the labor force of Chicago's slaughterhouses and worked on construction sites throughout the Northeast. According to one observer, the Slavs were considered desirable workers because of "their habit of silent submission, their amenability to discipline, and their willingness to work long hours and overtime without a murmur." The *Pittsburgh Leader* testified that the east European immigrant made "a better slave than the American."

Victor R. Greene (*The Slavic Community On Strike,* 1968), a student of the Slavic community in the anthracite coal region of Pennsylvania, suggests that such observations were based on a thorough misconception of the goals and values of these immigrants. The Slavs were "birds of passage" who viewed their stay in America as a brief visit, only long enough to earn money with which to purchase land in their native countries. As a group, Slavs were the most physically robust of the new immigrants, willing to tolerate the wretched working conditions of the mines in exchange for higher wages than other industries would pay. Emily Balch, who studied the Slavs in 1910, noted that even among the unskilled who spoke little English, miners were paid better than mill workers, receiving $2.40 to $3.00 for eight hours in the Pittsburgh mines as compared to $2.28 to $2.41 for a twelve-hour day in the mills.

Slavic laborers clung to the belief they would return home even after they had, in fact, become permanent residents. One Polish immigrant recalled that at the beginning of this century her parents had left her and her siblings in Poland when they went to work in America, "They both came with the idea that they're both gonna make a little money and go back, finish that new house. And of course we were there. . . ." However, even as they talked of return, a growing family and other circumstances kept her parents in America. "But the children kept comin' every twenty months here; then the war (World War I) broke out, so they stayed. . . ." (June Namias, ed., *First Generation,* 1978). Historians have often mistakenly assessed Slavic behavior as if the Slavs always knew they would never return home, rather than from the perspective that the Slavs had of their condition at a given time. The change in Slavic reaction to unionization, suggests a shift in perspective. Slavs resisted unions as long as they saw themselves as transient. However, once they realized they would be staying, they became amenable to organization. Historian John J. Bukowczyk, summarized the Polish workers' perspective as "Peasant to the bone, they treasured security, stability, and steady work. Such people yearned neither for money, status nor power in the 'land of opportunity.' What they sought was contentment in the things they prized: family, faith and fatherland." Those Slavs who arrived with capital elected to purchase or rent small plots of land in the Northeast or Midwest. About one-third of the Poles arriving in the United States engaged in truck farming in these regions. On New York's Long Island, Polish truck farmers grew tomatoes and other vegetables. In the Connecticut Valley, they cultivated tobacco, onions, and asparagus; and in the north central Midwest, corn and wheat.

Like the Slavs, many Italian immigrants planned to be birds of passage and acquire enough money to return to their home villages with a measure of status and wealth. Males often arrived in large numbers in the early spring, finding jobs on construction gangs and living sparsely until the late fall. They spent the winter months in Italy, returning to America the next spring. Families came over later, once a little money had been accumulated or when it was apparent that being strangers in the United States was preferable to being political and social peons in the Mezzogiorno.

Arriving with strong backs, few skills, and little or no capital, most Italians turned to manual labor wherever they settled. In New York, Italian labor built the subways and bridges linking the boroughs. In 1897, over 75 percent of the workers on New York City construction projects were Italian. They rolled cigars by hand in Florida. They mined coal in Pennsylvania and Illinois. They groomed vineyards in California. On the prairies they laid the track linking coast to coast. Though many worked in factories, especially in New England textile mills and New York garment factories, most Italian males preferred working outdoors. Those Italian women who joined the workforce took jobs as factory operatives.

Josef Barton's study of Italians, Romanians, and Slovaks in Cleveland (*Peasants and Strangers,* 1975) suggests that those immigrants who had developed skills as artisans or merchants in their home culture adapted most easily to urban environments in the United States. Barton observed that among Italians, social background prior to emigration "strongly influenced both their first job and their subsequent work experience." Italian immigrants had not all been peasants or fishermen. Those from certain social milieux were better prepared than others to enter America's industrialized economy. Almost half of the artisans traced by Barton, for example, entered skilled positions after emigration to the United States and an additional 40 percent found their first jobs in white-collar occupations. Moreover, artisans experienced the most important long-term gains. Twenty years after their arrival in Cleveland, almost two-thirds of all Italian artisans studied by Barton were middle class. Laborers, peasants, and their sons had much greater difficulty transforming themselves into prosperous Americans.

Italians who had been laborers in Italy often retained old work habits and preferences in their new American environment. They sought jobs with steady hours and a set salary, not jobs offering rapid advancement at the price of irregular or excessive hours of labor. Work was important, but must not intrude upon family life, especially upon the interaction of parents and children. Social historian Stephan Thernstrom (*The Other Bostonians,* 1973) suggests that Italians—even in the second generation—were frequently unfamiliar with "the idea that work can be a central purpose of life, and that it should be organized into a series of related jobs that make up a career. . . ." There was little hunger for promotions or fear of losing face if they became plasterers or plumbers rather than professionals or independent entrepreneurs.

Unlike rural Italians who sent males first, Italian fishermen usually emigrated with their families and thus were better able to deal with the dislocation and disruption of traditional life-patterns in the cities of America. Often Sicilian fishermen and their sons made remarkably rapid adjustments to American urban life because a fishing job in the Mediterranean was a business enterprise. After a catch, fishermen had always marketed their wares directly to consumers.

Like the Italians, Greek immigrants preferred outdoor work but generally avoided agriculture. Only a few turned to farming or herding and migrated to the western states, where, according to historian Theodore Saloutos, "The mountains, valleys, shores, and skies reminded them of their birthplaces." Most became factory laborers or worked on railroad construction gangs, where they could at least remain out of doors. The textile mills of New England, long a source of jobs for immigrants, also attracted many Greeks. By 1910, Lowell, Massachusetts, had 20,000 Greeks among its 100,000 inhabitants. Following earlier waves of Irish and French Canadians into the mills, Greeks underbid the wages of their predecessors and had the reputation for being less inclined to drink and therefore more reliable laborers. Wages were low, less than $4 per week, but the work was steady.

The areas of settlement and occupational preferences of east European Jews were also affected by a combination of historic experience, cultural preferences, expectations, and individual abilities. Unlike most of the Slavic, Italian, and Greek immigrants mentioned above, Jews arriving at the turn of the century tended to be skilled artisans or experienced merchants. Because many east European countries had laws proscribing Jews from owning land, they developed nonagrarian skills easily transferable should it become necessary to move quickly. Since medieval times, Jews had been moneylenders, tax collectors, innkeepers, grain merchants, stewards, artisans, and commercial middlemen. In the Pale of Settlement in Russia, Jews predominated among the tanners, tailors, blacksmiths, carpenters, furriers, jewelers, bakers, and butchers. By 1900, many eastern European towns had workshops and sweatshops where varied craftsmen worked side by side to produce ready-made goods for the urban market. Many Jews were retailers, peddlers, and shopkeepers. And even before the turn of the century, Jews constituted over one-fifth of the factory operatives in the Pale and almost 28 percent in Poland.

Sixty-six percent of the Jewish males who arrived in the United States between 1899 and 1914 were classified as skilled workers compared to an average of 20 percent for all other male immigrants combined. For Jewish immigrants, then, the transition from their cities and villages to the urban industrial centers of the United States was eased because they carried with them valuable skills. Jews who had been tailors in rural villages or labored in town workshops found a ready place in New York's garment industry. They dominated the industry, doing piecework in their tenement apartments on their own sewing machines or on machines rented from employers. In such cases every family member regardless of age or sex contributed his or her labor. Thus, in New York City the garment industry employed approximately 50 percent of all the city's Jewish males and two-thirds of the city's Jewish wage earners. In New York and other port cities, Jewish workers also found positions in cigar factories, print shops, and book binderies.

Just as cultural values brought from home villages influenced the occupational choices of male immigrants, so too they determined roles of immigrant women and children. All immigrants relied on the cooperation of family members, regardless of gender, to supplement the earnings of the male head of household, but the nature of that help varied from group to group.

The role of the immigrant woman worker was neglected by all but a few historians until the 1980s. In *From the Other Side: Women, Gender and Immigrant Life in the United States, 1820–1990* (1994), Donna R. Gabaccia makes clear that immigrant women joined the American workforce and that these women played crucial roles in the economics of the immigrant family. Available data suggest that "Foreign-born women and their daughters constituted over half of the American workforce of female wage-earners before 1900, slightly less than half of all female wage-earners in 1920." The reason they worked was that few immigrant men earned a wage sufficient to sustain their families. Thus female newcomers worked to support families, rather than to sustain independence as self-sufficient single women living alone. With little training, experience, or education, most immigrant women labored at the bottom of the occupational ladder, succeeding native-born women in jobs at the base of a "female occupational hierarchy." Jobs in industries such as textiles, shoes, and clothing were gender segregated, with men generally holding the more skilled positions. Foreign-born women replaced native-born women as machine operatives and in other semiskilled or unskilled occupations. The same gendered pattern pertained to agriculture. In California, about one-fourth of   Japanese women worked in the fields. On Louisiana sugar plantations, Sicilian women grew gardens of fruits and vegetables that fed landowners and workers alike.

At times, women were restricted in their occupations and working conditions by their particular group's cultural traditions and taboos as well as by the well-intentioned efforts of American reformers to protect all women from the evils of industrial exploitation. Many groups discouraged women working outside of the home, believing that such labor undercut male authority, a cornerstone of "traditional" American family life. According to Mario Garcia (*Desert Immigrants, The Mexicans of El Paso, 1880–1920*, 1981), "The 1900 El Paso [Texas] census sample shows that no mothers and almost no daughters, most being too young, worked outside the home in a [Mexican] immigrant family headed by the father (although no data exist, some women may have worked part-time)." However, survival often took precedence over cultural tradition and the pattern eroded in El Paso as elsewhere. Approximately one-fifth of all Mexican immigrant women worked. Most often those who did so were unmarried daughters, widows, and abandoned or single women. Historian of the Latina experience, Vicki Ruiz (*Cannery Women, Cannery Lives,* 1987), points out that "Whether living in a labor camp, a boxcar settlement, mining town, or urban barrio," Mexican women both "nurtured families" and "worked for wages" when necessity demanded.

Italian and eastern European Jewish married women, too, were discouraged from working outside of the home, although garment piecework at the family's dinner table was permitted. Women from the Mediterranean countries frequently helped their husbands or fathers sell goods at markets or peddle them in the streets. In small shops they might manage the bills and inventory. Slovak and Bohemian women did domestic work as had Irish women of a previous immigrant generation. Census data suggests the uneven pattern of domestic employment across groups. Scandinavian women were often employed as servants, as suggested by the 1920 census listing over 85 percent of employed Swedish and Norwegian women, respectively, as servants, but only 8 percent of

Italian and 7 percent Yiddish-speaking Jewish women as servants. Some scholars argue that the lower percentage of Italian and Jewish women in service was the result of family migration patterns among these groups that led to a preference for work in the home, while still others argue that these groups rejected domestic service to take advantage of higher wages in factory work. This taboo had nothing to do with the arduousness of the work. Italian and Jewish women were permitted to become sewing-machine operators in garment factories, and, by 1910, thousands of Greek women labored in New England's textile and shoe factories. In the Southwest, Mexican women preferred jobs as domestics, but when such employment was unavailable they tended crops in the fields, as did the men.

At times women found themselves in desperate straits. Older children cared for their younger siblings while mothers worked as cooks or domestics or labored in the fields. Women, impoverished and unable to cope with the stresses of life in America, sometimes turned to the oldest profession for their livelihoods. Prostitutes were not confined to isolated corners of cities as they had been in eastern Europe or southern Italy. They lived in the same streets and in the same tenements where families lived and children cavorted. They were regarded with a combination of shame and sympathy by their respective groups. Italians, Jews, and Slavs blamed hardship in America for driving young, unmarried women to the streets. As sociologist Kathie Friedman-Kasaba observes, "Among the prostitutes surveyed in New York City in 1912, the overwhelming majority (68 percent) had been born in the United States." However, some proportion may have been the native-born daughters of immigrant parents. Although police records for the years from 1913 to 1930 indicate that only approximately 17 percent of all prostitutes arrested in Manhattan were Jewish, far less than the Jewish proportion of Manhattan's population, Jewish reformers were concerned. German-Jewish reformer Julia Richman led raids on Lower East Side brothels, demanded the assignment of special agents to Ellis Island to protect new arrivals from pimps seeking to recruit them, and organized the Working Girls Club to encourage and protect immigrant shop girls. In collaboration with the Young Ladies Charitable Union and the United Hebrew Charities of New York, Richman developed an industrial school for impoverished immigrant girls. In the West, Chinese prostitutes first started to arrive in the 1850s when the high proportion of laborers and gold miners created a large market for their services. In *Unbound Feet* (1995), Judy Yung explains that Chinese prostitutes were often kidnaped or purchased from their parents. In 1892, one young woman testified before American authorities, "I was kidnaped in China and brought over here [eighteen months ago]. The man who kidnaped me sold me for four hundred dollars to a San Francisco slave-dealer; and he sold me here for seventeen hundred dollars. I have been a brothel slave ever since." Christian missionaries in San Francisco opened up shelters and urged state and municipal officials in California to battle those who profited from the suffering of young Chinese women immigrants.

Single women sought solutions to their plights through activism. Labor organizer Rose Schneiderman, who arrived in 1889, recalled that when her father died, her pregnant mother became the family's sole support. After weaning her baby, Rose's mother took a job in a fur factory, leaving Rose to stay with the infant. Two other brothers were temporarily placed in the Hebrew Orphan Asylum. Later, her mother, concerned about Rose's schooling, sent her to the orphanage too. But within a year Rose and the baby were again living with their mother in a one-room apartment. Her mother worked all day and brought home bundles to sew at night. On weekends they visited the boys at the orphanage (Rose Schneiderman and Lucy Goldthwaite, *All for One,* 1967).

Young Jewish single women, such as Rose Schneiderman, were the backbone of the garment industry unions, often emerging as leaders. Some had been active in the Jewish labor movement in Russia. At first, the Yiddish-speaking women trade unionists had difficulty communicating with their Italian coworkers. In 1907, an effort to organize artificial flower makers failed because the Italian immigrant women dominating the industry could not understand the speeches the union leaders made. One observer remarked that "the only time there was a large turnout for mass meetings was when English and Italian speakers were on the platform." Other cultural differences separated female immigrants as well. Meetings planned for Saturday nights interfered with Italian family home life and were poorly attended. Also, Italian males usually escorted their wives or sisters to and from work and intervened to "protect" their women from union organizers who, they feared, were keeping Italian women from home responsibilities. However, increasing contact bred understanding and by the turn of the century, Italian and Jewish immigrant women were in the vanguard of labor unionization in the garment trades. Other groups followed similar patterns. Mexican women in the California food-processing industry eventually organized, according to historian Vicki Ruiz. Chinese women, confined by family and external patterns of discrimination limiting their employment opportunities, needed several additional generations in America before they were able to join the labor movement. Women too frail to work in factories or tied to their homes by the duties of motherhood frequently supplemented their family's income through piecework done at the kitchen table, taking in male or female boarders who paid them rent, and cooking meals and doing laundry for boarders. At times, such services yielded more income than the woman's husband made as a laborer.

Women immigrants who managed to acquire some education were not limited to labor in factory or home. Some became teachers in public or parochial schools. As it had in Europe, the Catholic Church offered women opportunity for education and advancement. Catholic women who became nuns could teach or join one of the renowned nursing orders such as the Sisters of Charity.

State legislation limited the working hours for all women working outside the home. The first such legislation was passed in New Hampshire as early as 1847, and by the turn of the century many other states had followed suit, responding to pressure from social reformers. A law enacted in Oregon in 1903 provided that "no female (shall) be employed in any mechanical establishment, or factory or laundry in this State more than ten hours during any one day." The legislation was later upheld in the 1908 landmark case *Muller* v. *Oregon*. Louis Brandeis, arguing for the state, persuaded the Supreme Court that long hours impaired the health, safety, and morals of working women. The majority of the justices concurred that women's "physical structure and a proper discharge of her maternal functions—having in view not merely her own health but the well-being of the race—justify the legislation to protect her from the greed as well as the passion of man." By 1913, thirty-nine states either enacted new laws protecting women workers or improved existing statutes.

Enforcement of female labor legislation varied from state to state. Ironically, the efforts of social reformers often hurt those they were trying hardest to help—immigrant women. Wages were so low, and life so marginal, that limiting the working hours of immigrant women could spell economic disaster for the family. Thus, many immigrant women were forced to evade the very laws written to protect them. And they were readily aided in this by exploitative employers.

Child labor, like female labor, was initially determined by the cultural norms of each particular new immigrant group. Not until the twentieth century would the intervention of humanitarian reformers alter child employment patterns. According to Virginia Yans-McLaughlin's study of immigrants in Buffalo, Italian girls rarely left home to accept jobs as domestics or factory laborers. Boys, however, could accept whatever kind of employment they were capable of performing. Older boys often duplicated their father's salaries in seasonal labor, while the younger ones worked in street trades as newsboys or shoeshiners. Among the Slavic miners, girls were permitted to work in local textile mills, while boys went down into the mines as soon as they were able. Before the age of twelve, Slavic boys worked on the surface, but by their midteens they were riding the elevators below ground.

East European Jews generally preferred to keep daughters at home and permitted sons to work in shops and factories as they were able. However, the piecework that was available in the garment trades often allowed the entire family to work together. In 1902, reformer and journalist Hutchins Hapgood wrote (*Spirit of the Ghetto*) that the homes of Jews on New York's Lower East Side typically were turned into workrooms. "During the day the front room, bedroom, and kitchen became a whirling, churning factory, where men, women and children worked at the sewing and pressing machines." Hapgood and others were often surprised and dismayed to see the extent to which child labor was used in homes and in factories, where young children worked elbow to elbow with adults under confined conditions. "In one room," Hapgood discovered, "would be four men, one or two women, a couple of young girls, aged nine to fourteen, and perhaps an eleven-year old boy, working on knickerbockers or knee pants." Another observer described how mothers, too busy sewing, often relegated to a female child "the work and care of the family . . . washing, scrubbing, cooking. . . ." Home labor, with everyone in the family employed, was often no more profitable than piecework in factories. Rapacious employers reduced the amount paid for each finished piece. Workers were thereby forced to work faster and faster to receive the same low wage. By the 1920s, laws in most states fixed a minimum age for employment and compelled school attendance. Compliance was not immediate, but advancing mechanization, an adequate adult labor supply, and rising personnel standards in industry increasingly made child labor less profitable to employers. However, immigrant families in need of supplementary income continued to violate the law whenever economic necessity demanded.

II

Even as immigrants profited from opportunities in America, the United States benefited from the immigrants' presence. As industrial capitalism took center stage, these new arrivals were becoming the chief source of labor in almost every area of industrial production. Southern and eastern European languages and English spoken with the accents of the Mezzogiorno, eastern European villages, Mexican border towns, and French Canada echoed in factories and mines in concentrated regional pockets. The Dillingham Commission's report published in 1910 states that, in a twenty-one industry survey, it found 57.9 percent of all employees were foreign born, approximately two-thirds being of southern and eastern European origin. In industries such as garment manufacturing,

coal mining, slaughtering, meat packing, construction, and confectionery, the proportion of new immigrant to native-born labor
was even higher.

The arrival of millions of skilled, semiskilled, and unskilled
workers added a crucial ingredient to America's recipe for industrialization, a plentiful supply of low-cost labor and a dramatic expansion of the domestic market for the goods and services produced by American fields and factories. However, native-born
American workers and those born abroad who arrived in an earlier era were skeptical of how the newcomers were affecting their
own lot. It is impossible to gauge precisely the immediate impact
of this abundant immigrant labor force on American-born and earlier immigrants. Nativist literature published after 1890 suggested
that new immigrant laborers were displacing American workers at
every work site. Though not completely accurate, these charges do
appear to have some basis in fact for particular industries, such as
coal mining and iron and steel manufacturing. Low-paid Poles and
Slavs were nudging out workers of English or Irish heritage. After
the Chinese Exclusion Law of 1882, Mexican labor replaced Chinese workers on railroad section gangs.

Rapid expansion of American industry kept foreign and
American workers from actually colliding. Lateral movement and
vertical promotion kept many native-born workers clear of the
newcomers. New mines in the western states absorbed displaced
miners from Pennsylvania and Ohio. Though the evidence is still
vague and impressionistic, there is also some indication that
American workers were elevated into managerial and technical
positions created in industries by the growth new immigrant labor
helped generate. In some factories and plants, the native-born
American managers and foremen owed a debt to the newcomers,
whose presence was responsible for their own ascent into white-
collar jobs.

The availability of cheap immigrant labor afforded the United
States a decided competitive advantage over its European industrial rivals. And the owners of America's mines, large factories,
and small sweatshops did not hesitate to exploit their inexpensive
and abundant supply of immigrant labor. Twelve- to sixteen-hour

days were normal in factories and mines. Unventilated shops with inadequate exhaust systems and improper safety equipment exposed workers to noxious fumes and other health hazards. Mine workers often died prematurely of respiratory diseases, while those in factories suffered loss of limbs or eyes in industrial accidents. While employers blamed workers' carelessness or inexperience for the accidents, investigators such as Cyril Eastman, in 1910, pointed to ignored safety hazards and malfunctioning equipment. Workers injured on the job and unable to earn a living received no compensation. Medical or funeral expenses were left to impoverished workers and their families. Neither employers nor the government aided those unable to work as the result of sickness or industrial accidents. In describing the high incidence of industrial injury, reformer Rose Schneiderman told a crowd, "The old Inquisition had its rack and its thumbscrews and its instruments of torture with iron teeth. We know what these things are today; the iron teeth are our necessities, the thumbscrews are the high-powered and swift machinery close to which we must work, and the rack is here in the firetrap structures that will destroy us the minute they catch on fire."

The earliest attempts at labor organization, however, were aimed as much against immigrant workers as against exploitative employers. In organized labor's view, the huge pool of immigrant labor threatened to undermine the status of all American workers by rapidly decreasing wages and encouraging managers to think of employees as more easily replaceable than pieces of machinery. Organizations such as the National Labor Union, begun by iron-molder William Sylvis in 1868, had restricted its membership to workers skilled in a craft, but the Knights of Labor, founded in 1869, opened its membership to all workers who would join. High on the agenda of both unions was to protect the wages of American-born workers from foreign competition, especially immigrants willing to labor for lower wages. Ironically, labor organizations eventually were forced to turn to the immigrants for survival. Machines increasingly replaced skilled craftsmen, and industrialists were quick to realize that, whereas they were required to compensate each skilled employee individually commensurate with his or her abilities, they could impose a uniform set of hours, working conditions, and wages upon production-line labor. Eventually, the millions of unskilled, immigrant laborers hired to work on production lines were courted by union organizers who relished the thought of increased strength through numbers.

The 1880s witnessed both extreme labor unrest and the emergence of a new type of labor union. In 1886, alone, an estimated 610,000 men and women were out of work because of strikes, lockouts, or shutdowns that sometimes erupted in violence. The extreme violence in the labor movement was epitomized by the Haymarket Riot in 1886. In Chicago, a city known for radical and anarchist activity, unemployed workers, many of whom were Irish and German immigrants, gathered for a rally in the city's Haymarket Square. Someone threw a bomb, killing a policeman and several bystanders. A bloody melee ensued. Club-swinging policemen waded into the crowd, injuring hundreds, and members of the crowd retaliated in kind. The police blamed the riot on eight alleged anarchists, most of whom were immigrants of German background. After jury trials, four of the eight were hanged. As a terrible legacy, the Haymarket Riot was associated in many American minds with the organized labor movement, immigrant workers, dangerous wild-eyed radicals, and anarchists. For many, the incident fueled fears of the "reckless foreign wretches," as one newspaper termed the protesting workers.

Despite Haymarket and other violent incidents, many of which were instigated by employers, the American labor movement expanded and drew followers from among skilled workers, both native- and foreign-born, during the last two decades of the nineteenth century. Especially attractive was the new American Federation of Labor (AFL) founded in 1881, which grew as the Knights of Labor declined in influence and membership. Recognizing the unique problems affecting workers in different occupations, the AFL encouraged the development of separate craft unions. It decided to represent all these unions, amassing strength in numbers while permitting each member union to preserve its autonomy, including the power to call strikes. Samuel Gompers, a Jewish immigrant born in London, became the first president of the AFL. For forty years he sought to win recognition for organized labor as a legitimate interest group within American society. More immediately, Gompers sought higher wages, shorter hours, and equitable treatment for the Federation's members.

The AFL was anxious to enlist newcomers in the union movement, but most southern and eastern Europeans were unskilled laborers and thus ineligible for membership in a craft union. Even many of the skilled workers among the immigrants were difficult to recruit because of the system of home production popular among many groups.

Both men and women engaged in home production. While home production may have precluded union membership, it did offer immigrant workers other comforts; as historian Eileen Boris (*Home to Work, Motherhood and the Politics of Industrial Homework in the United States,* 1994) observes, "At home, women could fulfill their duties as mothers. They could look after children, care for illnesses, and cook." They could also "protect virtue," as one Italian mother observed, noting that as her daughter matured, there was greater need to keep an eye on the behavior of male borders in the small tenement apartment. Maternal duties often took precedence over piecework. One Mexican woman reported that she "work[ed] very brokenly when babies are awake." As Boris concludes, "Although mothering dictated for these women where their labor would occur, the state of the family economy determined that they must earn wages of some kind." Male and female Bohemian cigarmakers worked side by side in their apartments as teams to produce the popular stogies. Union organizing committees found homeworkers hard to recruit because they lacked the manpower to go through apartment buildings door-to-door to reach such workers.

But whether at home or in the shop, immigrants both skilled and unskilled initially rejected unions as irrelevant to their plans and expectations for the future. Likewise, both national and regional differences kept workers apart. And businessmen anxious to break unions were quick to exploit these differences. In 1903, the first large group of Greek workers was sent west to break a strike of Italian coal miners in Utah. Nine years later, in 1912, striking Greek miners from the island of Crete clashed with mainland Greeks brought in to smash a strike by copper miners in

Bingham County, Utah. These nonunion strikebreakers were then trotted out as evidence that the unions were unrepresentative of the workforce. Those newcomers who chose to join a labor union did not take lightly the role that scab labor played in breaking the union. Nor was resistance to scabs confined to the strikers. At times, entire communities joined in the protest. In 1913, Greek women at Ludlow, Colorado, punished scabs with clubs studded with spikes as their husbands and brothers stood against the state militiamen summoned to quell the miners' protest.

Why did the newcomers reject labor organization at first? For some it was a matter of time. Those who had tilled the soil in their homelands were still living on agrarian time. They rejected the discipline of unionization even as they despised the industrial clock requiring them to report to work at a certain time, to eat at the same time every day, and to cease working at a given hour. Another reason that immigrants seemed initially indifferent to the growing confrontation between capital and labor in the United States was because their own needs were being by met by customs and commercial arrangements carried over from their home countries. Just as newcomers brought their cuisines and cures to America, their cultural baggage included patterns of labor relations. Mediterranean immigrants, unable to speak English and unfamiliar with American customs, were suspicious of union organizers. They placed their confidence in their own labor brokers, or *padrones,* to secure jobs for them on the construction sites of buildings, bridges, and roads and to negotiate working conditions and wages.

Italian padrones operated in European cities as well as in the Italian enclaves of American cities. According to historian Humbert Nelli, the padrone was the Italian immigrant's intermediary—"someone who spoke both languages, understood old-world traditions, and new-world business operations, and could get in touch with American employers who needed unskilled workers." While the padrone served a crucial function in the immigrant community, enough of these ethnic labor bosses made illegal profits at the expense of workers to give a bad name to the entire group. At times, the padrone charged workers first-class transportation rates, though the employer had provided free passage. At other times, a contractor might pay the laborers' wages directly to the boss, who then paid workers whatever he wished, keeping the difference for himself. Some padrones accepted brokers' fees but never delivered the promised jobs. Yet, despite the risk of being duped, many unskilled ethnic workers relied on padrones to provide them with regular work. At the turn of the century, padrones controlled over 50 percent of New York City's Italian labor force. Not until the beginning of unionization in the construction industry, coupled with World War I labor shortages, did the power of the padrone diminish. Often padrones worked hand in glove with *banchieri,* entrepreneurs who had acquired some investment capital as a grocer, barber, or saloon keeper and used it to offer newcomers a variety of services at steep fees. Banchieri could function as moneychangers, moneylenders, travel agents, marriage brokers, or legal advisers. It was often the banchieri who contacted workers in Italy and transported them to the United States so that the padrones could provide the necessary laborers to construction managers and others in need of workers. Both padrones and banchieri were paid well for their services.

Greek immigrants, too, relied on padrones and suffered the exploitation that so frequently resulted from dealing with these powerful labor brokers. Among Greeks, the system was virtually a contemporary version of the indentured servant system popular in the late seventeenth and early eighteenth centuries. A Greek padrone, knowing shopkeepers in need of labor, wrote letters to relatives and friends in Greece telling them of the opportunities available to ambitious boys in America. In such correspondence the padrone would offer to arrange for transportation and accommodations for the young men for a time after arrival. Greek male adolescents whose families had accepted the padrone's offer were sent to America and apprenticed to grocers, restaurant keepers, shopowners, or bootblacks for a period of three months to a year with the padrone keeping the boy's wages during the apprenticeship. Only after the apprenticeship was over would the boy receive any salary—usually $10 to $20 per year. The peasant family had one less child at the table and often benefited from a son's earnings. The desire to live in America and the promise of advancement overshadowed harsh treatment and low wages; there was an inexhaustible supply of apprentices. American businessmen dealt with padrones because they could provide workers at a cost far below the market rate. If workers protested, the padrone could even provide strikebreakers for a fee. Leonidas G. Skliris, known as the "Czar of the Greeks," earned notoriety for his ability to serve his clients regardless of the amount of coercion and extortion required.

The Chinese Six Companies, a benevolent association in San Francisco, performed labor brokerage services for immigrant Chinese without exploiting them. The Six Companies derived its name from the six regions of China that produced the most emigrants to America. When a ship docked on the West Coast, representatives of the Six Companies boarded and offered the newcomers not only jobs but shelter, food, and other assistance. In return, immigrants paid dues to the Companies from their wages and were required to list on the Companies' books all loans and services for which they owed the organization. Should they return to China, members were required to first clear their account with the Companies. Few Chinese refused to join since there was no alternative source of assistance and protection for Chinese workers.

Caucasian workers often unfairly rendered the sweeping verdict that Chinese laborers were by their very nature scabs. Chinese workers found themselves in agrarian labor in America's fields and orchards. Others were domestics or restaurant service workers. Low paid farm workers doing seasonal labor and service workers, who were part of small staffs in private homes or restaurants, had long been difficult to organize, but easy to exploit and intimidate. Moreover, when Chinese workers and other Asians such as Japanese and Filipinos sought to join unions they often found themselves excluded on racial grounds. Some formed their own unions and cooperated across ethnic lines. In 1903, Japanese and Mexican farm workers struck jointly to demand higher wages to plant and harvest beets near Oxnard in California's Ventura County. The Japanese-Mexican Labor Association (JMLA) formed in response to the strike and elected a Japanese president and vice-president and a Mexican secretary. The new organization's demands included higher wages and an end to the monopoly in labor recruiting enjoyed by the Western Agricultural Contracting Compact. When the growers brought in scabs to break the strike, it led to violence. At this point, with the help of the American Federation of Labor, the JMLA achieved many of its objectives, including the right to bargain directly with most growers and higher wages. However, when the JMLA sought to join the AFL, Samuel Gompers, who harbored an impenetrable bias against Asia's "coolie labor," would not grant the charter unless all Japanese and Chinese were excluded from the local. The JMLA rejected Gomper's anti-Asian terms.

Even immigrant groups with a history of labor activism were slow to organize until some event galvanized them. Take, for instance, east European Jews engaged in the needle trades. In 1900, the United Brotherhood of Cloakmakers was formed. It was a small union, and by 1906 only 2,500 of the 42,500 cloakmakers were unionized. Soon the inhuman conditions in which the cloakmakers labored and resistance of employers to improve them triggered greater militancy among both male and female workers. Garment workers were encouraged by the successful strikes of shirtwaist makers in 1909 and cloakmakers in 1910. However, no single development galvanized workers more than the Triangle Shirtwaist fire of 1911.

The Triangle Shirtwaist factory, a nonunion shop employing 700 workers, occupied the top three floors of the Asch building located at the corner of Greene Street and Washington Place in New York City. At 4:35 P.M. on Saturday, March 25, 1911, a fire started on the eighth floor. It spread rapidly through the bolts of fabric to the floors above and below. As usual, the doors of the workrooms were locked from the outside, a practice followed by some employers to keep the young machine operators from leaving early to start the weekend. The fire escapes were inadequate to support the fleeing occupants, and the fire company ladders reached only to the seventh floor, too short to rescue workers who had fled to the roof. One hundred and forty-six persons perished in the blaze, many of them young women and men who did piecework at their sewing machines in the shop. Newspaper reports repeated the harrowing details of how those trapped inside crowded onto window ledges and then threw themselves to the street, their clothing on fire:

The hair of some of the girls streamed up aflame as they leaped. Thud after thud sounded on the pavements. . . . [O]n both the Greene Street and Washington Place sides of the building there grew mounds of dead and dying. And the worst horror of all was that in this heap of the dead now and then there stirred a limb or sounded a moan. When fire chief Croker could make his way into these three floors he found . . . bodies burned to bare bones . . . skeletons bending over sewing machines.

The horror of the Triangle Shirtwaist fire stimulated labor militants. As a result, the International Ladies Garment Workers' Union (ILGWU) and later the Amalgamated Clothing Workers of America (ACWA), each of which had a largely Jewish, Italian, and Polish membership, developed into two of the strongest labor unions in the United States. David Dubinsky (ILGWU) and Jacob Potofsky (ACWA) became nationally known as fighters for the right of all workers to have strong, honest unions.

On rare occasions, collective action prompted the founding of agricultural colonies. Eastern European Jews established such a colony in the early 1880s on a 2,400-acre tract on Sicily Island, in Catahoula Parish, Louisiana, seventy-four miles from Natchez, Mississippi. The commune could not conquer the swampy, malaria-ridden land, and the experiment failed. Of the sixteen such ventures launched by philanthropic organizations in the 1880s, only the community at Vineland, New Jersey, was a success. The Japanese faired similarly. In 1904, Jo Sakai, a Japanese student who had just earned a degree from New York University's School of Commerce, returned to his hometown of Miyazu, Japan, where he organized a small group of agricultural colonists to settle in Boca Raton, Florida. With aid from Florida pioneer Henry Flagler's Model Land Company, Sakai started the Yamato Colony. It struggled along until the early 1920s, by which time most of colony's members had left. One colonist remained, George Sukeji

Morikami, who continued to farm and work as an agricultural agent in South Florida, eventually acquiring several hundred acres of land. Shortly before his death in the mid-1970s, Morikami donated 200 acres to Palm Beach County and the State of Florida for a park and museum to honor the memory of Yamato Colony.

Of course, labor protest took years to improve conditions in many industries. And not all workers who ventured forth to labor in America prospered or even managed to sustain themselves. Upon returning to their countries of origin they believed their mistake was to have stayed in America too long. One such unfortunate, Peter Molek, a Slovenian repatriate, returned to his homeland sick and broken, warning another bent on finding his fortune abroad, "America the jungle swallows many people who go there to work. She squeezes the strength out of them, unless they are wise or lucky enough to escape before it is too late; unless they work in the mills or the mines only a few years and save every cent they can and return home, or buy themselves a piece of land where land is still cheap."

III

Those who chose to neither return home nor to join a union and spend their lives laboring for others found a third alternative. They could become independent entrepreneurs seeking the increased income and independent lifestyle of self-employment. Even in cases where the increase in real wages was minimal, the intangible benefits of being one's own boss in America attracted many newcomers. As in the case of all other immigrant economic activity, cultural values, historic experience, and future expectations were as critical as capitalism's marketplace conditions, if not more so, in determining the kind of business enterprises these new entrepreneurs would find attractive.

The newcomer who was fired with ambition to succeed but hamstrung by limited capital traditionally took up the peddler's pack, or its urban counterpart, the pushcart. The pushcart was a large wooden cart on two wheels that could be pushed from block to block and neighborhood to neighborhood. The pushcart peddler, his cart loaded with fruits, vegetables, fish packed in ice, or dry goods, had no overhead and needed only enough capital to purchase his wares. Peddlers were popular with immigrant consumers. Often catering specifically to their own ethnic group, these outdoor merchants carried delicacies and goods reminiscent of the old country. They spoke the old language and understood the old customs and mores. Also, pushcart peddlers sold food in small quantities for those with makeshift kitchens and limited funds. Profits were never great, but a pushcart peddler sometimes saved enough to open a small shop in the neighborhood where his customers lived.

Many Jewish immigrants had already been small merchants on the streets of towns and cities in Poland and Russia, so the grip of the American pushcart fit naturally in their hands. Religious Jews could arrange their business days to permit observance of holidays, attendance at religious services, or abstention from labor on Friday evening and Saturday. According to Charles Bernheimer, a contemporary writer, by 1905, New York City had almost 1,000 Jewish "peddlers and keepers of stands, the number varying according to the season of the year." On Fridays, Hester Street, a center of New York's pushcart trade, was alive with shouting vendors selling to housewives whatever they needed for the Sabbath. Everything from carp to coffee to candles was for sale in various quantities and at affordable prices. In the 1840s many of the "Yankee peddlers" who traveled the backroads of rural America, especially the South, were actually German Jews. By the end of the century, Russian Jews, particularly those who entered through the port of Baltimore, purchased backpacks or wagons and headed for the small towns of the South where the competition for business was far less than in northeastern cities.

Italians and Greeks also peddled. However, these groups found other jobs equally acceptable. Shoeshining was a popular entering wedge into the economy for Greeks and Italians. All that was needed were strong arms and backs, a minimal knowledge of English, and a willingness to work seven-day weeks, including holidays from morning to night. In 1894, Italians constituted all but one of New York City's 474 foreign-born bootblacks.

Greeks dominated the confectionery industry in the United States. Theodore Saloutos, in writing about Greek Americans, noted that many Greek entrepreneurs learned to make candies and cakes in Greece, "for the Greeks always have been known as a people with a sweet tooth." Once in the United States an individual could open a small shop in a Greek neighborhood and soon his kitchen might be supplying the needs of nearby coffeehouses, grocery stores, restaurants, and luncheonettes. Because Greeks celebrate religious and cultural occasions with feasts, a confectioner might cater the sweets at "wedding receptions, christenings, or the celebration of name days."

The experience of the pioneer Greek candy merchants who arrived even before 1880, as described by Saloutos, might well serve as an archetype of the new immigrant's entrance into the American world of free enterprise. "The pioneer confectioners were Eleutherios Pelalas of Sparta and Pangiotis Hatzideris of Smyrna, who established a *lukum* (sweet) shop shortly after their arrival in 1869. This partnership was terminated within a brief time; in 1877 Pelalas assumed the management of an American-owned establishment in Springfield, [Illinois] where he later opened a series of stores. Hatzideris, on the other hand, formed a partnership with another associate in New York, which handled more commercialized brands, such as 'Turkish Delight' and 'Greek Prince.' Hatzideris eventually returned to Smyrna, but his partner continued the business under the name of Higgis Greek-American Confectionery Company, with plants in New York, Memphis, and Pittsburgh." Pelalas's and Hatzideris's businesses employed the first immigrants from Sparta, providing training in a trade as well as a steady living. Chicago became "the Acropolis of the Greek-American candy business," according to Saloutos. The Greek newspaper, *Hellinikos Astir,* reported in 1904 that "practically every busy corner in Chicago is occupied by a Greek candy store." It was estimated that at one time, 70 percent of the Greek candy merchants in the United States were in Chicago and that Chicago money and training established candy stores throughout the South and West.

The Greeks were not alone in realizing Americans also had a sweet tooth. Albert J. Bonomo, a Sephardic Jew from Turkey began making candy at New York's Coney Island to supply amusement park concessions. After World War I, his son Victor joined him in a candy factory where they produced saltwater taffy and hard candies. Years later, Victor Bonomo's cooks concocted a recipe of corn syrup and egg whites that was cooked and then baked. Though not technically a taffy, this short nougat once cooled was cut into large sheets and sold at five and dime stores by clerks who used a ball peen hammer to break off pieces for customers. When Bonomo cut slabs the size of a candy bar and wrapped them individually, "Bonomo's Turkish Taffy" became one of America's most popular candy bars. The wrapper showed smiling men, presumably Turks, in fezzes, pouring batter into a large vat.

The immigrant's choice of occupation, while largely the product of group values and personal preferences, was also affected by local competition. Working on ladies' garments seemed unmanly to many native-born laborers, but not to Russian Jews and Italians. As a result these newcomers faced little native competition for jobs in a growing industry. Many Jews had already worked as tailors in the small towns of Russia's Pale and the Italians appreciated work that could be done at home or in nearby factories where relatives could work side by side.

Asian immigrants also were quick to capitalize on the prejudices of other ethnic groups. The Chinese did not define such domestic tasks as cooking, ironing, and washing as strictly "women's work." Nor were male Chinese repelled by performing these jobs as were most American workers. Instead, the Chinese discovered that laundering, especially in towns with many single men, could prove a lucrative trade. Only a scrub board, some soap, an iron, and an ironing board were needed. According to Paul C. P. Siu (*The Chinese Laundryman: A Study in Social Isolation,* 1987), there is anecdotal evidence that Wah Lee was the first Chinese laundryman in San Francisco and that in 1851 he hung a sign, "Wasn'ng and Iron'ng," over a corner store at Dupont Street (currently Grant Avenue) and Washington Street. Nine years later there were 890 Chinese laundrymen in town, 2.6 percent of the Chinese employed in California. Estimates suggest that by 1880, more than 5,000 Chinese in San Francisco earned their livings in laundries, 7.3 percent of the employed California Chinese. When the Chinese moved eastward, they continued to set up laundries, seeking out low-rent locations in towns or cities where they settled. The first Chinese laundry in Chicago opened in 1872; by 1893 there were 313 laundries in the city and 523 by 1918. While few Chinese grew wealthy as launderers, owning their means of livelihood insulated them to a degree from Americans terrified by the "Yellow Peril." Nor were the Chinese alone. According to Ricardo Romo, by the 1920s, cleaning establishments were only exceeded by grocery stores and restaurants in their popularity among East Los Angeles Mexican businessmen in the 1920s.

The food industry was the lever by which many immigrants pried open the door of American opportunity, according to historian Donna R. Gabaccia (*We Are What We Eat, Ethnic Foods and the Making of Americans,* 1998). A food store might broaden its stock to cater to the preferences or ritual necessities of specific ethnic groups. Other stores achieved success by capturing an exclusive clientele. The strict Jewish dietary laws concerning meat, for example, drew many east European Jews into the meat and poultry business. It is estimated that in 1888, approximately half of New York City's 4,000 meat retailers and 300 wholesalers were Jewish. By 1900, 80 percent of the wholesale and 50 percent of the retail meat trade was in Jewish hands. Bakery products were also important to Jews, and Jewish bakeries swelled to number almost 500 across the city. By contrast, Greeks and Italians handled most of the fruit and vegetable trade.

As immigrants became more prosperous, ethnic restaurants opened. The restaurateurs, often immigrants themselves, knew which recipes were popular with their particular group and the style of service that made the members of that group feel most comfortable. Some of the eateries, such as Mama Leone's (1906), specializing in Italian dishes, and Lüchow's (1882), a German restaurant, both in New York City, achieved national recognition for their cuisine. Until the palates of native-born Americans and other ethnic groups were trained to crave a particular cuisine, immigrant restaurateurs had to remain flexible. As Sucheng Chan (*Asian Americans, An Interpretive History,* 1991) observes, "Establishments in the larger towns and cities generally served only Chinese food and used only fellow Chinese as waiters and busboys, but those in the smaller communities dished up large plates of American-style beef stew, pork chops, or fried chicken as well as Chinese spare ribs, sweet and sour pork, fried rice, or chow mein, and relied on Euro-American waitresses for help."

Unlike the many immigrant groups pursuing opportunity in the streets of cities, the Japanese pursued it in the countryside, especially in California and the Pacific Northwest. When the law forbade alien land ownership, the Japanese leased land. They specialized in fruit and vegetable farming. Patterns of prejudice and the need to conduct business in an atmosphere of trust caused many Japanese agrarians to evolve vertical business structures grounded in their own ethnicity. Therefore, Japanese peddlers, stall owners, and storekeepers marketed what Japanese farmers grew. Only a small number of Japanese agrarians became wealthy agribusinessmen. Historian Roger Daniels (*Asian America, Chinese and Japanese in the United States since 1850,* 1988), describes how one Issei entrepreneur, George Shima, who had emigrated from Fukuoka Prefecture in 1889, arrived with some capital and worked as a common laborer to earn still more. Shima rapidly progressed from worker to labor contractor, to land lessee to major business figure and was elected president of the Japanese Association of America by 1909. Shima's empire was based on using the latest developments in agricultural science to develop the San Joaquin Delta and to raise potatoes for the California market. By 1913 he controlled 28,800 acres in production and even more through marketing agreements with other Japanese agrarians. He had over 500 employees, including engineers and university-trained agricultural experts. By 1920, he likely controlled 85 percent of the state's potato crop, valued at $18 million dollars.

Capital was scarce, and few immigrants were able to finance businesses after covering the cost of moving to America. So some followed in George Shima's footsteps and labored long hours, lived frugally, and hoarded the necessary funds. Others borrowed money from relatives. However, neither savings nor personal loans were realistic options for immigrants supporting large families or lacking affluent friends or relatives. Few banks were willing to lend money to immigrants, whose only collateral were skilled hands, strong backs, and steely nerves.

Thus, new immigrants formed self-help organizations to accumulate money. The Italians, Chinese, and Japanese each evolved mutual assistance organizations to provide business capital. According to sociologist Ivan Light, the decisive community ties among the Japanese in America were those created by *kenjinkai.* The kenjinkai, or *ken,* were social organizations based on the provincial origins of Japanese immigrants. Most Japanese were eligible for membership in some ken organization. Fellow members, or *kenjin,* celebrated holidays together, enjoyed parties and picnics, and provided needed economic and social aid such as legal services and direct relief to the destitute. The kenjinkai founded employment agencies for members, and ken fellows tended to congregate in the same trades.

A crucial aspect of ken operation was a paternalism making it the social obligation of an employer to enable a talented and loyal employee to open a business of his own; guild organizations regulated competition to prevent internal chaos. Japanese also had the *ko, tanomoshi,* or *mujin*—all names for rotating credit associations that assisted members in starting enterprises. As with kenjinkai, members were usually from the same provinces.

The Cantonese *hui* and its variations were the rotating credit institutions most often used by Chinese to acquire business capital. The basic principle of the hui is useful in understanding all similar associations of this type. An individual needing a lump sum of money gathered a group of friends, each of whom agreed to pay a stipulated amount, perhaps $10 per month, into a pool. In a hui of twelve members, the organizer himself received the first lump sum created, or $120. A month later, he held a feast in his home for the other contributors. At the feast, each member contributed another $10. A lottery decided which member (excluding the organizer) would get the total. Each member could get the lump sum only once, and the lottery continued at subsequent feasts until every participant received his lump sum of $120. The organizer never contributed to the pool, but did provide twelve feasts costing $10 per feast. At the end of the twelfth feast, each member had spent $120 over the year and received one lump sum of $120 plus twelve feasts. The organizer of the hui had received the interest-free use of $120 when he needed it, ten of the twelve members had received an advance on their contributions, and all had enjoyed twelve fine meals.

The Chinese, like the Japanese, typically associated with provincial neighbors in American cities. They, too, formed brotherhoods for benevolent and business purposes. In San Francisco, the Chinese Six Companies were later joined by other district associations and renamed the Chinese Consolidated Benevolent Association. There were also clan associations known by the last names of families. Thus, the Wong Association included all those in the city with the surname Wong. Everyone in these associations addressed each other as cousin, though they were not related as such in the western sense. Surname associations tended to care for the social and benevolent services, while the district associations were involved in business operations such as the extension of loans for new businesses. The *tongs* (literally translated as "halls"), known in American lore for their fierce wars in the streets of Chinatowns, were originally fraternal organizations transplanted from China. However, in the streets of America, some tongs turned into violent gangs selling protection to brothels and gambling houses. Various tongs battled for influence and territory, sidestepping control by American police and terrorizing Chinese communities. Tong wars did not cease until the 1930s when their function was usurped. Disputants within the Chinese community were granted hearings before the Chinese Benevolent Association and members of genuine fraternal organizations substituted the name "lodge" or "association" for tong to indicate their desire to dissociate their group from the gangs of racketeers.

The southern Italians also organized themselves by Old-World residential patterns. Historian John Briggs (*An Italian Passage, Immigrants to Three American Cities, 1890–1930,* 1978) found that Utica, New York, had a very active *Societa Calabria,* established in 1903. These natives of Calabria joined together to foster "concord, brotherhood, education, instruction, work, [and] honesty." In large cities, lodges kept their membership exclusive and were sometimes criticized by community leaders for encouraging divisiveness based on Old-World rivalries. However, in smaller cities and towns the territorial exclusiveness was abandoned in the competition for dues-paying members from a limited pool of Italians. Members' dues financed social affairs and aided the sick and destitute. Rarely, however, did such societies finance individual entrepreneurial activity. Joseph Lopreato contends that, "cooperative ethnic activity" came hard to the Italians because the "vicissitudes of their history" had left them with trust in family members only. Ties of blood far exceeded region in importance in Italy's southern provinces. After emigration, the blood ties of la famiglia endured. However, few families had the resources to invest in the start-up costs that a new enterprise demanded.

Most banks were hesitant to serve the needs of immigrants. Moreover, pride and fear of rejection deterred immigrants from entering the austere offices and risking the judgmental stares of native-born bankers. Even as pushcarts grew into department stores such as Macy's, fraternal organizations that extended loans to members became banks. Small ethnic banks were willing to make modest loans and prepared to send money overseas to relatives anxiously awaiting help. At times such banks were so informally arranged that transactions were conducted over the bar at the local tavern. Occasionally, one of those ethnic banks evolved into a major financial institution. Such was the experience of Amadeo Pietro Giannini's Bank of Italy in San Francisco. As historian Andrew Rolle has described him, Giannini became "the banker to a generation of immigrant fishermen, fruit peddlers, and small ranchers, and workmen."

Giannini, the son of a successful immigrant merchant, founded his bank to aid fellow Italians and to keep them from the teeth of loan sharks charging fantastic rates of interest. Giannini also hoped to teach Italian immigrants how to maneuver successfully in the American economy. He spoke publicly about the virtues of interest-bearing savings accounts and pledged that he would loan any worker up to $25 "with no better security than the calluses on the borrower's hands." Giannini's shrewd investments and faith in the small saver paid high dividends. After the San Francisco fire in 1906, he transacted business on the wharf, not waiting until a new building was prepared. By the time of his death in 1949, Giannini's bank, renamed the Bank of America, was the largest bank in the world. Historian and biographer Felice Bonadio (*A. P. Giannini: Banker of America,* 1994) recalls that one of Giannini's favorite aphorisms was "Be first in everything."

IV

Most new immigrants did not throw themselves wholeheartedly into the pursuit of wealth, as did A. P. Giannini; they were equally as interested in structuring their lives to protect family and religious customs brought from their native countries. However, few were content to remain impoverished and most made at least modest economic gains. It is this advancement from candy peddler to store owner, from delivery boy to launderer, from sewing machine operator to tailor—rather than from rags to riches—that has particularly intrigued historians and caused most of them to define upward mobility occupationally.

In his now classic study of social mobility in nineteenth-century Newburyport, Massachusetts (*Poverty and Progress,* 1964), historian Stephan Thernstrom described an "ideology of mobility" that operated to provide Americans with "a scheme for comprehending and accommodating themselves to a new social and economic order." According to this mobility ideology, the United States had a uniquely fluid society, the defining characteristic of which was its competitiveness. Each citizen who competed, according to the ideal, was guaranteed that his social status would be determined by his merit. The wealthy and prestigious could remain so only as long as they performed well; the talented born to lowly station could be certain to ascend quickly to the riches and social position befitting their demonstrated worth. Failure to succeed in such a system could only be interpreted as the product of an individual's inadequacy, most certainly not the result of social injustice as was the case in the Old World.

From early in the nineteenth century onward, this ideology of success was popularized and restated so that all Americans could comprehend it. Politicians, ministers, teachers, and journalists all reiterated the notion—especially when they addressed the poor— that in an open society there could be no obstacles that an industrious man could not surmount. One newspaper, the *Newburyport Herald,* reminded its readers that, "If Washington had whined away his time after the defeat on Long Island, he would never have been the victor at Yorktown; but he put himself to work to make up his losses." Such examples made the point and suggested that initial failure did not preclude eventual success, a valuable means of forestalling disillusionment and encouraging optimism among even the least affluent.

Success was most frequently defined as rising above the level of manual labor. In urban factories or mills, the laborer might become a foreman, clerk, manager, or even owner. However, increasingly, small business came to be viewed by Americans as the path to mobility. With a minimum of capital, the workman could become a businessman.

A second measure of success was more modest. Rather than a change in occupational level, success could be defined by the criterion of property ownership. Thus, it could be immaterial whether a man worked with his head or his hands, for himself or someone else. What mattered was whether a man owned the roof over his head or could purchase it with the money in his bank account.

By the end of the nineteenth century, the ideology of success was well ensconced in American mythology. The novels of Horatio Alger featuring tales of boys who went from rags to riches because of their own acumen and luck became manuals for the young. However, most immigrants arriving after 1880 had never been exposed to the ideology of success. Even more important, new immigrants brought with them their own definitions of success, or the good life, quite different from those set forth in America's mobility ideology.

Historians have mapped occupational changes intragenerationally and intergenerationally within and among immigrant groups and sometimes between newcomers and the native born. They discovered intriguing differences in mobility rates comparing one group to another. The studies seem to concur that while the southern Italians did eventually achieve occupational upward mobility, their rate of rise was somewhat sluggish compared to that of native-born blue-collar workers and other immigrant groups, especially the east European Jews. Some, such as historian Thomas Kessner, contend that southern Italian peasants suffered an initial disadvantage in the American economy because their agrarian skills and preferences for outdoor labor allowed them to do little more than wield pick and shovel on construction sites in America's industrial cities when they first arrived. However, historian John Briggs (*An Italian Passage,* 1978) points out that many of the Italian immigrants he studied had arrived in America with entrepreneurial experience gleaned in Italian towns and had never been peasants at all. He suggests that indecision over whether their move to America was a permanent one, not a lack of urban skills, resulted in lower rates of upward mobility.

In some groups, there was no upward occupational mobility at all. According to Ricardo Romo, "Among first-, second-, and third-generation semiskilled and unskilled male Mexican laborers in Los Angeles, not a single individual moved upward to a white-collar position during the ten years between 1918 and 1928." However, among all male Los Angeles workers, 20 percent of the unskilled workers moved up to white-collar ranks between 1910 and 1920.

The rate of occupational mobility for east European Jews was indisputably the highest among all immigrants. Many members of this group had learned trades or become entrepreneurs in Europe because they were denied land ownership and other economic opportunities. They valued their status as independent artisans and tradesmen because it freed them from the supervision of a potentially hostile Gentile boss, a sine qua non of survival in their countries of origin. Moreover, because the Jews were in flight from tsarist persecution after 1900, there was no doubt in most of their minds that they were in America to stay and should begin to focus their attention on their role in the American economy.

While mobility studies have been useful in assessing the agility of various immigrant groups on the occupational status ladder, such studies were not designed to assess whether immigrants themselves put great value on upward mobility. Cultural and social priorities as well as historical experience shaped occupational choices and other economic decisions. Newcomers sought to carve out satisfactory niches in the economy that did not require abandonment of essential habits, customs, and values—all non-economic but critical ingredients of the good life.

Among Greeks and southern Italians, education, job success, and even the acquisition of great wealth were not permitted to take precedence over the preservation of the family's integrity and the patterns of loyalty and support that the family engendered. To the southern Italian, work was something one did to acquire sufficient money to be comfortable and not for personal fulfillment or satisfaction. Those who expected anything more than a living from their jobs were often viewed by relatives and friends as self-indulgent and as an insult to the previous generation whose status they were striving to exceed. In his study of the Italian community of East Harlem, anthropologist Robert Orsi (*The Madonna of 115th Street, Faith and Community in Italian Harlem, 1880–1950*, 1985), describes each extended family and the apartments where blood and nonblood relatives lived as a *domus,* "the chief unit of social relationship and cultural transmission," a term first popularized by European scholar Emmanuel LeRoy Ladurie's study of Montaillou. According to Orsi, no job or profession could summon the attention and energies of an individual as could the needs of those who shared a domus and knelt before the Madonna of 115th Street, the image that embodied the community's values system. Individualism was not a priority. "In a very fundamental way the individual could not exist apart from the domus and remain a human being. ... The men and women of Italian Harlem spoke not of their own success or progress but that of the domus."

Even for the upwardly mobile east European Jews, pursuit of wealth was not paramount. For the Orthodox, the good life consisted of being able to live and worship in a manner consistent with Mosaic law and religious tradition. Not all Jews were equally religious, but most were imbued with a cultural respect for intellectual pursuits. Rabbis, teachers, and others who worked with their minds instead of their hands were highly regarded within the Jewish community. Increasingly drawn to secular occupations, Jews aspired to socially prestigious professional positions in law, medicine, or education for their children, sometimes even preferring such fields to more lucrative business careers. Nonetheless, the path to such professions required education well beyond the minimum amount required by U.S. law. To obtain such an education meant withdrawing a potential wage earner from the family. Historian Selma Berrol (*Immigrants at School: New York City, 1898–1914*, 1978) has demonstrated that only after Jewish parents had reached a lower middle-class status did school papers take precedence over work papers. Economic success, then, enabled Jewish children to reach parental expectations.

American reformer and journalist Jacob Riis credited Jewish immigrants with recognizing that, beyond its intrinsic value, knowledge is power: "The poorest Hebrew knows—the poorer he is the better he knows it—that knowledge is power, and power is the means for getting on in this world that has spurned him so long, [knowledge] is what his soul yearns for. He lets no opportunity slip to obtain it." Moreover, unlike the Italians, Mexicans, and some other groups, east European Jews were encouraged to surpass their parents. Work was supposed to bring satisfaction and respect as well as a living. And the honor accorded an individual was seen to reflect on the entire family. Success thus did not estrange the child from the parents, but elevated the entire family's social position.

The Chinese immigrant's notion of the good life, too, was more complex than the pursuit of either occupational advancement or the acquisition of property. According to historian Betty Lee Sung, emphasis was placed on "scholarship, official position, and an illustrious family." Like the east European Jews, the Chinese valued learning. A learned man regardless of occupation or income was the object of respect in the community. Official titles and a personal reputation for honor were important to Chinese immigrants. Like Jews, the Chinese were drawn to the learned professions. However, most often the Chinese path to mobility began in the mines, progressed to railroad labor, and culminated in entrepreneurship, a laundry or a restaurant. Not until well after World War II were Chinese able to vault the barriers of prejudice and enter the learned professions in substantial numbers.

Family responsibilities were as important among the Chinese as they were among the Italians. Filial piety was the cardinal rule.

And to the Chinese, the word "family" included more than just parents and siblings; it connoted a broader group of relatives, a kinship group or clan. The individual was expected to subordinate personal goals and purposes to those of the family. While the learned professions remained barred to most Chinese, many became respected members of their communities and created business opportunities and jobs for nuclear family members and other kin.

Occupational mobility statistics, then, indicate the slot various immigrant groups held in America's economy and how it changed over time. But from the immigrant's perspective, success or personal satisfaction often transcended the color of the collar—white or blue—and even the size of the bank account. The good life often depended on reconciling noneconomic values, traditions, and priorities with the material wealth he or she hoped to accumulate in the United States. Not all those who made the journey found satisfaction as well as wealth and position. And often their odyssey led them farther away from their past than they cared to go.

Contemporary novels in the immigrants' native language placed the quest for economic advancement within the context of the larger issue of assimilation. How American did the immigrants become? What were the costs and benefits of Americanization? Nowhere is the dilemma more starkly recreated than in *The Rise of David Levinsky* (1917) by Yiddish novelist and journalist Abraham Cahan. Cahan's novel traces the odyssey of a Russian Jewish immigrant who compromises his religious values and sacrifices his passion for scholarship for material success. Early in the novel, a young David laments that becoming "Americanized" undermined his daily religious practices. "The very clothes I wore and the very food I ate," David testified, "had a fatal effect on my religious habits." Much later in life, a weary Levinsky muses that "David, the poor lad swinging over a Talmud volume at the Preacher's Synagogue, seems to have more in common with my inner identity than David Levinsky, the well-known cloak-manufacturer."

Cahan's words touched a chord deep in the hearts of many immigrants who were, like David Levinsky, confronting their own transformation from alien to American.

CHAPTER FOUR

Integrating the Immigrant in City and Countryside: Newcomer and Nation Transformed

For many immigrants, the first reaction to the United States was a tremendous sense of isolation. They were greenhorns, uninitiated in the ways of their new country, unable even to speak the language. They were harassed and ridiculed by older immigrants and native Americans for not knowing how to behave appropriately in their new home. Even compared with members of their own immigrant group, newcomers were nervous misfits with odd clothing and hairstyles unsuitably reminiscent of the old country. Often, newcomers were pressured most heavily by members of their own group to become Americanized quickly and not remain embarrassingly different. The newcomers, meanwhile, felt awkward and were shocked by the changes that life in America had already wrought on earlier arrivals. One Jewish immigrant recalled his first days in America: "I felt as if on coals. No word could I think of but 'greenhorn.'" On city streets he was startled by the appearance of young Jewish men and women. "The girls had painted cheeks and greased netted hair with hidden pins. As if that weren't enough, they also flashed golden teeth. They seemed faded and withered. The males with stiff hats tipped over their foreheads and their plastered locks, gave off an aroma of vulgar, youthful virility." Nor was such surprise limited to city sidewalks. A Swedish immigrant in a rural upper Middle West community wrote home, "there are girls who doll themselves up enough to frighten you. They would be better as scarecrows than anything else, so if you need any of those I can send you a boatload." His culture shock was typical of that experienced by many new arrivals. So it became essential for each immigrant to rapidly figure out what it meant to be an American and to decide which changes were worthwhile and which customs and values were too important to relinquish.

Decisions about modifying values and behavior were never made in a vacuum. Newcomers were affected by previous experience, peers, and environment. What had already happened to them in their lives was crucial. Those who had tilled land belonging to others often wanted their own land. Others, disillusioned with life on the land hoped to earn a living in any way but farming. Immigrants frequently modeled themselves on those who had arrived earlier and seemed to them successful, seeking out relatives and friends from home.

Most decisive in the process of adjustment was where the immigrant had chosen to settle. The choice of city or countryside determined the kinds and quantity of economic and social options open to new arrivals. According to historian Kathleen Neils Conzen, even as immigrant urban dwellers sought to preserve the past in their neighborhoods, "localized" rural cultures also sought to cope with the pressures and possibilities of modern life "on a parallel trajectory of their own."

Books of advice to new immigrants about techniques of integrating themselves into American society and culture proliferated in the late nineteenth century. Some were published by Americans hoping to impose their own design on immigrant behavior. Others were the legacy of earlier settlers. One of the latter, written in Yiddish and published in Russia in 1891, advised readers to:

Forget your past, your customs and your ideals. Select a goal and pursue it with all your might. No matter what happens to you, hold on. You will experience a bad time but sooner or later you will achieve your goal. . . .

The new arrival was being encouraged to barter his or her past for a more satisfying future. However, for most immigrants it was not a casual exchange. Historians have largely rejected the notion of assimilation as an unsatisfactory way to describe the process of negotiation whereby newcomers became Americans. Assimilation implies that one group absorbs the other. Instead, today's scholars prefer the word *integration,* which suggests the process of groups merging, each group negotiating a place for some of its own values, customs, beliefs, and institutions in the relationship even as it accepts some of the values, customs, beliefs, and institutions of the other group. By the 1970s, historians such as Philip Taylor (*The Distant Magnet,* 1971) were already rejecting older depictions of the process as a smooth, almost mechanical progression. Instead, he contends that the struggle each newcomer faced after arrival was marked by a ". . . series of conflicts between competing influences from the wider American society battling with the entrenched leadership of heads of families or of ethnic institutions." Though some groups and individuals embraced American values and institutions more quickly and thoroughly than others, the weight of evidence tips the scales toward Taylor's contention that the integration of newcomers was not always smooth, swift, and direct.

Those who settled in ethnically homogeneous rural communities often had less access to the institutions and customs of American culture than those who lived in heterogeneous industrial cities where members of different groups mingled in the marketplace and labored shoulder to shoulder in the workplace. Racial barriers, too, placed constraints on patterns of integration. Dark-skinned immigrants, such as those from the West Indies or Asia, for example, found that American racism allowed a segmented assimilation, an integration only with those of similar hue, such as the native born, African-American descendants of slaves who had migrated in large numbers out of the rural South to northern and midwestern cities in the 1890s.

In cities and rural townships, immigrants received assistance and advice, frequently unsolicited, from many sources with varied agendas. Benevolent aid societies, some operated by American charities and others run by religious institutions or members of their own ethnic groups, were quick to extend newcomers a helping hand. Public schools not only taught immigrant children the "3 Rs" but assumed responsibility for socializing children and, indirectly, their parents, in the ways of American society. Even politicians, primarily concerned with acquiring the loyalty of new voters, became conduits for assistance and advice.

Various immigrant groups arriving at the turn of the century, with unique languages and cultural traditions, differed from one another and from the native-born, or core society, as to what constituted an acceptable level of integration. Even those of the same group negotiated different terms with America depending upon whether their new homes were tenement apartments or small farmhouses on the prairie. Conformity required compromise, but how could sacred values and traditions be cast by the wayside? For all immigrants, Americanization was a struggle to reconcile the ways of the Old World with life in the New.

I

The earliest casualty in the adjustment process was an immigrant's native language. It began with names. As mentioned, many an immigrant was given a new identity by an Immigration Bureau Officer who could not understand or spell his or her name. Many others jettisoned family names ending in "a," "o," "ski," "sky," or "wicz." Names difficult for American tongues became barriers to employment and acceptance and stigmatized the foreign born. Thus, Irving Abramowitz became Irwin Abbot "for business reasons" and Pietro Minotti was dubbed Peter Minor. However, immigrants and their children did not always Americanize their names. According to Eileen Tamura (*Americanization, Acculturation, and Ethnic Identity, The Nisei Generation in Hawaii,* 1994), Issei parents, native-born Japanese who emigrated to the United States, almost universally gave their children Japanese names.

These American-born youngsters, Nisei, kept those names. Among 985 Japanese eighth-graders in Hawaii in 1924, 91 percent were called by their Japanese names in school. However, even in Hawaii, exposure to other groups in the cosmopolitan environment of cities made a difference. Tamura observes that "In urban Honolulu, where exposure to American ways was greater than in rural Oahu and the neighbor islands, Nisei acquired English names earlier and more often." In matters of cultural adjustment, "Calling oneself 'Robert' or 'Mary' created a different self-identity from 'Chotoku' or 'Shizuko.'"

Language retention was related to residence. Hoping to minimize the change in their lives required by emigration, immigrants chose to live in as close proximity as they could to those who had emigrated from the same town or village as they themselves. In cities and countryside, new arrivals and their children tried to envelop themselves in a sort of cocoon, almost completely avoiding contact with other groups and the core society, although shopping and work often necessitated contact with strangers. A trans-Atlantic chain migration from the Norwegian fjord district of Balestrand established daughter settlements in the rural upper Middle West. There neighbors in the Old World could be neighbors in the New. Many large and midsized cities had little Italies, Chinatowns, Mexican barrios, and enclaves of Polish, Russian, and Ukrainian immigrants. On New York City's Lower East Side, members of particular immigrant groups even dominated specific tenement buildings. According to historian Albert Camarillo's study of Mexicans in California (*Chicanos in a Changing Society, From Mexican Pueblos to American Barrios in Santa Barbara and Southern California, 1848–1930,* 1979), Santa Barbara's barrio facilitated contact among Mexicans as mutual aid societies, or *mutualistas,* "helped perpetuate Mexican culture, language, and cohesiveness in an otherwise foreign society." Other groups had similar voluntary organizations. Surrounded by familiar faces, immigrants could continue to speak their native language, eat familiar foods, and conduct family and religious lives in traditional fashion, resisting the pressure to integrate.

However hard newcomers tried to avoid the discomfort of contact with those who did not speak their language, urban life forced them into such contact daily. In cities, it was necessary to speak English to get on a streetcar, ask directions, buy food, and obtain a job. Mastery of English would enable recent arrivals to mingle easily with the native-born and earlier immigrants. Italians, Poles, Mexicans, Chinese, and east European Jews learned English as their neighbors spoke it. Their speech echoed not only their mother tongues but the regional cadences and inflections common to native speakers in Charleston, New Orleans, El Paso, Boston, or New York. Often, immigrants spoke a hodgepodge of their native language and English. Richard Gambino (*Blood of My Blood*, 1974) recalls hearing his Italian immigrant neighbors call an automobile a "carra," a store a "storo," a bar a "barra," a job a "giobba," and a toilet a "baccausa" (because early tenements had been served by backhouses or outhouses).

In the more homogeneous communities of rural America, one might avoid learning English longer. According to historian Jon Gjerde (*The Minds of the West, Ethnocultural Evolution in the Rural Middle West, 1830–1917,* 1997), in rural communities many European immigrants, "particularly women," but men as well, lived their entire lives without learning English. In 1892, one resident of a community in Dodge County, Wisconsin, recalled that "very few" of the Germans in the town understood "a word of English." Because men generally had more contact with the outside, English-speaking community, they often mastered English before women in rural America. In 1900, in Arendahl township, Minnesota, non-English speakers composed 3.2 percent of its male population, but almost twice that, 6.3 percent, of its female residents. In Norwegian homes, women often hid rather than face the strain of trying to pronounce English words. English "loan words" that entered the vocabulary of midwestern Norwegians further demonstrates the gender difference. Over 70 percent of these words dealt with machinery and over 50 percent with farming, whereas just a little over 30 percent dealt with women's sphere of housekeeping.

In addition to retaining their mother tongues in their own lives, many newcomers wanted their children to speak the language of the old country, as well. To the foreign-born, retaining their language into the next generation was a matter of pride as well as comfort. Some groups such as the Japanese established special schools to teach their children the mother tongue. They defended their schools against attacks that such institutions blocked acculturation. To Issei, sound citizenship meant that their children, the Nisei, should merge the best of Japanese culture with the best that America had to offer. They contended that such schools promoted good citizenship because the schools taught moral values grounded in Japanese culture and yet resonated with what Americans believed.

One Italian newspaper editor wrote in 1903 that "in the civilization of the Italian language . . . [were] thousands of secrets for our future in America." Another, writing in the same period in Utica, New York, titled an editorial on the subject, "A Duty of the Heads of Families." He defined it as the duty of all Italian parents to be certain that their children learn Italian, because "although born here they are Italians and have, thus, the right to know the language of their homeland." He quickly added that since the children learned English at school, there could be little harm in a father insisting that Italian be spoken exclusively in the home.

But the more immigrant parents insisted that Yiddish, Italian, Chinese, or Spanish be spoken at home, the more their children rebelled. As they grew to adulthood, the children of the immigrants realized that a fluent command of the English language was a critical ingredient of socioeconomic mobility. English, spoken as if by a native-born American, was a prerequisite for gaining entrance to a prestigious college, getting a high-salaried job, meeting the right people, including the right marriage prospect, and becoming an authentic American. Occasionally, those of the second generation became hypersensitive, ashamed of the ethnic identities so clearly revealed in their parents' accents.

At times, there was generational conflict over language. An indignant son wrote a letter to Abraham Cahan, the editor of *The Forward,* a Yiddish-language newspaper, to complain of his father's public use of Yiddish, the language shared by most east European Jews. The son, a big success in America, had taken his father shopping in a fashionable Fifth Avenue shop and had become embarrassed to the point of anger when his father spoke Yiddish to a clerk whom he suspected of being Jewish. Cahan scolded the young man for berating his father, but also lectured the father on the importance of speaking English in America. Such were the pains inflicted by one generation upon another as both struggled to cope with the dilemma of Americanization. Cahan, himself an immigrant from Russia, encouraged newcomers to write letters which he published in *The Forward*'s *"Bintl Briv"* ("Bundle of Letters") column, a feature he inaugurated in 1906. Cahan believed that the immigrants should share with each other their problems and questions about America. He would try to offer advice that would help the newcomers adjust to their new life without sacrificing their dignity or their Jewish heritage. In the end, though, the children won the generational war. Their future success required them to embrace English, and they would not allow their parents' nostalgia to block the path.

Just as newcomers clung to their language, they often continued to embrace some of the prejudices and stereotypes common in the Old World communities they had so recently left. Just as language and loyalties linked those who had been neighbors before emigrating, traditional rivalries persisted. Some neighbors viewed each other with time-honored wariness. In the streets of America, Athenians still considered Spartans ignorant, slow, and pugnacious, while Spartans found the Athenians as effete and decadent as they had seemed in Greece. Northern Italians who removed to America brought with them their contempt for Il Mezzogiorno, while the distinctive dialects and attitudes of Neapolitans, Calabrians, and Genoese were so divisive, southerners had little more than their mutual distrust of the Sicilians in common. Jews from Galicia, a province of Austria, and those from Lithuania or neighboring regions shunned each other. *Galitzianers* regarded themselves as culturally German, generally better educated, and more secular than their less enlightened, often more orthodox co-religionists from farther east. However, the Lithuanians, or *Litvaks,* dismissed Galitzianers as pedants, a dry humorless lot who were hardly as shrewd or worldly wise as Litvaks for all the westerners' pretensions of superiority. Galitzianers, meanwhile, often quipped that Litvaks were so pious that they repented before they sinned.

Even when patterns of prejudice were responsible for patterns of neighborhood development as in the case of barrios in the Southwest, the effect was to strengthen premigration cultural patterns.

In the rural Midwest, Swedes and Norwegians harbored negative stereotypes of each other. An especially strong distaste existed between the Irish and the Norwegians. The former considered the latter arrogant interlopers, while Norwegians regarded the Irish as belligerent people of low-class habits and behavior.

The languages and prejudices of the Old World were sustained longest in those American communities where Old World neighbors again lived side by side. However, such residential patterns were not always detrimental to integration into American life. At times, the ethnic neighborhoods or homogeneous rural towns could be as much a help as a hindrance to integration. Such enclaves could function as incubators, providing immigrants and their children with a supportive environment until they were sufficiently prepared and confident to venture forth and mingle with the native born and members of other immigrant groups. Chinatowns allowed some newcomers to avoid work contracts with labor organizations that would exploit them, offering Chinese immigrants instead the chance to become "small, independent entrepreneurs, such as laundrymen, grocers, and restauranteurs," serving the needs of their kinsmen as described by historian Shih-Shan Henry Tsai (*The Chinese Experience in America,* 1986). Later, they might move their businesses to non-Chinese neighborhoods and offer these services to members of other ethnic groups. In rural California, Chinese farm laborers typically lived with Chinese farmers until they saved enough to become farmers themselves. According to Sucheng Chan (*This Bittersweet Soil, The Chinese in California Agriculture, 1860–1910,* 1986), "Few real Chinese families existed in nineteenth century California because even though there were Chinese women present, the great majority of them were women who had been brought to America to work as prostitutes." Why? Poor men headed for America to earn higher wages could not afford to take their wives. Married women who did come, often found America not to their liking and returned.

After 1882, the Chinese Exclusion law made sending for wives difficult and American-born Chinese women of childbearing age were not numerous.

Ethnic enclaves in urban and rural America developed, then, sometimes by choice, sometimes by the compulsion born of prejudice, and often by both. Immigrants chose to live close to their work and among others who shared their culture and lifestyle, and, therefore, would not despise them. According to historian Caroline Golab (*Immigrant Destinations,* 1977), "If the conditions of work remained favorable long enough to keep the newcomers rooted to their piece of city-space, the ethnic neighborhood and community could be formed, complete with its unique industrial and occupational structures." In New York, the garment factories where most Jews and Italians worked were within walking distance from Lower East Side tenements. In Golab's study of Philadelphia, she discovered that "Jews and Italians settled in central parts of the city next to the major wholesale and retail markets that employed them in large numbers." The factories in which most of Philadelphia's Poles worked utilized the latest in industrial technology and required ample room for plant and transportation facilities. They were located in the newer or less settled areas of the city—Nicetown, Port Richmond, Bridesburg, southwest Philadelphia, and northwest Philadelphia—surrounded by the homes of their workers.

In most cities, no single ethnic group resided exclusively in a neighborhood or enclave. Usually three or four groups shared a corner of the city, but each group would be more concentrated on particular streets or even in specific buildings than the others. In Philadelphia's areas of high Polish concentration, Poles occupied most of the houses on particular streets or avenues, block after block. Similarly, on New York's Lower East Side, Jews and Italians shared the neighborhood, each group holding domain over particular blocks. Thus, different groups could live in close geographical proximity and yet be socially isolated. Provincialism within each ethnic enclave echoed provincial and village configurations in the Old World. In Italian communities, families who were Sicilian, Calabrian, or Neapolitan—often from the same village in these provinces—again took up residence near one another in an American city. There they could purchase familiar foods, prepared in traditional fashion, from merchants who might even haggle over the price or sell the merchandise in amounts small enough to fit every budget. In the neighborhood of an American city, an immigrant might find that group taboos and traditional codes of personal behavior derived from Old-World experiences and wisdom continued to have relevance. Richard Gambino recalls that after a fight he had with a childhood playmate, his Italian-born grandmother and the mother of the other young pugilist confronted each other and with a combination of body language and *passatella* (ritualized oratory) battled for their respective family's honor on a street in Red Hook, Brooklyn. No mere trans-Atlantic voyage could make proper decorum superfluous as determined by time-honored custom.

Neighborhoods changed character as different immigrant groups deserted them and moved on to better housing in less congested parts of the city. Newcomers then crowded into the empty buildings, bringing with them their own unique customs and culture. This process of ethnic succession in a neighborhood took several generations. Moreover, even when economic prosperity permitted geographic mobility within the city, emigrants returned periodically to "the old neighborhood." In New York, Chicago, and Philadelphia, immigrants followed expanding subway and bus lines into new neighborhoods. The subway offered not only an escape route, but a ride back home. Some returned daily, commuting from new homes to old jobs. Others came just on weekends to visit friends and relatives, to shop and to eat. In her description of Chinese communities in the United States (*Mountain of Gold,* 1967), Betty Lee Sung contends that Chinese cuisine preserved "Chinatowns" even after improved economic conditions had permitted some families to move away. Those families continued to serve traditional Chinese dishes in their homes; and the basic ingredients could only be purchased in Chinatown, "for where else can one buy soy sauce, bean curd, dried mushrooms, snow peas, and bamboo shoots?"

Patterns of shopping and consumption were important markers on the path toward integration. On farms and city streets, consumerism might reflect traditional patterns of interaction among family and friends sharing dinners on weekends. However, just as often what newcomers chose to purchase marked their progress toward integration into American society. During the 1980s and 1990s, scholars demonstrated that patterns of consumption offer a barometer of cultural change, or acculturation, an important dimension of the larger process of national integration. An elderly Norwegian immigrant described her pastor's parlor as heavenly. The room's windows bore the mark of middle-class respectability, "lace curtains." Also, "there was a carpet on the floor, a corner sofa, one round and one oblong table, a what-not filled with knick-knacks, cane-seated chairs, and a rocker." According to Andrew R. Heinze (*Adapting to Abundance, Jewish Immigrants, Mass Consumption, and the Search for American Identity,* 1990), eastern European Jews on New York's Lower East Side established their identities as Americans by their spending practices, especially at holiday times. During the Passover holiday in 1902, an article in the *New York Tribune* reported that Jews who had purchased new furniture and bedding abandoned their used goods on the street for collection by Sanitation Department workers. In Russia's shtetlakh, families had hauled furniture to the banks of nearby rivers for a cleaning. However, in the United States, replacement, not restoration of possessions, was the rule as increasingly higher wages increased disposable income. Throughout the year, the most popular mark of middle-class attainment was the piano in the parlor. Yiddish newspapers were filled with advertisements by companies selling pianos and parlor furnishings. Heinze describes Jewish immigrants as "mesmerized by the idea of a room devoted simply to 'living.'" No matter how small the tenement apartment, Jews sought to carve out a parlor space. Whether in rural towns or urban enclaves, newcomers of every group believed that middle-class respectability was as close as the nearest store or mail-order catalogue.

The nucleus of community and the link between traditional lifestyle and membership in the American middle-class was the house of worship. As Jon Gjerde (*The Minds of the West,* 1997) observes, "the church served as the principle vehicle through which cultural patterns were re-established." Nor was it just the language or style of worship. Church edifices attested to the community's commitment to both ethnocultural tradition and the pursuit of material success. "Whether the edifice was a gothic wood structure built by Swedish Lutherans, a white frame chapel constructed by New England Congregationalists, or a large lime-stone or brick basilica erected by German Catholics, rural ethnic communities often expended considerable resources to witness their faiths." One German-language newspaper described the brick edifice of St. Joseph's Church in Iowa as "in the middle of a lovely prairie," identifying itself "as Catholic afar by its cross." Inside such churches, a variety of traditions, rituals, and sacred objects of religious import were part of the cultural baggage newcomers brought from their native lands. Religious fealty was intertwined with regional and national identities. A distinctive feature of late-nineteenth-century immigration was the multiplicity of diverse Catholic groups that joined the already heterogeneous American Catholic community, especially in sizable cities. Sometimes these urban-dwelling immigrants worshiped together, common faith transcending their differences. More often, these differences were obstacles to cohesion. Each group preferred its own clergy, who could conduct worship and serve congregants in the familiar pat-terns of their native communities. In neighborhoods where immi-grant Catholics of different ethnic groups resided, newcomers felt most at home worshiping in their own churches. Both Irish and French Canadians were Roman Catholics. However, in the New England parishes where Irish priests delivered their sermons in English, French-speaking Canadians were ill at ease; they viewed the insistence on English as an attempt by Irish clergymen at Americanization, undermining French heritage. Irish parishioners treated newcomers speaking a foreign tongue as suspicious inter-lopers with designs on the Church.

More than language, contrasting traditions and unique styles of worship accented national distinctions among Catholics. John J. Bukowczyk describes the special role that the Blessed Virgin

Mary had in Polish Catholic tradition. "Throughout Poland, the faithful frequented local Marian pilgrimage sites; in America, Polish immigrants eventually built one of their own in Doylestown, Pennsylvania. Each Polish church had its cadre of Marylike nuns, its Marian alter, and its image of the sacred "Black Madonna, Our Lady of Czestochowa, Poland's patroness." According to Helen Znaniecki Lopata (*Polish Americans,* 1976), "Polish peasants, particularly during the decades of heavy migration, combined a Polish version of Catholicism with pagan and magical beliefs in animated natural objects and spirits." A Polish immigrant far from his familiar church building and sacred objects, in need of spiritual comfort but repelled by the formalism of the Irish-dominated American Catholic Church, might turn to pagan superstitions acquired in his home village, cherishing amulets having no place in Catholic iconography. He might sprinkle the floors of a newly acquired apartment with salt or coins before moving in to ensure his family's prosperity in their abode. Charms to ward off illness, assure fertility, or attract a particular member of the opposite sex were used in tandem with lighting candles in church or praying with rosary beads in hand.

Historians Josef Barton and Rudolph Vecoli have published essays that demonstrate how folk religion and community life deeply colored the Catholicism of Czech and Italian Catholic immigrants, respectively. The contadini described by Vecoli, for example, subscribed to a system of *clientelismo.* While God was a "lofty, distant figure," a local saint, a "friend of God," could be a poor peasant's intermediary. Therefore, Italians prayed directly to particular saints—Santa Lucia, San Gennaro, San Michele, and others. Each saint had special jurisdiction over illness, business, or other particular fields of endeavor. In Italy the high point of a peasant's year was the celebration, or *festa,* in honor of the saint who looked after the town. The statue of the saint was carried through the town as part of a long and colorful procession complete with brass bands and weeping women.

These vibrant religious festivities were not immediately abandoned when villagers left for the New World. They maintained a transnational link between southern Italian villages and neighborhoods where those villagers now lived. In New York's East Harlem Italian community annual festas celebrated the Madonna of Mount Carmel on East 115th Street. Anthropologist Robert Orsi (*The Madonna of 115th Street,* 1985) describes how the women of the community knelt before the image of the Madonna and confided their special concerns to her for the health and prosperity of family members. In the Little Italies of urban America, immigrants celebrated the patron saints of their native villages with the same parades, bands, and delicacies they had enjoyed in Italy. Such goings-on were deplored by American Catholics who watched the religious processions clanging through the streets of Italian neighborhoods. To non-Italian Catholics these festivities seemed little more than pre-Christian pagan rites. Over time and several generations, these festas and other such customs were usually modified or abandoned by Italians hoping to blend in with other more assimilated, non-Italian Catholics. However, in some Italian neighborhoods, such as New York's Little Italy, festas in honor of St. Anthony and St. Gennaro continue to be celebrated with traditional enthusiasm.

Dissimilarities among Catholic immigrants significantly reduced the quality and quantity of emotional and material support rendered newcomers by the Church. Irish and German churchmen who arrived earlier or were native born looked unsympathetically upon ethnic parishes, embarrassed by newcomers' eclectic styles of Catholicism and apprehensive that ethnic rivalries might fracture the Church or, worse, dilute their own influence within it. Therefore, Church assistance was often contingent upon Americanization, a condition unsatisfactory to most immigrants, who preferred whenever possible to build and direct their own parish churches, parochial schools, and hospitals. Immigrants hoped to simultaneously preserve their particular version of Catholicism and their group's identity. George J. Sanchez (*Becoming Mexican American,* 1993) studying Mexican immigrants in Los Angeles observed that "the North American Church exhibited a form of Catholicism which appealed little to the Mexican populace. Consequently, Mexican immigrants often felt alienated from the institutional Church. Anti-clericalism remained high and may have escalated among the Mexican American population because Irish American priests were rarely found to be sensitive enough to the needs of a working class people from a different culture." Sanchez quotes one immigrant woman's unmistakable anti-clericalism, "I don't believe in the sanctity or in the purity of the priests, or that they are invested with superhuman powers. To me they are men like all the rest. That is why I don't pay attention to their preachings." The Italians of Buffalo, New York, reports Virginia Yans-McLaughlin, viewed the Church as "an Irish-American institution" and therefore, "remained either nominal Roman Catholics or without Church ties of any kind," until they could afford their own churches and priests. In Buffalo, the immigrants "generally avoided the parochial schools" for similar reasons, though some parents found the Irish brand of Catholic education a lesser evil than Protestant-flavored public education.

The oldest fissure in Catholicism had occurred in 1054, resulting in a complete separation between the Roman Catholic and Greek Orthodox Churches. In the United States, Greek immigrants clung to their own church, with priests clearly distinguished by their full beards, tall hats, and flowing robes. Whenever a *kinotis* (community) became sufficiently large and affluent it imported a priest from Greece and built a church, hoping to resist assimilation of its members by the more highly organized and affluent Roman Catholic Church.

Despite internecine discord, new immigrants clung to their religions, while adjusting the style of their religious practices to reflect their experience in America. Second-generation Greek immigrants worshiped in chapels that were but bland versions of the elaborate, ornate churches of their homeland. East European Jews, Orthodox in their native Russia or Poland, shaved their beards and sat next to their wives and daughters in the "Conservative" synagogues they now preferred rather than the Orthodox houses of worship where women sat mostly secluded in balconies or behind curtains. Others who rarely attended services in their villages now became members of churches or synagogues to maintain close contact with those from home and to draw spiritual strength necessary to confront the adversities of immigrant life. On New York City's Lower East Side, rabbis were known by the village in Russia or Poland from which they had emigrated, and were sought out by former neighbors for advice.

Statistics on changes in religious practice are notoriously unreliable. However, a consensus among sociologists suggests that the religious lives of the children and grandchildren of immigrants were generally less conventionally pious than the lives of most newcomers. As the children of the immigrants rebelled against their parents' piety—which seemed old-fashioned and stifling— they expressed their rebellion by shunning traditional religious expressions. Others, merely hoping to embrace America more quickly, readily abandoned any religious customs and rituals that conflicted with the economic or social demands of American life. Many second-generation east European Jews worked on Saturday, which was their Sabbath, but a regular business day for their Gentile neighbors and employers.

Despite the fears of priests and rabbis, there was never a rush of second-generation Catholic or Jewish immigrants to Protestant churches as a means to Americanization—not that there was a lack of proselytizing on the part of the Protestants. Many Protestant groups did invade immigrant enclaves with honed conversion techniques. In local hospitals, Protestant chaplains or staff attempted the deathbed conversions of terminally ill Roman Catholic and Jewish patients. The founding of Catholic hospitals such as St. Vincent's Hospital in New York and St. Joseph's in Philadelphia, and Jewish hospitals in various cities with names such as Mt. Sinai or Beth Israel, suggests the determination of Catholic and Jewish communities to resist Protestant proselytizing and tend to the souls as well as to the bodies of ill members of their congregations. In some cities Catholic hospitals proliferated because of language differences. In Philadelphia, St. Mary's Hospital served the German immigrant community, which felt uncomfortable at St. Joseph's Hospital, founded by the Irish.

Still, Protestants were indefatigable in their pursuit of souls among the newcomers. Tract societies updated their publications to address a new generation of foreign-born readers and the Sunday School movement sought to make their weekly classes in Christianity appealing to the urban poor. Albert Camarillo found that in Santa Barbara, California, Protestant missionary work among the Chinese took precedence over work conducted among Chicanos. However, by the early part of the twentieth century, proselytizers were scheduling regular evangelical services in the Pueblo Viejo barrio. The Santa Barbara First Baptist Church launched the first permanent missionary effort among Chicanos in 1902. Seventeen years later, sufficient numbers of Mexican Americans and newly arrived Mexicans had joined to justify making it a permanent church rather than just a mission. However, prior to the 1930s, the two Baptist churches in the city practiced segregation of Anglo and Mexican congregations.

Even as traditional religious identities were challenged in the American environment, so were other values, customs, and lifestyles. Even personal appearance and gender relationships were affected. In 1892, some of the German farmers in Dodge County, Wisconsin, were noticed as still wearing wooden shoes in the stable and yard, but removing them upon entering the house because the American-style parlor had to be kept free of dirt. Use of newer technology threatened to change gendered work obligations. Traditional divisions of labor, with men doing the tilling of fields and women milking cows and tending to gardens and kitchens, had to be encoded in state law to be preserved. In 1886, a Swedish-American woman, Anna Lindquist, was arrested in Minnesota. This "poor Swede girl," as the newspaper described her, was arrested for wearing men's clothing. A farm laborer hired to "herd cattle and do a man's work," Lindquist found her dress "inconvenient in the brush" and so dressed in male clothing, not realizing it was illegal. Another woman, Annie Hedstrom, not only dressed as a man but took a job under the alias Charlie Parker because she said, "she did not like woman's work around the kitchen, and besides, she could earn more money as a man."

Traditional clothing was abandoned by other young women anxious to appear as attractive and stylish as their American sisters. According to historian George Sanchez, female Mexican immigrants "of all ages typically wore cotton house dresses." However, "Since their personal appearance was more strictly supervised by parents, young Mexican women were often the first to conflict with their families over fashion." Swimwear, skirt length, and cosmetics were always points of friction as young women tested the "boundaries of tradition and their own personal freedom through experimentation and innovation in dress and image." In her study of two generations of Italian women in New York, Miriam Cohen observes that although daughters usually turned their earned incomes over to their mothers, they "openly set aside a portion of their income for personal clothing expenses." Warm, sturdy clothing was important, but working-class women in New York dressed well as a way of maintaining self-respect and "in hopes of attracting a beau."

For some groups, such as Orthodox Jews, changes in dress conflicted with religious law. Married women were required to wear a *sheytl,* or wig, publicly as a sign of modesty. Yet, many young wives changed their fashion to conform to the American style their husbands found alluring. In 1902, Hutchins Hapgood observed, "If she is young when she comes to America, she soon lays aside her wig, and sometimes assumes the rakish American hat, (and) prides herself on her bad English. . . ." Shedding their wigs was for women, as shaving their beards was for men, an outward concession to America.

Women changed more than their appearance in America. Free public schools encouraged many new immigrant parents to allow their daughters at least an elementary school education. Compulsory attendance laws after 1918 persuaded the hesitant. Young women too old for school usually acquired knowledge of American ways informally from coworkers. In cities, many took evening classes to improve their English and learn American housekeeping, an opportunity not always available to immigrant farm women.

One lesson women learned quickly was that in America marriages were not prearranged by parents. In traditional societies, marriages were the products of family agreements, sometimes with the assistance of a marriage broker who was a member of the community and hired by one or both families to make a match. With a favorable match, a family gained prestige or wealth through its new tie to a family of equal or greater reputation and resources. The happiness of the bride and groom was a lesser consideration and marriage for love alone was unthinkable—indicating an abdication of parental responsibility or the absence of filial respect. In Greece, a dowry was paid to the groom by the bride's family. Fathers and brothers labored hard to secure money for dowries lest the family be dishonored by unmarriageable daughters. A dutiful brother often postponed his own marriage until his sisters had dowries sufficient to attract husbands. During the height of emigration from Greece, marriages were frequently arranged across the sea by a system of picture brides. These young ladies, betrothed by mail to men already in America, often came from the same village as their prospective mates and knew their families well. After the arrangement was struck, the bride would be sent to America by herself to meet and marry the man to whom she was promised. Few unengaged Greek women emigrated on their own, but those who did and later married in America spared their families the burden of the dowry.

Arranged marriages were routine in China. The poorer the family, the more crucial the bride price. Judy Yung describes the situation of nineteen-year-old Wong Ah So, whose family betrothed her to a "Gold Mountain man," as men who already had been to America were often called. The groom, a laundryman, paid the family 450 Mexican dollars. An apprehensive and very nervous Wong Ah So emigrated with this laundryman, Huey Yow, in 1922 even before a wedding ceremony had taken place. Failure to go would have brought dishonor to her relatives by breaking a family agreement.

Among east European Jews, village *shadkans* or matchmakers often brought the "lucky" boy and girl together. After the marriage, the male ruled the family, while his wife managed both household and consumption decisions; there was little egalitarianism in such homes. Husband and wife had been socialized since childhood to fit these roles, and their "acceptable behavior" bore little resemblance to that in American marriages, even during the rigid Victorian era. Increasingly, immigrant women from societies where marriages were arranged demanded to choose their own mates on the basis of romantic love, an option that males were equally anxious to exercise.

Norwegian immigrants migrating from Balestrand, Norway, to the upper Middle West had already experienced courting and brought with them the practice of "night courting," or bundling, which occasionally led to premarital births, as documented by Jon Gjerde (*From Peasants to Farmers,* 1985). In the United States, Norwegians found themselves criticized by pastors for night courting, but the abundance of land allowed marriage at an earlier age and often resulted in larger families.

As new immigrants modified marriage patterns, they found that traditional childrearing patterns were likewise altered. Italian, Greek, Slavic, and Asian households were traditionally parent-centered. Age implied wisdom and the young were expected to show appropriate deference. Jewish households were more "child-centered," and parents tended to be more indulgent toward offspring than in other ethnic households. In general, however, new immigrant families resisted the comparative permissiveness of American family life as long as possible. Until the family achieved economic security, which frequently did not occur until the second or third generation, children were expected to perform tasks as if they were little adults. Childishness and play were put aside by immigrant children at a much earlier age than by American children.

Still, childrearing practices differed considerably among new immigrant groups. Greek, Slavic, and Italian children were permitted to spend more time learning from their peers than Jewish, Chinese, or Japanese children, who were more closely supervised by parents. Asian, Mexican, and Slavic boys were taught that manliness involved veiling their emotions, while Italian and Jewish boys were encouraged to express their feelings; even tears were permissible in certain contexts. These characteristics of childrearing, while modified somewhat by American schools and social workers, nevertheless proved remarkably resistant to change several generations after arrival.

Gradually, each immigrant altered what historian Maxine Sellers (*To Seek America,* 1977) described as the "values and priorities, ways of expressing (or not expressing) emotion, subtle preferences, and unconscious practices that affected the texture of life in the home, on the job, and in the neighborhood." Many new immigrants living in neighborhood replicas of Old-World towns, served by familiar merchants and worshiping in the customary style of their groups, felt an intense attachment to their old ways. Others were just as intensely refashioning themselves in the mode of the American Anglo-Saxon Protestant middle class. However, most immigrants found themselves being pulled in both directions as they tried to negotiate a compromise between total absorption and total alienation.

In the peak immigration era between 1880 and 1921, the federal government neither aided nor interfered with the lives of newcomers after the initial inspection at immigrant reception centers. Immigrants in need of advice or assistance were dependent on private charities, usually supported by ethnic or religious institutions or by the generosity of individual philanthropists. At first, most of that assistance came from welfare organizations established by Protestant reformers inspired by the Social Gospel movement or by assimilated members of an ethnic group now hoping to aid others in making the transition from alien to American.

Operating on the theory that immigrants would be more likely to embrace traditional American values if they were well-fed and well-housed, social reformers set out to remedy the problems of urban life. Protestant Social Gospel reformers established libraries, gymnasiums, soup kitchens, clinics, employment offices, and instructional facilities in a wide variety of subjects. Christians hoping to spread the Gospel through good works reached out to newcomers through the YMCA and YWCA, the Salvation Army, local agencies that provided a broad range of services, from emergency food and shelter to health services, and rescue missions for prostitutes, unwed mothers, alcoholics, and other troubled souls.

Church-related programs, by their very nature, often repelled new immigrants. Many social welfare programs designed for the immigrants were thinly disguised missionary efforts. Rather than successfully proselytizing the newcomers, such programs succeeded only in alienating many of them, especially those of Roman Catholic or Jewish faiths. While immigrants hoped to reconcile their ethnic cultural heritage with the new American lifestyle, most Protestant reformers were bent upon persuading the immigrants to abandon their past and relinquish their Old-World habits, customs, and native languages. Reformers feared that the divisiveness of a culturally pluralistic society would destroy American democracy, and they considered the religions and values of their clients primitive compared to progressive Protestant Christianity.

Secular middle-class reformers were frequently more successful in attracting immigrants. In cities, the fortresses from which they launched their assault on poverty and ignorance were the settlement houses. These buildings, located in the midst of immigrant enclaves, were run by idealistic social workers dispensing a wide variety of services to the surrounding neighborhood in the late-nineteenth- and early-twentieth-centuries. Jane Addams's Hull House in Chicago (1889), the New York City University Settlement of James B. Reynolds (1886), and the Henry Street Settlement of Lillian Wald (1893) were renowned for their community service.

Reform was often as transnational as the newcomers, according to Daniel T. Rodgers in *Atlantic Crossings, Social Politics in a Progressive Age* (1998). Founded in nineteenth-century England by young, idealistic Cambridge and Oxford men, the settlement movement in the United States was dominated by young college-trained women. These women, often from wealthy backgrounds and of genteel breeding, initially hoped to uplift American society through cultural enrichment of the urban poor. However, music and painting made way for more practical arts in the face of new immigrants' tremendous needs. Settlements captured the imagination and harnessed the energies of those trained in teaching, social work, nursing, architecture, and urban planning.

The Henry Street Settlement began in 1893 when philanthropists asked a recently graduated nurse, Lillian Wald, to help minister to the needs of poor immigrants on New York's Lower East Side. Wald's experience with poor families visiting patients in the hospital ward where she worked inspired her to draft a course of instruction in home nursing. Her course, first offered in an old building on Henry Street that had been used as a technical school, inaugurated an expanding program of service. Other settlements had similar beginnings.

Settlement houses provided a comprehensive array of services including counseling, employment bureaus, and emergency relief to those in need of food, clothing, or shelter. There were social clubs for young and old, and full schedules of classes in every subject from "Shakespeare" to "English for Beginners," with a wide selection of vocational programs in the industrial arts.

Immigrant children and the American-born children of immigrants were of particular concern to settlement workers, and reformers ventured far ahead of their time in developing quality day-care centers to aid working mothers. At settlement houses, children received medical and dental care, nutritious meals, and education. At times, settlement workers carried their efforts into the local public schools as well, teaching immigrant children English and dramatics. Many social workers believed that involving children in theater remedied shyness and helped the children to express their anxieties about life in America. An early friend of the Henry Street Settlement was Yiddish playwright Jacob Gordin, who helped aspiring young actors. "The stage during this period," according to Lillian Wald, "performed its time-honored function of teaching and moralizing."

Classes in cooking helped to acquaint immigrants with American foods and patterns of eating and served as a culinary exchange. In Milwaukee, settlement workers helped their pupils compile family recipes from Germany, Russia, Poland, and elsewhere into *The Settlement Cook Book*. This cookbook, which has been repeatedly revised and reprinted, raised thousands of dollars for the Milwaukee settlement house and is still on the shelf in many American kitchens. But, too frequently, settlement workers ignored the cultural heritages in which immigrants took great pride. Ethnic customs and practices were considered remnants of an Old-World culture with no place in America. Too frequently, there was a patronizing, condescending quality to the advice and assistance offered.

Insensitivity to the ethnic rituals and traditions of each respective immigrant group did severe damage to reformers' credibility. In 1910, Jane Addams described one such incident that occurred at Hull House when an abandoned infant died.

A delicate little child was deserted in the Hull House nursery. An investigation showed that it had been born 10 days previously in the Cook

County Hospital, but no trace could be found of the unfortunate mother. The little thing lived for several weeks and then, in spite of every care, died. We decided to have it buried by the county and the wagon was to arrive by 11 o'clock. About 9 o'clock in the morning, the rumor of this awful deed reached the neighbors. A half-dozen of them came in a very excited state of mind to protest. They took up a collection out of their poverty with which to defray a funeral. We did not realize that we were really shocking a genuine moral sentiment in the community. In our crudeness, we described the care and tenderness which had been expended upon the little creature while it was alive; that it had every attention from a skilled physician and trained nurse; we even intimated that the excited members of the group had not taken part in this and that it now lay with us to decide that the child should be buried, as it had been born, at the county's expense.

Very quickly Addams and the staff realized their error. Addams lamented,

It is doubtful whether Hull House has ever done anything which injured it so deeply in the minds of some of its neighbors. No one born and reared in the community could possibly have made a mistake like that. No one who had studied the ethical standards with any care could have bungled so completely.

Such cultural bungling was insufficient comfort for many Catholic clergy who feared losing their flock to secular and Protestant reformers. They organized their own settlement houses. In Los Angeles, two settlement houses were erected in the developing barrio to serve the Mexican population by 1905. One of them, El Hohar Feliz, was a children's home established by Catholic women whose stated purpose was to "devise ways and means of saving these little wanderers from the fate that threatened them," loss of their souls. In 1917, Bishop John J. Cantwell organized an Immigrant Welfare Department within the Associated Catholic Charities to coordinate efforts to serve the foreign-born population of Los Angeles. By 1920, the Los Angeles Bureau of Catholic Charities reported that 82 percent of those its programs serviced were either Mexican or Mexican American. That same year Cantwell established the first medical clinic in the diocese within the Santa Rita Settlement House, in a neighborhood which was 89 percent Mexican American.

Frequently immigrants viewed the efforts of private agencies and philanthropists as unwarranted interference in their lives. Historic experiences aroused suspicion of strangers' altruism. Virginia Yans-McLaughlin, who studied the Italians of Buffalo (*Family and Community,* 1977), explained that the contadini were unaccustomed to "getting something for nothing. Peasants, familiar with poverty, and used to considering it a common problem that everyone in the community shared, considered reliance upon charity even more disgraceful than destitution." The contadini regarded any public or institutional intervention in family life as an intrusion. Charity was a matter for individuals, not institutions—even the Church.

Immigrant groups generally shared the Italians' repugnance toward charity. However, some groups such as the Greeks and east European Jews, did distinguish between charitable institutions run by members of one's ethnic group and those controlled by outsiders. Only aid from the former was acceptable.

East European Jews were frequently given assistance by organizations established by German Jews who had arrived several generations earlier and were now well-off financially and quite well integrated. German Jews such as the Schiffs, Lewisohns, and Guggenheims designed their philanthropy to foster rapid integration. They wished to eliminate the embarrassing, scruffy, primitive appearance of many east European Jews, especially those who refused to shave their beards and clip their side locks.

German philanthropists were generous toward the Hebrew Immigrant Aid Society, but were even more concerned with founding educational institutions. The most famous of these is the Educational Alliance, a synthesis of night school, day-care center, gymnasium, public forum, and settlement house. Irving Howe described the Alliance as, "a tangible embodiment of the German Jews' desire to help to uplift, clean up, and quiet down their 'coreligionist[s].'" Some of America's most prominent entertainers and educators, such as comedian Eddie Cantor and philosopher Morris Raphael Cohen, owed a debt of gratitude to the Alliance.

Still, east European Jews were not unaware that the charity of German Jews came at a cost. One Russian Jew complained in a letter to the *Yiddishe Gazetten* in 1894:

In the philanthropic institutions of our aristocratic German Jews you see beautiful offices, desks, all decorated, but strict and angry faces. Every poor man is questioned like a criminal, is looked down upon; every unfortunate suffers self-degradation and shivers like a leaf, just as if he were standing before a Russian official. When the same Russian Jew is in an institution of Russian Jews, no matter how poor and small the building, it will seem to him big and comfortable. He feels at home among his own brothers who speak his tongue, understand his thoughts and feel his heart.

For the destitute, the house of worship was a source of immediate assistance. Religion was often the glue keeping their communities and their own lives together. The Polish Catholic parish in the United States became analogous to the small Polish village or town in the homeland. In addition to providing immigrants with spiritual comfort, houses of worship served as social service centers for ethnic groups. Parish priests became administrators of assistance as well as teachers and spiritual leaders. Community churches took on the task of helping newcomers to adjust emotionally and to find jobs and adequate housing.

In rural communities, aside from churches, much assistance came from family to family. Those who had been neighbors in their home country now came to each others' assistance in the United States. Rural life was not conducive to settlement houses or other agencies, but voluntary associations often offered assistance.

Mutual assistance societies frequently extended more than financial aid to immigrants. Members gave one another advice on the practical problems of living in America and the moral support to combat feelings of loneliness and alienation. Some functioned as burial societies and sponsored insurance plans for members and college scholarships for their children. A fund collected from members' dues aided the unemployed, the ill, and the widows and orphans of deceased members. The burial responsibilities of mutual assistance societies were especially important to immigrants. Newcomers often feared that if they died in America, far from family and friends, they would be laid to rest without the rites of their religion, possibly in an unmarked grave. Such organizations, and others that were exclusively burial societies, drew members who had been neighbors in the Old World. Now in America, they organized to protect each other from the disgrace of an anonymous grave. Burial society dues were collected—fifty cents, a dollar, at regular intervals—and used to buy a large cemetery plot for members and their families. A modest funeral would also be arranged by the society with appropriate clergy and some society members in attendance. Roman Catholics and Orthodox Jews were especially concerned with ritually correct burial because both religions required burial in consecrated ground. The east European Jewish *landsmanshaftn,* or organizations of Old-Country neighbors in America, usually included burial among the services performed for dues-paying members. According to historian Daniel Soyer (*Jewish Immigrant Associations and American Identity in New York, 1880–1939,* 1997), landsmanshaftn turned Old-World communal affiliations and feelings of nostalgia into important networks fostering integration into American society. In New York alone, there were 3,000 such associations with over half a million members. Lodge halls were located in the community where most of the members lived. Meetings were held Sunday afternoon or evening for the benefit of the majority of members who worked six-day weeks, and dues were modest, sometimes supplemented by a large donation from a member who had become financially successful. Lodge halls became places for former neighbors to celebrate ethnic holidays, share news of their home towns, and feel at ease. Such was the case in Florida's Ybor City, according to Gary Mormino and George Pozzetta. Spaniards involved in the cigar industry founded El Centro Español in 1891, which became the model for other such organizations. In 1902, El Centro Asturiano de Tampa attracted Spaniards from Cuba who had also come to the United States to work in the cigar industry.

Whether they belonged to a society or not, immigrants found a corner to meet and share news. They gathered informally in taverns, coffeehouses, shops, and in each other's homes to wrestle with the problems of life in America. They sought advice from those whose success in America qualified them to offer it. In Slavic neighborhoods, tavernkeepers were usually the most prosperous. They were often ex-miners or factory workers who acquired sufficient capital to purchase their own business. New businessmen, politicians, and neighbors patronized their establishments, sharing ideas and information. Whether they turned to brother or uncle, local businessman or social reformer, the immigrants ferreted out the information they needed to make a success of this life in America. Having left their familiar culture behind, they created one in the United States, pulling together pieces of the old and pieces of the new, developing community institutions as the need arose and modifying existing ones to suit their requirements. There were many compromises, but few newcomers surrendered quietly to the dictates of those guidebooks that urged the immigrant to relinquish the past.

III

By the late nineteenth century, most states had compulsory school-attendance laws, though enforcement was erratic. Young newcomers were thus legally required to be in the classroom by day, and frequently their elders voluntarily attended school during the evening. By studying reading, writing, and arithmetic, the children were being tooled to compete for the material rewards America offered. Adults were tutored in English and civics in order to qualify for citizenship. Some enrolled in vocational programs hoping to acquire skills more immediately applicable to their daily struggle for survival. Both young and old were subjected to heavy doses of socialization in the classroom, including the importance of cleanliness, hard work, perseverance, individualism, and patriotism. From early morning until late every evening, the public school educators labored to promote assimilation.

Those immigrants who chose to attend formal classes often found the classroom uncomfortable. In 1912, social worker Peter Roberts noted that the young women who taught children during the day often taught adults in the evening but were "not as sympathetic with them as they should be." Too often, Roberts found, "the foreigner contracts the habit of thinking in his mother tongue and then translates his sentences into English," an inefficient method. The teachers did not perceive that immigrants thought in their own language and attributed newcomers' slowness to learn English to stupidity. Immigrants, repelled by the condescending tone with which such teachers addressed their foreign students, resisted instruction, clinging to their mother tongues for security. Roberts called for greater sensitivity to the immigrants' needs on the part of educators. As he watched immigrant children enter American classrooms, Roberts was convinced that, "When the public school does (its) work in an efficient manner, it will be one of the most efficient agencies for the assimilation of the men of the new immigration who live in industrial centers."

Many of the immigrants themselves recognized the link between education and Americanization. In her 1912 autobiography, immigrant Mary Antin movingly describes being taken to school, along with her brother and sister, by their father. He knew "no surer way to their advancement and happiness" than education. Antin believed that, for her father, taking his children to school was both a pragmatic and a symbolic gesture. He brought his children to school "as if it were an act of consecration," his way of "taking possession of America."

Not all new immigrants embraced public education with the confidence of Mary Antin's father. Some regarded the schools as American institutions designed to undermine traditional patterns of religion and family life. In the rural Middle West, religion and nationality were crucial determinants of how neighbors divided over public schools. Immigrants who felt favorably about their government before emigration tended to accept public schools and their role in fostering Americanization far more frequently than immigrants who had regarded the state as oppressive prior to their departure. According to Jon Gjerde, "Because they carried a favorable attitude toward inclusion in the state from Europe and developed a less deeply rooted particularist ideal in the United States, Scandinavian Lutherans were better able to to make the transformation to a liberal, pluralist political world." They could support public education, unlike German Lutherans and Roman Catholic immigrants from Germany who "built intellectual walls guarding against intrusions," such as public schools, which they regarded as "powerful institutional structures within the community."

But try as immigrant groups would to resist the incursions of the public school on the family, the cultural tug of war was usually won by the school. Indeed, the public school had powerful champions at the highest level of government. In an 1875 speech, Presi-

dent Ulysses S. Grant celebrated the public school as the defender
of freedom in the face of an "enemy who tries to hinder the
progress of our free institutions," a thinly veiled reference to the
foreign-born, but especially to Roman Catholics whose parochial
schools Grant and others saw as perpetuating superstition and ignorance. He urged that Americans support secular schools, leaving
religion to "the family, the altar, and the church." Within months
after his speech, Grant introduced an amendment to the Constitution that made public education mandatory in all states and prohibited using public funds for any religious institutions, which included schools, of course.

Although Grant's amendment never became law, the school
wars for the hearts and minds of immigrants were fought with ve-
hemence at the state level. In midwestern states with large rural
ethnic populations that made certain towns all but homogeneous,
the battle seethed. The Wisconsin state legislature passed the
Bennett Law in 1889, modeled on an Illinois law passed the previous year that required instruction in English. According to the
Bennett Law, all children aged seven to fourteen were required to
attend school for at least sixteen weeks per year. In a direct assault
on the state's immigrant population, which often preferred education for their children in their own languages, the Bennet law required that all of the state's elementary school children be instructed in "reading, writing, arithmetic, and United States history
in the English language." Responsibility for children's education
was thus removed from parents and given to boards of education.
After a bitter political fight in which a newly elected Republican
governor met defeat in his bid for re-election, the law was re-
pealed. However, other states such as Texas and Massachusetts
managed the same policy by just requiring the use of English in all
public schools as the language of instruction.

In addition to the struggle over language and religion, immigrants whose children attended public schools recoiled from the
cultural biases teachers brought to their jobs. In Texas, Mexicans
were segregated from Caucasians as were African Americans
throughout the South. In Los Angeles, Mexican immigrants faced
stereotypical depictions of themselves by well-meaning but culturally naive educators such as Helen Heffernan, who believed that,

"Our Mexican population had leisureliness, gay lighthearted enjoyment of the present; a spirituality and quiet devotion; a passionate love of color, music, and dancing." In Heffernan's judgment, schools had the responsibility of replacing at least some of the charm with sensible middle-class habits. In her estimation, the school had a mandate to reform "these little foreign children, many of whom have had no opportunity for warm water, soap, or a comb at home, with the added fact that no one cared whether they were clean or dirty."

Language as well as personal hygiene was an issue for Mexican immigrants as with other newcomers. The schools insisted on English and only English. However, as historian Ricardo Romo has observed, Mexicans reasoned that Los Angeles, like other southwestern border areas, was simply a geographic extension of the homeland, and "were no doubt encouraged by the survival in this area of thousands of Spanish place names and streets as well as by the persistence of Mexican culture." Moreover, many Mexican parents understood that the preservation of Spanish culture in the home depended on language maintenance. Others saw teaching their children English alone as being overly submissive to a foreign culture. At best they were open to bilingualism and appreciation of both Mexican and American customs and traditions.

Within immigrant groups, discussions over education included debates over education for women. In 1910, a woman wrote to editor Abraham Cahan in *The Forward* complaining that her husband disapproved of her going to school two evenings a week, and in retaliation, had imposed strict financial restraints on her. Cahan scolded the husband severely for his behavior and insisted that, "the wife absolutely has the right to go to school two evenings a week." Cahan recognized the role of education in the integration process and encouraged his readers to use schools to their own best advantage, as corridors to the opportunities of American life.

Even school programs that seemed unexceptional triggered opposition from immigrants who perceived much of what occurred at school as an assault on their ways of preserving family and tradition. For instance, state-supported hot lunch programs violated the traditional Italian noontime meal, or *colazione*. It was

customary for contadini families to eat together at noon, in the
fields or in the home. Lunch programs, designed in particular to
help impoverished immigrants, violated the Italian tradition by
keeping children away from the family. Often Italian parents insisted that their children come home at noon. Even Richard
Gambino, growing up in the 1930s, fondly remembers coming
home to a "good home-cooked lunch of the *paise* (old country),
for example, fried eggs and potatoes on Italian bread." To
Gambino, and to many other youngsters raised in immigrant
households, this fare was "indescribably delicious" and much preferred to the school's institutional "balanced meals." Gradually
peer pressure and the insistence of school officials undermined the
way of the paise, and Italian children learned to eat away from
home.

When affronted, immigrants protested, even engaging in
spontaneous riots. On one occasion, school officials' attentions to
children erupted into violence. In *Silent Travelers, Germs, Genes,
and the "Immigrant Menace,"* historian Alan M. Kraut describes
the 1906 riots that occurred in Jewish and Italian immigrant neighborhoods on New York's Lower East Side when school principals
trying to improve the health of their students allowed physicians to
perform adenoidectomies in school clinics. Swelling of the lym-
phoid tissue in the nose above the throat resulted in a blockage that
caused mouth-breathing and, some physicians of the day thought,
could lead to insufficient oxygen reaching the brain. Feeble-
mindedness was the feared result. Although permission slips were
sent home, many parents did not fully understand what they had
signed. When the operations were performed, there was normal
but abundant bleeding. Wild rumors—perhaps circulated by physicians angry about losing fees to school physicians doing the sur-
gery—circulated through the streets that children were being murdered. Only large numbers of police eventually quelled the
disturbance.

Overcrowded schools in immigrant neighborhoods often required rezoning. Such redistricting could place severe constraints
on an immigrant group. In 1904, New York City's Board of Education proposed shifting 1,500 children from overcrowded schools in

the Lower East Side to less crowded schools on the West Side, according to education historian Diane Ravitch. In angry protest, 2,000 Jewish parents gathered at a settlement house meeting. Of primary concern was the fear that their children would miss morning prayers and afternoon religious school. Jewish parents felt that untempered secular education would inevitably alienate children from their elders.

Often objections raised by an immigrant parent extended to schoolyard activities. To a man who objected to his son playing baseball with public school friends in 1903, Yiddish newspaper editor Abraham Cahan wrote, "It is a mistake to keep children locked up in the house. . . . Bring them up to be educated, ethical and decent, but also to be physically strong, so they should not feel inferior." Baseball was an important part of education because it seemed so American. The game gave Jewish boys a vigorous tie to their fellow countrymen without demanding a sacrifice of Jewish belief and tradition.

Italians, Greeks, and east European Jews sometimes forestalled the Americanization of their children in public school by classes held after school. The Greek community organized such programs of instruction. These classes, held in church basements and community centers, were designed to teach the Greek language to American-born children. Parents who sent their children to such schools were struggling to temper integration so that their children would not become completely alienated from their past. However, according to historian Theodore Saloutos (*The Greeks in the United States,* 1963), the child, "attending public school during the day, in which he was taught by an American-born, American-educated teacher, and then attending a Greek school in the late afternoon, presided over by a Greek-born, Greek-educated teacher, was often confused by the seemingly contradictory experiences." Moreover, most newcomers could not afford the expense of such private schools.

Among east European Jews, Hebrew schools were opened free of charge by philanthropic institutions such as New York's University Settlement and the Educational Alliance. Classes at these Hebrew schools, usually held after public school classes were over for the day, added ethical and religious debate to children's educations through the study of Bible and Jewish traditions. Hebrew schools were a compromise between completely dispensing with Jewish education altogether, and *yeshivah* training, where the emphasis was on Orthodox Jewish custom and law, taught by rabbis often more fluent in Yiddish than English. Thus, even in the institutions designed to preserve the immigrants' past, the need to adapt to America modified the content and style of education. Similarly, the Roman Catholic Church often sponsored religious instruction for Catholic children attending public schools. In many cities the Church succeeded in getting release time changed so that children could leave their public school classes early one afternoon per week to receive religious instruction.

Did the public schools actually serve as effective academies of integration for immigrants? Traditionally, schools have been regarded by historians as the bridge between the Old World and American society. Idealistic teachers guided immigrant children and their parents through the early, difficult stages of acculturation, outfitting students with the intellectual paraphernalia necessary for upward mobility. However, long after the end of the peak period of immigration, some historians embarked on a revision of this benevolent perspective of the school promoting the immigrant's welfare.

In 1972, historian Colin Greer debunked this "Great School Legend," suggesting that success in the classroom was not the lever that pried open the door to wealth and prestige in the United States. Greer contended that economic prosperity preceded academic success with "cultural background and economic status being reflected and reinforced in the school, not caused by it." Greer suggested, moreover, that the fundamental purpose of the school was to maintain the relative social positions of groups in the society. Rather than being an agent of Americanization, schools preserved the status quo among socioeconomic classes. School performance, Greer found, consistently depended on the socioeconomic position of the pupil's family. Immigrant children frequently flunked out of school because the curriculum was designed to weed out those unable to conform to the white Protestant model of success and achievement.

On balance, the public school system was neither the only path to economic and social opportunities nor a reactionary institution designed to perpetuate the existing class structure. It is important to note that education had a different significance and usefulness for each new immigrant group. And the nature of the relationship between the child and the school was perhaps more a function of the immigrant's unique cultural attitudes than the design of the institution. As with mobility studies, historians have been as yet unable to adequately measure the attitudes of immigrant groups toward education. Figures on school attendance or academic failures for each group are insufficient measures of immigrant attitudes toward the schools. Such data may reveal more about a group's success in surmounting obstacles to education than they do about whether group members regarded the educational process as benign or detrimental to their best interests in America.

The importance of cultural perspective was pointed out in a study of the scholastic achievement of immigrant children in urban schools between 1900 and 1930 by Michael R. Olneck and Marvin Lazerson ("The School Achievement of Immigrant Children: 1900–1930," *History of Education Quarterly,* Winter 1974). In the east European Jewish community, study and learning were highly valued. The practice of Judaism required literacy, and a mark of family success was the ability to educate the male children in Talmudic law and the rabbinic commentaries on the law. Religious schools were scattered throughout the Pale in Russia and, in larger cities, there were often great *yeshivat,* centers of Jewish learning. Stephan F. Brumberg in his 1986 volume, *Going to America, Going to School, The Jewish Immigrant Public School Encounter in Turn-of-the-Century New York,* concurs with Olneck's and Lazerson's observation that traditional respect for learning and confidence in educational institutions survived the journey to America and expanded to include secular public schools.

In contrast to the east European Jews, southern Italian culture placed low priority on formal education, according to Olneck and

Lazerson. In the Mezzogiorno, family loyalty was the greatest virtue and the most important duty. The outside influence of school—encouraging individualistic success and upward mobility—appeared to be a direct challenge to family values and parental control. Contadini in the streets of America reminded each other of the southern Italian proverb: "Stupid and contemptible is he who makes his children better than himself." Moreover, long hours in the classroom prevented the young from contributing to the family coffers, as had been the custom in Italy. As one resentful parent said, "The schools (make) of our children persons of leisure—little gentlemen. They (lose) the dignity of good children to think just of the parents, to help them. . . ." However, later studies suggest that southern Italian views of education became increasingly positive once those who were birds of passage chose to remain in the United States permanently. Italians soon encouraged their sons to pursue college education as a path to both prosperity and respectability. Parental approval of higher education for women often took a generation or two longer.

Thomas Kessner's study of mobility among New York's Italian and east European Jewish immigrants (1977) examines New York City public school surveys from 1908 and 1910 to suggest the influence of cultural attitudes upon performance. In 1908, a survey of fifteen Manhattan schools showed a disproportionately high number of immigrant children kept behind one or more grades. Among the new immigrants, 23 percent of the east European Jewish children were kept behind as compared with 36 percent of the Italian children. The study focusing on those who successfully completed high school found that none of the Italians who entered high school graduated, while 16 percent of the east European children received diplomas. A 1910 survey of New York's slums cited by Kessner found more Jews above age sixteen still in school than any other ethnic group. Six years later, a census of local colleges revealed that the Jewish enrollment constituted 73 percent of the City College student body. If Jews's cultural attitudes inclined them toward higher education, the improved economic status of many families by 1910 permitted them to sacrifice the income of their sons and daughters who were bending over books rather than sewing machines.

More than any other immigrant group, Jews took advantage of New York's free city colleges. Newspapers reported that "The thirst for knowledge . . . fills our city colleges and Columbia's halls with the sons of Hebrews who came over in steerage. . . ." Aware of the trend, Italian journalists and educators urged their *compari*, "Let us do as the Jews . . . invade the schools, teach ourselves, have our children taught, open to them the school paths by means of the hatchet of knowledge and genius. . . ."

Historian John W. Briggs (*An Italian Passage,* 1978) observes that in some cities the Italian immigrants' embrace of education was no less enthusiastic than any other group's. Spotlighting elementary-school children in two midsized New York cities, Rochester and Utica, and one large midwestern city, Kansas City, Missouri, Briggs found that Italian children had roughly the same attendance patterns as other immigrant and native-born students. In Rochester, where much school data were available, Briggs found that Italian children did not experience unusually high rates of failure.

Again, as with studies of upward mobility, much of the debate over education may result from historians asking the wrong questions. Scholars have assumed that a link existed between education and an individual's ability to make good in America. It has also been assumed that immigrants saw this connection clearly. Thus the debate on education eventually dovetails back into the debate over mobility, with much counting of students and comparisons between ethnic groups. Instead, historians should consider education within the context of the overall cultural perspective of each immigrant group. The issue is not as much school attendance of Italians as compared to Jews, but school attendance of Italians in Italy as compared to those immediately after coming to America, and later in ensuing generations.

Only the research of Joel Perlmann grapples with the complexity of determining the role of education in the relative success of different ethnic groups. Perlmann's 1988 study explores the differences in educational patterns and economic success in a sample of almost 12,000 Irish, Italian, Jews, African Americans, and nonimmigrants in Providence, Rhode Island, between 1880 and 1935. His research reveals a close relationship between premigration ethnic differences and postmigration behavior with respect to education and advancement. When he compares the two largest immigrant groups to arrive during the peak of migration at the turn of the century, the Italians and the Jews, he finds that premigration cultural attitudes are crucial in shaping the groups' views of education and the effect those views have on their achievement of material success. However, the relationship between premigration attitudes and economic success is hard to study with precision. While the origin of these cultural attitudes remains unclear, they persisted after arrival and often for several generations in the Providence sample, shaping success in school and patterns of upward mobility, according to Perlmann.

Scholars who have long treated the public school as a powerful engine of upward mobility capable of recasting aliens as Americans may have overstated the case. Premigration cultural perspectives appear to have determined how much influence the schools could have on particular groups and their children. Each immigrant group may have entered the United States with its own cultural perspective on the value of education, as well as a shopping list and timetable, picking and choosing, and paying for its successes in the coinage of compromise in the negotiation between traditional values and the American way.

IV

Told to speak a new language, learn a new skill, let the children play baseball, keep house like an American, eat differently, dress differently—it seemed as though nothing short of total transformation would make the immigrant acceptable in this alien society. In midwestern states the struggle over integrating the foreign born and their children into American society and culture was often at the base of partisan political battles at the state and local levels. During the 1960s and 1970s, political historians such as Paul

Kleppner and Richard Jensen, armed with electoral and legislative voting data and the high-speed mainframe computers needed to analyze such data, described two opposing ethnoreligious bundles of values that underlay partisan affiliation. On one side stood voters and politicians committed to a "ritualist" or "liturgical" perspective, grounded in *right belief.* These ritualists tended to support the Democratic Party and oppose legislation and administrative decisions that would employ the power of the state to force a particular kind of behavior that the majority defined as proper and moral. Thus, German Catholics defined a religious individual as one who believed in the tenets of Catholicism and practiced them, but did not insist that state power be used in support of those beliefs among the general population. They often supported Democrats who opposed temperance legislation limiting or eliminating the sale, distribution, or public consumption of alcoholic beverages.

On the other side, stood "pietists," those who measured religiosity according to *right behavior.* Swedish Lutherans were quite willing to support laws defining what public behavior was acceptable and what was unacceptable on Sunday, the day they recognized as the Sabbath. Republicans supported the kind of activist moral posture that pietists could support. By 1896, pietists in the Midwest joined with Southern Democrats to push aside the preferences of urban Catholic voters and give the Democratic presidential nomination to William Jennings Bryan, who lost to Republican William McKinley.

In the towns and counties of rural America, in states such as Nebraska or Wisconsin or Minnesota, ethnic politics could be impassioned. In Nebraska, according to historian Frederick C. Luebke, clashes over prohibition, women's suffrage, and the regulation of parochial schools often divided the state's ethnic communities. However, "By 1890 intense antagonisms generated by the liquor question as well as by an attack on German-language schools fused the heterogeneous German community into a nearly solid bloc of support for the Democratic party as the political defender of German ethnocultural interests." Though some Germans found Populist reforms appealing, many Germans saw a nativist element in Populism and jumped to the Republican Party in 1892 and 1896 when they felt Nebraska Democrats were too enamored of the Populists. In 1916, Iowa voters barely rejected a women's suffrage amendment to the state constitution. While towns dominated by Swedish Americans overwhelmingly supported the amendment, those in which the Dutch and Czechs were more numerous remained lukewarm in their support. The heavily German-American, foreign-born, and Roman Catholic Iowa counties opposed the suffrage amendment most vehemently.

In cities, the masters of party politics liked the newcomers just fine. In the districts and wards that made up the immigrant neighborhood, urban bosses and their associates attended lodge meetings, festas, and funerals. They mingled in bars and coffeehouses frequented by particular immigrant groups. In addition to taking stands on issues of interest to particular ethnic groups, urban ethnic politics was often about immediate material assistance to needy newcomers. Urban political bosses provided food to the hungry and shelter to the homeless. Newcomers low on cash were more than willing to repay the boss—at the ballot box. It was the American quid pro quo.

The immigrant's importance to the urban politician was established long before the onset of the new immigration in 1880. During the 1840s and 1850s, urban politicians in both major parties looked greedily at the millions of Irish and German immigrants, knowing that most of the males would soon be casting ballots. The Irish vote soon became the cornerstone of Democratic support in New York and many other large eastern cities. In the cities of the Midwest, especially large cities such as Chicago, both major parties contended for the German vote. For politicians, the immigrant ballot became the key to partisan hegemony.

The first bosses late-nineteenth-century immigrants encountered in the cities of the Northeast were often Irish. These successful heirs of white Protestant politicians seemed to have an instinctive understanding for their varied constituencies. Bosses such as New York's Honest John Kelly and Richard Croker, Philadelphia's James McManus, and Pittsburgh's Christopher Magee and William Finn, all immigrants or the sons of immigrants themselves, recognized the economic and psychological needs of the newcomers. Tammany Hall, New York's Democratic headquarters run by Mayor Fernando Wood in the 1850s, offered Irish immigrants baskets of coal in winter, turkeys at Thanksgiving, and most important, patronage jobs on the police force and on publicly financed construction projects. Now, forty years later, ward bosses provided the same services to Italians, Slavs, and east European Jews: emergency food and fuel, legal assistance, and, of course, jobs that new arrivals could get nowhere else as quickly or with as few explanations.

The pattern in the Northeast was replicated in the Southwest in cities such as El Paso, Texas. There, according to historian Mario T. Garcia, the local Democratic organization, sometimes called the Ring, depended mightily on the Mexican immigrant vote. The Ring recognized that within the Mexican population were those sufficiently acculturated and politicized that they could play crucial roles as mediators and ward bosses in Chihuahuita and other Mexican El Paso enclaves. Mexicans supporting the Ring were rewarded with patronage jobs as policemen and sanitation workers. The Ring solidified its Mexican vote by occasionally supporting Mexican candidates, such as O. A. Larrazolo for district attorney. Ironically, Larrazolo would become the Republican governor of New Mexico in 1918 and a U.S. senator in 1928.

Urban bosses throughout the country were especially sensitive to the diverse ethnic customs and traditions in their wards. George Washington Plunkitt, a Tammany boss in New York City at the turn of the century, gave a series of humorous, colorful, and highly informative interviews on machine politics that were published in newspapers and later as a book. Plunkitt acknowledged the need to accept ethnic differences among his constituents and act accordingly. One of his functionaries was Johnnie Ahearn of the fourth district with a constituency that was half Irish and half Jewish. Plunkitt admired Ahearn's ability to remain popular with both groups: "He eats corned beef and kosher meat with equal nonchalance, and it's all the same to him whether he takes off his hat in the church or pulls it down over his ears in the synagogue." Both Ahearn and Plunkitt understood that Americanization was a slow, halting, and painful process. They knew that immigrants were most supportive of politicians who appreciated their desire to retain their ethnic identities as they adjusted to life in America.

Unpleasant memories of those who made and enforced the law in their native countries made many new immigrants hesitant at first to have any contact with politics or politicians. However, the humane assistance and warm, personal style of many bosses and their associates worked to dispel such wariness. Bosses tempered economic assistance with friendship and respect; those who accepted their aid did not, therefore, feel diminished by it. The machine thus eased the strain of integration. Soon members of newer immigrant groups themselves tested the political waters, often using the machine to launch their own careers.

Aside from smoothing the newcomers' paths to political activism, the machines may have also played a role in dissipating ethnic conflict in American cities. In *The Triumph of Ethnic Progressivism: Urban Political Culture in Boston, 1900–1925* (1998), James J. Connolly argues that political parties run by urban machines moderated ethnic conflict and sought to reconcile ethnic differences in the interest of preserving the atmosphere of coalition-building so essential to electoral success. According to Connolly, "as long as parties remained entrenched in the city's political process, social conflict was channeled into partisan competition."

Many opposition politicians, journalists, and public-spirited reformers deplored what they regarded as the opportunism of urban bosses. In *Shame of the Cities* (1904), reformer Lincoln Steffens condemned bossism as undemocratic. However, social workers aiding the urban poor perceived the important function of the boss and his machine at the community level. Jane Addams, in the early twentieth century, understood why bosses succeeded where reformers failed:

Primitive people such as the southern Italian peasants who live in the 9th ward, deep down in their hearts admire nothing so much as a good man. The successful candidate must be a good man according to the standards of his constituents. He must not attempt to hold up a morality beyond them, nor must he attempt to reform or change the standard.

Still many reformers, concerned more about preserving morality in government than assisting new arrivals, pursued efforts to
curb the power of the machine. As machine politicians sought to
educate newcomers in their style of politics, Andrew Dickson
White, president of Cornell University said, "With very few exceptions, the city governments of the United States are the worst
in Christendom—the most expensive, the most inefficient, and the
most corrupt." White and others demanded reform. In 1883, the
National Civil Service Reform League and other reform groups
succeeded in gaining passage of the Pendleton Act, which organized civil service appointments on a merit system in an effort to
curb federal patronage positions, the meat sustaining the machine.
However, bosses and their allies were strong enough to manipulate
the civil service lists to keep their friends in office and prevent
their enemies from enjoying the spoils of office after a victory.

As a Progressive reformer in the 1890s, Theodore Roosevelt
studied the machine and concluded that urban reformers would
have to create whole social agencies to fulfill the role of urban
bosses before they could be displaced. Not until the New Deal was
created by Roosevelt's distant cousin Franklin, did this idea of social agencies become a reality. Meanwhile, the machine thrived.

Opportunists or not, political bosses usually provided urban
groups with badly needed services and used their power to stimu-
late urban growth even as they enriched themselves and enhanced
their party's political fortunes. These partisan warriors and their
morally ambiguous machinations have defied all efforts to render
a clear-cut judgment of their record. Many an urban boss derived
money and patronage while meeting the needs of the city for expanded public utilities—water, gas, transportation, and electric-
ity—as well as the construction of public buildings, sewage systems, docks, and street and sidewalk pavements. Many also
markedly increased the number of schools, hospitals, museums,
and other institutions and services needed by an expanding city. In
the process, bosses had to circumvent city charters that saddled
city government with archaic legislative machinery, weak executive authority, and disorganized courts. Whether they were scoundrels masquerading as angels of mercy or urban Robin Hoods,

bosses surmounted obstacles to their constituents' welfare. And often those whom they served best were the newest, neediest, and most numerous of their constituents—the immigrants.

At the ballot box, in the neighborhood, at worship, and at work, the pace of change for the immigrants was dizzying. Yet to native-born Americans the metamorphosis was almost imperceptible. Many found the appearance and behavior of the newcomers repulsive—and very frightening. Just the vast size of the immigration was altering the nation in a rapid, uncontrolled fashion. At best, immigrants appeared to be naive greenhorns; at worst, foreign interlopers. To many Americans, the new immigrants would always be aliens. And to many immigrants the native born would always seem reluctant hosts.

These divergent perceptions of the immigrants' entry into American society were reflected in the mixed reviews that greeted Israel Zangwill's play, *The Melting Pot,* when it opened before its first American audience at Washington, D.C.'s Columbia Theater in 1908. Zangwill, a British Jew, told the story of young David Quixano, a Jewish immigrant who fled to the United States from Russia following his family's slaughter in a pogrom. As the plot unfolds, David writes a great symphony and falls in love with another immigrant, a Gentile Russian noblewoman. In the final scene, the symphony receives great acclaim and the young immigrant wins the lady. Despite the injunctions of Jewish law against intermarriage, the hero decides to follow the dictates of his heart and marry her.

Advocates of an American melting pot praised the play, especially President Theodore Roosevelt, seated next to the playwright's wife on opening night. To Roosevelt, immigrant languages and cultures were obstacles to American nationalism and impediments to the welfare of newcomers in their new country. He contended that:

The man who becomes completely Americanized—who celebrates our constitutional Centennial instead of the Queen's Jubilee, or the Fourth of July rather than St. Patrick's Day and who talks "United States" instead of the dialect of the country which he has of his own free will abandoned—is not only doing his plain duty by his adopted land, but is also rendering himself a service of immeasurable value.

The melting-pot concept flattered American vanity. It suggested not only that the nation was a haven for the oppressed, but that when refugees were exposed to American democracy they underwent a dramatic metamorphosis for the better. There emerged a distinctly new type—the American—who was culturally and biologically superior to the people of Europe, Latin America, and Asia from whom the American was distilled.

However, praise for Zangwill's *Melting Pot* was less than unanimous. Immigrant newspapers panned the play as an overly idealized version of the assimilation process. The Jewish immigrant press, in particular, took exception to the endorsement of intermarriage as an acceptable vehicle of assimilation. These critics were irritated by the image of newly arrived immigrants standing down at the docks with those of their own kind—each group with its language and history, its particular hatreds and rivalries—soon to be mixed together indiscriminately for the good of all. As early as the first act, Zangwill has David observe that "America is God's Crucible, the great Melting Pot where all the races of Europe are melting and reforming!" By the last act the melting pot is touted as Americanism as David exclaims, "A fig for your feuds and vendettas! Germans and Frenchmen, Irishmen and Englishmen, Jews and Russians—into the Crucible with you all! God is making the American." To those who had experienced religious prejudice and discrimination or who had witnessed conflict among immigrants of diverse background, the melting-pot image hardly seemed to reflect their experience in the United States. And it offended millions of immigrants who hoped to amicably reconcile their native culture with their new surroundings, not to drown their past and resurface as Americans.

Equally outraged by Zangwill's play were those native-born Americans who did not share President Roosevelt's confidence in the melting process. Even as the immigrants rejected the concept of a melting pot as undesirable and threatening, Americans intimidated by the size and character of the immigration at America's doorstep denounced the policy of inclusion. They wanted protection from this foreign intrusion that they perceived as a menace to their values, institutions, economic stability, and self-image.

Both immigrants and native-born saw themselves as engaged in a struggle. The newcomers took the measure of America and made the choices that best suited their needs and expectations. However, as hard as they pushed to enter the "golden door" on their own terms, there were always those on the other side of the threshold pushing back.

The Huddled Masses:
An Essay in Photographs

by Alan M. Kraut and Sarah Larson

I / Europe

Jewish fusgeyers *(Yiddish: travelers on foot) emigrating from Kovno, Lithuania with their belongings on their backs.* Yivo Institute for Jewish Research.

Top: Travelers of many economic classes gather near the docks outside of the Hall of the Hamburg-Amerika shipping line, c. 1900. U.S. National Archives #131-SSA-1A.

Bottom: Beneath an inscription that reads, "My field is the World," emigrants queue up to secure passage on a Hamburg-Amerika steamer, c. 1900. U. S. National Archives # 131-SSA-7.

Bottom: On the deck of the S.S. Patricia *in 1902, trans-Atlantic immigrants meet to chat, court, and play.* Museum of the City of New York.

III / Arrival

Top: The Statue of Liberty went unnoticed by many immigrants who were busy collecting belongings and children as their ships docked in New York Harbor. Others mistook it for the tomb of Columbus. Library of Congress.

Bottom: Immigration reception at Ellis Island. Library of Congress.

Opposite top: Landing card of Lari Schanker from Russia, who arrived in America neatly tagged with all other third-class passengers. Mrs. Hassa F. Schanker.

Opposite bottom: Checking for highly contagious trachoma, an official pries up a woman's eyelid with a buttonhook normally used for fastening gloves. Those with the illness were detained for treatment. The hook was not sterilized between inspections, but merely wiped on a towel draped over the railing. U.S. National Archives #90-G-125-12.

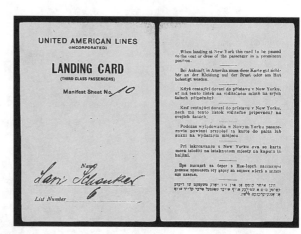

UNITED AMERICAN LINES
(INCORPORATED)

LANDING CARD
(THIRD CLASS PASSENGERS)

Manifest Sheet No. 10

When landing at New York this card to be pinned to the coat or dress of the passenger in a prominent position.

Bei Ankunft in Amerika muss diese Karte gut sichtbar an der Kleidung auf der Brust oder am Hut befestigt werden.

Když cestující dorazí do přístavu v New Yorku, ať má tento lístek na viditelném místě na svých šatech připevněný.

Keď cestujúci dorazí do prístavu v New Yorku, nech má tento lístok viditeľne pripevnený na svojich šatách.

Podczas wylądowania w Nowym-Yorku pasażerowie powinni przypiąć tą kartę do palta lub sukni na wydatnym miejscu.

Pri iskrcavanju u New Yorku ova se karta mora isložiti na istaknutom mjestu na kaputu ili haljini.

При высадкѣ въ Нью-Іоркѣ пассажиры должны прикѣпить эту карту на видномъ мѣстѣ к пальто или платью.

[Yiddish text]

Name _Sam Schenker_

List Number ____6____

Opposite top: Health inspection of Asian immigrants at Angel Island depot off the coast of California. U.S. National Archives # 90-G-125-45.

Opposite bottom: After 1882, immigrants suspected of being "mentally defective" were subjected to intelligence tests; failure meant deportation. Posted on the rear wall are the photographs of European heads of state, national flags, and playing cards, probably used in questioning. U.S. National Archives # 90-G-125-10.

Above: On Ellis Island for Christmas, these somewhat bemused newcomers were gathered before a Christmas tree to be issued an apple and formally photographed, c. 1900. State Historical Society of Wisconsin.

Top: In an attempt to protect Ellis Island immigrants from dishonest money exchangers, the American Express Company was given sole concession in 1905. Brown Brothers.

Bottom: With their bundles and string-tied boxes, immigrants gaze across New York Harbor from the Ellis Island pier. Library of Congress.

Pushcart peddlers,
canny shoppers,
and idle strollers
leave little room
for the horse-
drawn wagons on
one of New York's
Lower East Side's
many narrow
streets, c. 1910.
U.S. National
Archives
196-GS-369.

Above: The average seven-story dumbbell tenement could house as many as 150 people and a shop on the ground floor; in warm weather tenants and merchants spilled out onto the front steps and sidewalk, c. 1900. Library of Congress.

Top: As American cities burgeoned, some immigrant families could only find affordable living quarters in alley shanties, c. 1900. Library of Congress.

Bottom: Ironically, the tenement inspectors sent out by urban reformers to protect the poor from exploitative landlords were hated by the immigrants, who feared eviction on the basis of overcrowding. U.S. National Archives # 196-GS-75.

V / Jobs

Opposite top: As the newcomers scattered across the country, they put their hands to any work they could find, such as this Polish family who labored on the Bottomley berry farm near Rock Creek, Maryland, from 4:00 A.M. to sunset on July 7, 1909. U.S. National Archives #102-LH-837.

Opposite bottom: Nine-year-old Johnnie, who was brought from Baltimore to shuck oysters in Dunbar, Lousiana, is closely watched by his padrone, March 2, 1911. U.S. National Archives.

Top: Some newcomers made their way in America by catering to the unique tastes and preferences of their own ethnic group, such as this Italian pasta maker, c. 1910. Library of Congress.

Bottom: Joseph Severio, an eleven-year-old peanut vendor in Wilmington, Delaware, worked six hours a day at his curbside pushcart, May 21, 1910. U.S. National Archives #102-LH-1501.

Above: Most of the employees in the spinning room of the Cornell Mill in Fall River, Massachusetts, were children, January 11, 1912. U.S. National Archives.

Opposite top: Using a skill they brought from Italy, the Maletestra family makes artificial flowers in New York, averaging ten to twelve gross a day at six cents a gross, 1908. U.S. National Archives.

Opposite bottom: In sweatshops such as those in the New York City garment district, immigrants established a camaraderie that overcame differences of language and culture, 1914. Mr. & Mrs. Jacob Heskes.`

Above: As more immigrants realized that their stay in America would be permanent, the fledgling labor movement took on a multiethnic flavor. Yivo Institute for Jewish Research.

Opposite top: Even as they protested working conditions, these striking immigrant clothing makers tried to look as American as their native-born customers. Library of Congress.

Opposite bottom: Anxious to help newcomers to become self-supporting, reformers established free classes that were often taught at night, c. 1910. Library of Congress.

VI / Assimilation

Top: Reformers also taught immigrant women how to make a good American home, to maintain middle-class standards of hygiene, and cook American food, c. 1910. Library of Congress.

Bottom: A class of immigrant mothers learning English, c. 1910. Museum of the City of New York.

Above: Coming full circle, eastern and southern European immigrants perform the maypole dance in New York City's Central Park, a rite of spring imported by English immigrants almost three centuries earlier, May 1, 1913. Library of Congress.

Right: T. Kartman of Samara, Russia, as he appeared in his home town, 1918, and as he appeared twelve years later in Brooklyn, New York. Yivo Institute for Jewish Research.

VII / Retention

Right: Most immigrants made their own choices as to how rapidly and to what degree they would take on the trappings of American culture. Library of Congress.

Top: The priest blessing holiday breads baked in the new land exemplifies how organized religion served as a familiar focus for many immigrants struggling to adapt to America, Easter, 1920. Library of Congress.

Bottom: For immigrants living far from the large cities, such as most Mexican immigrants of the nineteenth century, retention of old habits and values was not difficult. Library of Congress.

Top: In urban neighborhoods, immigrants of the same national group often formed clubs, such as this Slavic dance society, in a deliberate attempt to preserve ethnic customs, c. 1920. Library of Congress.

Bottom: No matter how assimilated the immigrant, inherited ethnic customs assumed great significance at rites of passage such as birth, marriage, and death, as suggested by this Chinese funeral procession, c. 1910. Library of Congress.

Above: The Ku Klux Klan protested the "mongrelization" of American society, c. 1920. U.S. National Archives #306-NT-150-910C.

THE AMERICANESE WALL, AS CONGRESSMAN
BURNETT WOULD BUILD IT.

UNCLE SAM: You're welcome in — if you can climb it!

Above: Nativists argued that "undesirable" foreigners could be weeded out by administering a literacy test at all immigration depots. Library of Congress.

THE ONLY WAY TO HANDLE IT.

Above: Immigration based upon a quota system was widely applauded around the country, as this editorial cartoon suggests, c. 1921. Library of Congress.

Above: Restrictionists won only a Pyrrhic victory in 1921; over twenty-three million immigrants had entered the country since 1880 and would unalterably change the nature of American society and culture. Mr. & Mrs. Harry Kraut.

CHAPTER FIVE

Nativism and the End of Unlimited Entry

A popular immigrant slogan ran, "America beckons, but Americans repel." Immigrants confronted substantial and escalating hostility from 1880 to 1921, even as urban politicians plotted to capture the immigrant vote and industrialists relished the abundance of cheap, unskilled immigrant labor for their factories. Ever since the mass migration of Irish and Germans to the United States and other countries in the mid-nineteenth century, immigrants who chose the United States had encountered the suspicion and trepidation of those already in America. The opposition that the newest immigrants faced was thus an extension of an already established pattern.

As the immigration stream to the United States began to swell in the last decades of the nineteenth century, so did anti-immigrant sentiment, or nativism. Most broadly defined, nativists were those Americans who believed that the immigrants posed an imminent danger to their way of life and who spoke out or acted against this "alien menace." Increasingly, migrants who chose the United States as their destination were the targets of nativist intellectuals concerned with such issues as how best to preserve the distinctiveness of the national state, sustain political democracy, defend individual liberties, maintain respect for the law, protect the public health, and preserve the purity of the Anglo-Saxon race. Immigrants were denounced in articles and books most newcomers could not yet read and derided in sermons from church pulpits and in addresses from university lecterns few of them ever heard.

Nativists were not merely a small coterie of mindless bigots. Millions of Americans who were not ideologically opposed to immigration were intimidated by the size and diversity of the foreign intrusion and by 1921 welcomed federal legislation that finally dammed the flow from abroad. They feared the threat they believed aliens posed to their economic and social position. These were not wild-eyed reactionaries, but a broad spectrum of sober, middle-class Americans who often had very specific grounds for objecting to these newcomers. One such ground was economics. Many American workers feared for their jobs in the wake of competition from low-paid foreign labor. A second ground for opposition was religious differences. The majority of immigrants were either Catholic or Jewish, especially frightening to a predominantly Protestant America. A third reason why some Americans looked askance at the newcomers concerned politics. Almost all newcomers came from nondemocratic societies, where republicanism and personal liberty were not time-honored traditions. Many immigrants were leery of the law and the government— institutions that had always catered to their rulers. To Americans, for whom the law was a sacred trust and a legacy from the patriots of the Revolution, the unfamiliarity of the immigrants with the ways of democracy and their general mistrust of government loomed as a tangible threat to the continuation of American republican government.

The health and physical appearance of the newcomers was perhaps most frightening to the native born and constituted a fourth reason for opposition to them. Pathogens recognize no borders and their movement across populations are a truly transnational phenomenon. Of special concern was the threat to the public health posed by international migrants who might be carrying germs that could infect Americans with epidemic diseases such as cholera, typhus fever, typhoid, or yellow fever. The response to the migration of microorganisms was both national and local. As historian Alan M. Kraut (*Silent Travelers,* 1994) observed, the discovery of germ theory in the late nineteenth century caused federal and state health officers to craft measures that would exclude these "silent travelers" that arrived on the bodies of newcomers. Still, as Kraut and historian of medicine Howard Markel (*Quarantine! East European Jewish Immigrants and the New York City Epidemics of 1892,* 1997) have demonstrated, particular groups of newcomers were stigmatized as the carriers of specific diseases. Even as cholera had been identified with Irish Catholic immigrants in the 1830s, tuberculosis was often called the Jewish disease, and the Italians were accused of bringing polio to the United States. However, the health of immigrants was at issue for another reason as well.

Among the immigrants were men, women, and children weakened by malnutrition, their bodies deformed by vitamin deficiencies. Critics of immigration feared that these wracked bodies would never be able to withstand the physical strain of agricultural or industrial labor. The United States might not only become the hospital of the nations of the earth, but a charity hospital at that. Some opponents of immigration raised the specter of millions of enfeebled foreign born in need of medical care and alms to survive.

Finally, newcomers' different appearance, including clothes and skin tone, also aroused apprehensions. Those continuing to wear their native garb for a time appeared out of place and even a bit ominous in the streets of America's new modern cities. Just as the ragged Irish of an earlier era had made proper Bostonians cringe, so the new immigrants of every hue and body type met anxious glances as they tramped down gangplanks into a New World long dominated by Anglo-Saxons. With each succeeding boatload, Americans worried about the influence of foreign blood on the vitality of the American population.

Even as immigrants found employment and made their peace with their strange, new environment, they faced the distrust and animosity of both the native born and the immigrants of an earlier era. While newcomers sought to broaden their options and opportunities in the United States, immigration's opponents moved to narrow choices and choke off possibilities of advancement. In 1921, it seemed that the immigrants had lost the last round; the imposition of federal immigration quotas by frightened Americans abruptly curtailed the growth of the immigrant community. However, the immigrants won the bout. Neither the Congress nor those who had lobbied against immigration could oust those already here, nor could they arrest the changes these newcomers had already initiated in their adopted homeland.

I

Strangers are regarded with suspicion in all societies. From the period of colonial settlement through the Civil War, European arrivals regarded native Americans and African slaves, brought as part of a great forced migration, as the "other." Neither group was eligible to fully participate in decisionmaking about the political, economic, and social direction the American national state would take. Those who governed were remarkably homogeneous: white, Anglo-Saxon, Protestant, and, consistent with the assumptions about gender in that era, male. Euro-Americans in the United States attributed their cherished liberties to twin roots: the Anglo-Saxon tradition embodied in the Magna Carta, that primal expression of political democracy later expanded upon by European Enlightenment thinkers, and the Protestant Reformation, the spiritual rebellion against an oppressive Roman Catholic Church. From America's shores, what were perceived as the tyrannical imperialist monarchies of Europe and the oppressive influence of a transnational Roman Catholic Church seemed too distant to be threatening. Then, in the middle of the nineteenth century, Irish Catholics arrived in large numbers, making native Americans uneasy. Perhaps the Atlantic Ocean was not wide enough after all to protect the American nation from threats to its autonomy. This unease grew to absolute anxiety with the mass migration at the end of the century.

From the colonial era on, natives and newcomers viewed each other through a prism of racial, religious, and cultural rivalries. Still, most Americans and most early-nineteenth-century immigrants were willing to coexist, however warily. But the latest arrivals, even more alien to established Americans than the Irish had been, stirred latent fears that a time was coming when a majority of the population would no longer be of Anglo-Saxon Protestant stock. Nativism, then, was the response of those Americans who, latching onto this fear, regarded themselves as an endangered species and were prepared to be ruthless in their own self-defense. Often those fears found cultural expression in newspapers, pamphlets, and books.

John Higham, in his now classic study of nativism, *Strangers in the Land* (1955), identified three strains of anti-immigrant venom—racial nativism, anti-Catholicism, and anti-radical nativism—most common in the treatises of nativists who hated newcomers on ideological grounds. However, anti-Semitism, its origins buried deep in the culture of Western civilization, might well be treated as a fourth strain, as Higham would later contend. Then, too, immigrants encountered the hatred of those who blamed the newcomers for unemployment, low wages, epidemic disease, or urban problems such as violent crime and vice.

The racial nativism that new immigrants inspired in their hesitant hosts was most frequently expressed in the books written by self-appointed guardians of America's Anglo-Saxon heritage, who were frequently scientists or college professors. Many of these scholars were inspired by Charles Darwin's biological research, arguing that Darwin's hypothesis on the physical evolution of plants and animals was applicable to the evolution of human society as well. They mistakenly related Darwin's biological theories to the human condition, applying "survival of the fittest" to society. Though Darwin posited only that those species better adapted to a particular environment had a better chance at perpetuating themselves through reproduction, nativists interpreted "fittest" and "best" to suit their anti-foreign, racist predisposition. Confident that certain races would triumph over inferior competitors due to the laws of nature, social Darwinists insisted that heredity alone determined which races could and which could not adapt to democratic forms of government and the competition of the free enterprise system. When Mexican immigration was criticized, it was often on racial grounds. The "Indian" or "Negro" blood in Mexicans was often cited as the reason why Mexicans posed a danger to the vitality of those north of the Rio Grande. To establish which members of the species were most fit, some researchers compared the cranial volumes of human skulls from members of various ethnic groups. Others used Intelligence Quotient tests. While not deliberately biased, these measurements and observations were decidedly culture-bound, favoring people most like the individual who had designed the questions and tasks. Nevertheless, investigators used the results of such examinations to contend that science ratified their prejudices.

At the turn of the century, economist Francis Walker, president of the Massachusetts Institute of Technology, described the newcomers as "beaten men from beaten races," and quite unlike "those who are descended from the tribes that met under the oak trees of Old Germany to make laws and choose chieftains."

Edward Alsworth Ross described sexual relationships between natives of sturdy Anglo-Saxon and Teutonic stock and newcomers as "race suicide." A professor of sociology at the University of Wisconsin, Ross wrote in *The Old World in the New* (1914) that the immigrants were subcommon, and that they would racially cripple the American population if permitted unrestricted entry. His investigation consisted primarily of observation, and he drew an absolute connection between "different" and "inferior."

Observe immigrants not as they come travel-worn up to the gangplank, nor as they issue toil-begrimed from pit's mouth or mill gate, but in their gatherings, washed, combed, and in their Sunday best. You are struck by the fact that from ten to twenty percent are hirsute, lowbrowed, big-faced persons of obviously low mentality. . . . These oxlike men are descendants of those who always stayed behind.

Ross's observations and conclusions were echoed by many others with similar credentials and equally primitive research methods.

Madison Grant's *The Passing of the Great Race* (1916) synthesized many racial nativist arguments into a masterful and widely read treatise on the superiority of hereditary over environmental factors in shaping mankind. Grant amassed much scientific data but interpreted it through the prism of his own prejudices. He insisted that interracial unions produced a hybrid race that reverted to a "more ancient, generalized and lower type." The lowest type among the immigrants was the east European Jew. The antithesis of the tall, fair Nordic type most admired by Grant, east European Jews could only sap the Anglo-Saxon race of its vitality if permitted to enter the United States and intermarry.

Lothrop Stoddard, a New England attorney trained in history, echoed Grant, claiming that yellow- and brown-skinned peoples were inherently inferior to Caucasians. In *The Rising Tide of Color* (1920) he warned that racially inferior nonwhites actively sought to undermine the civilization created by whites of Teutonic and Anglo-Saxon heritage. Other nativists claimed to have confirmed Grant's hypothesis with their own primitive I.Q. tests. However, they ignored evidence contradicting their assumptions, such as test results demonstrating that the longer a group lived in the United States, the higher its members scored on I.Q. tests.

Warnings from Grant and other nativists that the newest arrivals from abroad represented a clear and present danger to the physical vitality of Americans and to the survival of American institutions did not go unchallenged. In 1911, Columbia University anthropologist Franz Boas, himself a German Jewish immigrant, published *The Mind of Primitive Man,* an extensive refutation of racial nativism. In one series of experiments, Boas demonstrated that the American environment was modifying the very "racial characteristics" that nativists found so detestable in the immigrants. Because the slope of the cranium was often regarded as a reliable index of race, he measured the skulls of second-generation immigrants and discovered that many no longer physically resembled their parents' generation. Long-headed types grew shorter and round-headed types often developed elongated heads. Boas concluded that nutrition and other aspects of living conditions determined these "racial characteristics" more than heredity. Though Boas was acclaimed in the scientific community, he never convinced lay readers who preferred studies that supported rather than refuted their rationale for nativism.

Catholic immigrants from Italy, Poland, Greece, Mexico, and Canada were confronted by hatred distilled from faith and history, rather than science. Anti-Catholicism in the United States was part of a much larger transnational rivalry for power and souls. It was imported by the first English Protestants who had settled along the Atlantic coast in the seventeenth century. Themselves the products of the Protestant Reformation, these Englishmen regarded the Pope as a foreign tyrant wielding dangerous international influence. The authoritarian organization of the Roman Catholic Church, its link to feudal or monarchical governments in Spain and France, and Henry VIII's schism with the Church during the sixteenth century all contributed to America's anti-Catholic heritage.

The publication in 1885 of *Our Country: Its Possible Future and Its Present Crisis* by Protestant minister Josiah Strong stoked anti-Catholic nativism. Strong identified "an irreconcilable difference between papal principles and the fundamental principles of our free institutions." He viewed the urban political machine, often run by Irish Catholic politicians courting the votes of immigrants, as just the first of many pernicious influences that the newcomers would exert on American society.

Anti-Catholicism declined in the 1890s, but Jewish immigrants from eastern Europe continued to experience a nativism grounded in ancient religious antipathies. Traditionally, anti-Semitism was based on the orthodox Christian view of Jews as God's Chosen People who betrayed their Lord. In the late nineteenth century, however, anti-Semitic nativism in the United States was more economic and xenophobic than religious in origin. The Shylock image of the usurious Jew, popularized by Shakespeare's *Merchant of Venice,* peppered the speeches and writings of American agrarian and labor leaders, as well as the stewards of established wealth fearing the social changes brought about by industrialization, urbanization, and immigration. Driven from country to country by violent anti-Semitism, many Jews were seen by American nationalists as a rootless international community that would undermine a national state. There was also a racial component to anti-Semitic nativism. Sociologist E. A. Ross suggested in 1914 that Jews might be unable to compete as equals in the American economy because they were "the polar opposite of our pioneer breed." He and others complained that not only were Jews undersized and weak-muscled, but "they shun bodily activity and are exceedingly sensitive to pain." Economics and racial inferiority were linked by anti-Semites who claimed that the physically inferior Jew compensated for his difference with cunning and avariciousness in the marketplace.

Anti-Semitism was voiced by many early-twentieth-century educators, including Goldwin Smith, Cornell University's distinguished historian. Smith defended Europe's exclusion of Jews from political equality with Gentiles. According to Smith, "It may be fairly asked whether the member of a parasitic race, preserving his tribalism and tribal interests, had a plain and unmistakable right to a share of political power in a community to which he could hardly be said to belong." Smith's opposition to Jewish immigration was echoed by Henry Adams, Henry Cabot Lodge, and many contemporaries.

Immigrants occasionally found themselves under attack for political as well as racial and religious reasons. Though there was no evidence that most immigrants were radicals or came to America to foment revolution, the handful who did participate in labor protests or wrote in support of socialism or anarchism only seemed to confirm preexisting nativist apprehensions. Thomas Jefferson in *Notes on the State of Virginia* (1781) had observed that most immigrants would necessarily come from despotic countries and would either retain undemocratic principles of government or would pass to the other extreme and degenerate into anarchy. Though Jefferson and other Americans applauded the French Revolution in 1789 and avidly followed other revolutionary movements, especially in Latin America, it was feared that political refugees seeking sanctuary in the United States might be either too reactionary or too radical to nourish the gains of the American Revolution. By the late nineteenth century, anti-radical nativism had become an American perennial.

The Haymarket Riot of 1886, which followed a protest meeting called by labor organizers and anarchist agitators, involved many of Chicago's immigrant workers. It called attention to the radicalism of some immigrants. The incident heightened the fears of those already leery of working side by side with "strangers." Despite apprehensions, most newcomers were too preoccupied

with adjusting to their new environment to consider subversive political activity of any kind. Moreover, many immigrants abhorred
radical socialism; socialists advocated curbing immigration to prevent cheap immigrant labor from depressing American wages.

Anti-radical nativism often found expression in the streets as
well as in books and newspapers. The majority of immigrants entered the American economy as unskilled laborers, competing for
jobs with native-born workers and immigrants from northern and
western Europe. Factories and mines, thus, became tinderboxes
scattered over the American landscape. Labor strikes and work
shortages were the sparks that ignited nativist violence. American
workers cared little about the esoteric arguments of nativist scientists and college professors. They found their own practical reasons for hating the newcomers.

How did those who did not publish their denunciations of the
foreign-born express their opposition to immigrants? A particularly systematic campaign was mounted on the West Coast against
the Chinese. Nineteenth-century Americans regarded Chinese culture as primitive, Chinese society as backward, and Chinese influence on democratic institutions as corrosive. Considered racially
inferior heathens, the Chinese were stigmatized as the "Yellow
Peril" as they began to settle in some numbers on the Pacific
Coast. It required only an economic crisis to transform latent
prejudices into an all-out anti-Chinese crusade. During the national depression of 1870, easterners traveled west on the newly
completed transcontinental railroad, hoping to buy farm land or
claim mining stakes. Instead they found themselves confronted
with speculative land prices and in competition with Chinese immigrants for a handful of unpalatable jobs. In 1871, rioters killed
twenty-one Chinese in San Francisco; in 1877, twenty-five Chinese laundries were burned. Such violence was echoed in Colorado and Wyoming and during the following decade reverberated
throughout the western states.

Other immigrant groups were also targets of violent reactions
to economic stress. In 1895, during a labor strike in the southern
Colorado coal fields, a gang of miners and townspeople killed six
Italian laborers implicated in the death of a native-born saloon
keeper. Heavily indebted Louisiana farmers went on a rampage

against Jewish merchants, while in Mississippi local hoodlums burned and destroyed the homes of Jewish landlords.

The Leo Frank case demonstrates how economic tensions could be fused with other genres of nativism. Leo Frank was the Cornell University–educated son of Russian Jews. His father was a New York manufacturer, and Leo went south to manage an Atlanta pencil factory. Despite thin evidence, Frank was found guilty of murdering a young factory worker, Mary Phagan, in 1914. He was denounced by local residents, journalists, and politicians for exploiting southern workers and besmirching the South's womanhood. When the governor commuted his sentence to life, some Georgians boycotted Jewish-owned stores; others formed an explosive mob, stormed the prison farm where Frank was incarcerated and lynched him. Not until 1983, did Alonzo Mann, eighty-four years old, who had been an office boy in the factory sixty-eight years earlier, come forward to identify Jim Conley, the plant's African-American janitor, as the culprit.

Immigrants were blamed for social as well as economic disorders burdening American society, especially those in urban areas where most of the newcomers settled. Statistics on soaring crime rates in neighborhoods with high concentrations of immigrants were held up by nativist journalists, reformers, and politicians as proof positive of the deleterious influence of the immigrant on his environment. However, further investigation has suggested to historians a more complex interpretation of such figures.

Because taverns, gambling houses, and brothels were usually not tolerated in the more refined neighborhoods of the native born, they often could exist untroubled by the law only in immigrant enclaves. In such establishments, immigrants sought temporary escape from cramped quarters and gray, depressing lives. Each group had a favorite vice. Slavs and Italians favored drinking more than Jews, who preferred gambling, as did the Chinese. But no group had a monopoly on any particular vice. Though approximately 50 percent of the prostitutes in large urban areas were immigrants or the daughters of immigrants, they numbered many native born among their customers. Some saw the international trade in prostitutes as a transnational threat to American morality.

Settlement workers were perhaps more realistic than journalists or policemen in acknowledging that abominable living conditions, sickness, fear, and loneliness were the real causes of crime.
Most of the arrests were for crimes of poverty such as drunken-
ness, vagrancy, or petty theft. Social workers argued that the thief
who stole small amounts of food, clothing, or money was desper-
ately attempting to cope with poverty and hopelessness, rather
than responding to an innate criminality. Often the American press
did not probe deeply into the reasons for criminal activity. In 1904,
the *Times* of El Paso, Texas, reported the arrest of a female shop-
lifter, observing that "The evil of shoplifting is growing by leaps
and bounds in El Paso." Although most of those arrested were
Mexican women, the newspaper pointed out that "one or two
Mexican men have been arrested within the past week for this of-
fense." Despite charges by some native Americans, the facts suggest that the criminality of the foreign born in America was no
greater than that of the native born. In September 1909, only 25
percent of the prisoners in New York's Sing Sing Prison were foreign born, although immigrants composed over 43 percent of New
York City's total population. Moreover, at least some immigrants
who were arrested ended up going to prison because they did not
understand their rights or have the confidence to assert their right
to counsel and defend themselves against bogus charges. Historian
Mario T. Garcia quotes a reporter's investigation of jail conditions
in El Paso in 1900. The journalist found that "the Mexicans are
more inclined to plead guilty and throw themselves on the mercy
of the courts than the Americans. The Americans usually arrange
to fight their cases."

Yet the myth of immigrant criminality persisted. In 1913, social reformer and sociologist Peter Roberts traced the cause
of immigrant criminality to "drink and housing conditions." Roberts, an advocate of temperance, condemned those who "sacrifice
their reason to Bacchus." Different immigrant groups were stereo-
typically linked by the native born to certain kinds of crimes. The
Italians and Greeks were accused of "a distinct tendency to abduc-
tion and kidnaping"; the Russians, to "larceny and receiving stolen

goods." The 1911 report of the United States Immigration Commission charged that "certain kinds of criminality are inherent in the Italian race." The criminal activities of the mafia, or Black Hand, had led undiscriminating investigators to make a sweeping generalization defaming an entire group.

In his 1970 study of the Italian community in Chicago, historian Humbert Nelli contended that organized crime existed in Chicago long before the arrival of the Italians. The city's organized crime began in the 1870s under the leadership of Irish hoodlums such as Michael Cassius McDonald. The Black Hand was not a vast Italian syndicate, according to Nelli, but a style of extortion used by small groups of Italian hoodlums to squeeze money out of superstitious, frightened Italian workers. Only later, in the 1920s, did Chicago Italians play a major role in syndicate criminal activities, profiting from prohibition violations, prostitution, gambling, and drug sales. In another book (*The Business of Crime,* 1976), Nelli demonstrated that the story of Italian crime began as a transnational tale with strong links between families in specific regions of Italy and those who had migrated to the United States and other countries. However, as the original Sicilian mafia floundered in the United States, only "the secrecy, rituals, and exotic behavior" of the Old-World criminal societies remained. But these Old-World criminal rites and symbols titillated the American imagination and caused the press to credit the hoodlums with "wondrous evil power," far beyond their real capabilities. Despite the newspaper headlines and movies, few young Italians were in any way connected to organized crime.

The persistence of the stereotype of Italians as enmeshed in mafia activities notwithstanding, every group claimed their own thugs—unwillingly. Jews, too, found a place in the criminal underworld. Condemned and feared by their coreligionists and cited by native Americans as part of the high cost of Jewish immigration, a modest number of young Jews turned to crime when other opportunities seemed beyond their reach. Waxy Gordon and Dutch Schultz (nee Arthur Flegenheimer) stirred as much controversy as any mafia don.

Throughout the period 1880–1921, then, those who had migrated to the United States met with criticism and resistance. Traditional prejudice rooted in racial and religious differences survived the journey to the New World, though the ancient hatreds were frequently cloaked in the modern jargon of science. Self-appointed guardians of the American nation, democracy, and the national morality armed themselves with arguments borrowed from the founding fathers, Biblical text, and even science. Rational discourse and biblical parable, appropriately tailored to suit the audience, thus fueled hostility between native and newcomer. However, American workers, justifiably fearful of immigrant job competition and contemptuous of alien strikebreakers hardly needed science or religion to feed their animosity toward the new immigrants. Many Americans, dissatisfied with individually denouncing the newcomers or joining in random incidents of resistance, turned to collective efforts to halt immigration and limit the influence of those already here.

II

Newly arrived immigrants found that even as many charities, churches, political parties, and immigrant aid societies welcomed them, other groups were equally dedicated to slamming America's "golden door" in their faces. Nativists lobbied in the halls of Congress and state legislatures, sometimes running political candidates on anti-immigrant platforms. Often terrorist intimidation was substituted for political opposition. Organized anti-immigrant campaigns were limited neither geographically nor socioeconomically. In various regions of the United States, nativist groups and leaders stepped forward to oppose immigration, often focusing their efforts on a particular immigrant group settled in their region of the country.

One of immigration's most inflammatory opponents was himself an immigrant. Dennis Kearney, an Irish-born sailor who had dabbled unsuccessfully in mining speculation, saw Chinese immigrants as scapegoats for his personal debacle and targeted them for a demagogic crusade in the late 1870s. Kearney's racist campaign began in San Francisco's sandlots but soon spread as newspapers thundered his anti-Chinese rhetoric. He charged that the Chinese were in deliberate collusion with large corporate enterprises against white workers, accepting slave wages in return for a monopoly on jobs. Kearney always ended his diatribes by proclaiming, "The Chinese must go!" and his audiences responded with alacrity.

In 1877, Kearney organized the Workingmen's Party to harness to politics the vigor of his reactionary movement. Too small to actually field its own candidates, the Workingmen's Party operated as a voting bloc just large enough to hold the balance of power in California, a state crucial to both Republicans and Democrats in national elections. The demands of Kearney's party were specific: cut off Chinese immigration and curtail the legal and economic rights of those Chinese already in the United States.

At first, politicians hesitated to associate themselves with the fanatically racist Workingmen's Party. Moreover, they were hampered by the 1868 Burlingame Treaty with China, which guaranteed extensive privileges to Chinese citizens in the United States in return for highly favorable trade concessions to American merchants. Still, in 1876, a California legislative committee had proclaimed the Chinese racially inferior, people without souls or with souls not worth saving. In 1879, Congress passed (but President Rutherford B. Hayes vetoed) the Fifteen Passenger Bill, which would have limited to fifteen the number of Chinese passengers on any ship headed for the United States. And, in 1880, the Burlingame Treaty was revised so that the United States could regulate, limit, or suspend Chinese immigration, though it could not technically prohibit it. To circumvent the treaty, proponents of exclusion introduced a bill suspending the immigration of Chinese laborers for ten years; this became the Chinese Exclusion Act of 1882. The law was renewed periodically until 1943. Andrew Gyory's prize-winning history of the Act (*Closing the Gate: Race, Politics, and the Chinese Exclusion Act,* 1998) suggests that its passage signified more than simple hatred of the Chinese or pressure from the strong anti-Chinese lobby in California, though both were certainly factors. Surprisingly, the Act's passage cannot be simply attributed to successful agitation from organized labor either. Gyory sees greater complexity. He argues that economic depression, including unemployment, worker discontent, and politicians' need for an issue that involved little risk, but high dividend, *all* led to Chinese exclusion. Both Democrats and Republicans curried voters' favor with exclusion, a measure promoted as a cure-all to remedy the increasing amount of poverty and class polarization accompanying industrialization. Sentiment was hardly unanimous. In the Senate, the vote was thirty-two to fifteen with twenty-nine not voting. All fifteen votes against exclusion were Republicans. And another eleven Republicans did not vote. However, in the House the bill passed easily and with little debate. President Chester Alan Arthur, who had vetoed a similar bill a month earlier, signed this one on May 6, 1882. Now, even those with no love for the Chinese wondered if exclusion did not set a dangerous precedent. The *New York Times* seemed less concerned with the precedent than with sweeping aside an irritating issue. An editorialist simply stated, "It is to be hoped that this will settle the much-vexed Chinese question for a time at least."

The hopes of the *Times* editorialist were in vain. With the passage of each new bill, the anti-Chinese crusade grew stronger and its nativist missionaries more exultant. All Chinese coming to the United States were required to obtain a certificate of eligibility to be in the United States from the Chinese government. Should a Chinese immigrant already in the U.S. desire to leave temporarily, he or she had to secure a second document from the immigration inspector at San Francisco. This document certified residence in the U.S. and was to be surrendered to immigration officials upon the traveler's return. Any error in the paperwork generally meant exclusion or deportation. Three years later Congress satisfied concern over contract labor whatever its source. In 1885, Congress passed the Foran Act outlawing contract labor from China or anywhere else.

Though only ten Chinese were admitted into the United States in 1887, Republicans pushed through passage of the Scott Act in 1888, which expressly prohibited Chinese laborers from entering the country and limited acceptable immigrants to five classes: officials, teachers, students, merchants, and tourists. More important, the Act broadly defined "Chinese" as any member of the "Chinese race," whether or not they were Chinese nationals. And, most tragically, the Act prohibited the return of any Chinese who had left the United States. Thereby, despite their ownership of American property and their families' residence in this country, 20,000 Chinese laborers who had returned to China for a visit were denied readmission. Many never saw their families again.

Chinese living in the United States endured unofficial abuses and indignities as well. Discrimination in housing and occupations was unrelenting, and slanderous images of the Chinese were splashed through the newspapers. The American public was told that the Chinese were opium merchants, prostitutes, gamblers, and members of frightening, illegal, and secret societies. Those who wore queues (pigtails) were the objects of scorn. Nativists gave a new twist to the expression, "Not a Chinaman's chance."

Perhaps the crowning indignity came in 1892 with the passage of the Geary Act, which oddly resembled southern slave codes abolished not thirty years earlier. This Act denied bail to the Chinese in habeas corpus cases and required all Chinese to obtain a certificate of eligibility to remain in the United States. If a Chinese person was arrested without such a certificate on his person, the burden of proof fell on him to demonstrate his right to remain in the United States. Much to the surprise of the Chinese Consul General and many Americans, the U.S. Supreme Court declared the Geary Act constitutional on the grounds of public interest and necessity.

If politicians found anti-Chinese sentiment a convenient diversion to draw the public's attention from the need for more thorough-going reform, most nativists stood outside the political arena, manipulating public opinion and pressuring politicians behind a comfortable shield of anonymity. Their organizations had names—the American Protective Association, the Immigration Restriction League, and the Ku Klux Klan—but their members usually had no faces.

The American Protective Association (A.P.A.) was organized in Clinton, Iowa, in 1887 by Henry F. Bowers, who devoted his energies to ferreting out Catholic conspiracies. Bowers, a self-educated attorney from Baltimore, believed that he and many others had been deprived of a sound education by a Jesuit conspiracy against the public schools. Likewise, he felt that a Catholic conspiracy had undermined the re-election campaign of his friend, Mayor Arnold Walliker.

Fired by these imagined indignities, Bowers was quite successful, securing a membership for the A.P.A. in the Midwest and Rocky Mountain states. Alerted to the "Roman menace," new members swore never to cast ballots for Catholic candidates, never to employ Catholics when Protestant workers were available, and never to join Catholic workers on a picket line. The A.P.A. attracted disenchanted union members and laborers who felt particularly threatened by the competition of cheap Irish labor. It served its members as both a vehicle for political activity and as a fraternal order, with secret rituals, elaborate initiations, and a social activities program for members and their families. Though not a political party, the A.P.A. usually supported Republican candidates, which crippled its recruiting efforts in the white, Democratic South.

The A.P.A. faded away in the mid-1890s, but not before leaving behind a reputation for violence and exaggerated fears. A.P.A. members battled Catholics through the saloons of a Montana mining town during a day-long fracas in 1893. This incident was followed soon after by a shooting at a polling place in Kansas City, Missouri, during a municipal election. Rumors of full-scale warfare between the A.P.A. and Catholic groups were rampant in the early 1890s. The mayor of Toledo, Ohio, purchased a quantity of Winchester rifles for Protestants to repel an anticipated Catholic invasion that never materialized.

But by the second half of the 1890s, Irish and German Roman Catholics, once so frightening, had become prominent and crucial members of the electorate. Even a hint of anti-Catholicism became a liability for politicians with national aspirations. Yet, even as the membership of the somewhat aimless A.P.A. was trickling away, the much more sophisticated Immigration Restriction League was being organized in the East.

Founded by Boston patricians in 1894, the Immigration Restriction League set out to limit, but not completely end, immigration to the United States. On the rationale that open immigration allowed people of dubious background and limited capabilities into the country, the League proposed a literacy test as a means of ensuring that those admitted would not become a burden on the society. Ostensibly, the League's proposal that every immigrant over sixteen years of age be literate in a language was not discriminatory. However, a higher proportion of northern and western Europeans had access to at least minimal education. Literacy tests, therefore, would effectively exclude a higher proportion of immigrants from southeastern Europe and from Latin America.

The League operated as a highly organized, extraordinarily tenacious lobbying group. Into the early 1900s, the literacy test was incorporated into congressional bills and tacked on as a rider to amendments only to be vetoed or dropped. However, though League supporters might not publicly flaunt their xenophobia, they were influential individuals, roaming freely through the corridors of power. They kept the issue of a literacy requirement before the Congress until literacy tests for immigrants were established by federal law just before World War I.

Far from patrician and far from sophisticated was the Ku Klux Klan, which caught its second wind after World War I, taking up the cudgels for Americans who hoped to actively discourage immigrants from settling in their communities and competing for their jobs. Actually, the Klan was revived in 1915 by an ex-Methodist minister, Colonel Joseph Simmons, at a torchlight meeting on Georgia's Stone Mountain. The Colonel (an honorary title) hoped to profit by the opening of D. W. Griffith's movie, *Birth of a Nation,* by creating a fraternal lodge with secret rituals and a selective membership modeled on the old Klan of Reconstruction days as depicted in the film. But the ashes of Reconstruction resentments proved difficult to stir, and by 1920 Simmons had enrolled only 2,000 members. That year, the Colonel entered partnership with Edward Young Clark and Elizabeth Tyler, two public

relations experts who had learned their trade during World War I
Red Cross drives and now wished to apply their skills to a finan-
cially profitable venture. Under their combined leadership, the
Klan flourished.

The new Klan branded immigrants, especially Roman Catholics and Jews, subversives, directly threatening the American way
of life. Klansmen led in a renewed call for an end to open immigration, derisively labeling the ideal of a melting pot, a "mess of
sentimental pottage." Kenneth T. Jackson (*The Ku Klux Klan in
the City, 1915–1930,* 1967) has argued that "the greatest source of
Klan support came from rank-and-file nonunion blue-collar employees of large businesses and factories." A substantial minority
of white-collar Klansmen were marginally successful independent
businessmen, poorly paid clerks, and struggling dentists and chiro-
practors. A few unprincipled urban politicians also sought Klan
support to bolster their sagging careers. However, in some states,
such as Indiana, Klan membership included a wide cross-section
of white Protestant society. Historian Leonard J. Moore (*Citizen
Klansmen, The Ku Klux Klan in Indiana, 1921–1928,* 1991) suggests more than one-quarter of native-born men in the state became card-carrying Klan members, more than the state's largest
denomination, the Methodist Church. All members of the Klan
shared a desire to find an explanation external to themselves for
the changes taking place in American society and for their lack of
success in riding the crest of those changes. Recent immigrants, so
alien, so strange to life in America, seemed convenient scapegoats.
However, as Leonard Moore observes, the Klan in Indiana saw immigration as just one of a number of changes endangering cherished family and community values. The Klan became an engine
of political and social action for those who felt threatened by mon-
ied elites as much as by the foreign born.

The Klan proudly claimed credit for the eventual passage of
restrictive immigration legislation in 1921 and 1924, though other
groups had agitated for the laws with equal fervor and great profi-
ciency. Klansmen supported local candidates who seemed sufficiently nativist and pledged to work for the passage of restrictive

immigration laws. By and large, however, the Klan preferred public demonstration and catharsis to political manipulation and lobbying. White-robed, hooded Klansmen held public meetings, burned crosses, and committed occasional acts of violence such as the public flogging of immigrants or those assisting the newcomers. Women's auxiliaries often joined in the marches and other less violent attempts at intimidation.

Ironically, the final enactment of restrictive legislation seemed to dissipate the enthusiasm of organized nativists, no matter what their class or strategy. Immigration was all but choked off, yet the transformation of American society so repugnant to nativists proceeded. Throughout the era, immigrants actively resisted nativist verbal, legal, and physical assaults. These people who had traveled halfway around the globe refused to passively capitulate to nativist coercion.

III

Immigrants resisted the prejudiced behavior of native-born Americans in ways both psychological and physical. At the end of the twentieth century, scholars such as David Roediger, Noel Ignatiev, Karen Brodkin, and Matthew Frye Jacobson have argued that ever since the mid-nineteenth century, immigrants resisted the imposition of negative racial stereotypes as well as patterns of oppression. These scholars, whose books have been collectively described as "whiteness studies," contend that immigrant workers had a great deal in common with the suffering of slaves and later free black workers but rejected class-based alliances. Instead they pursued their own best interests by identifying with the concerns of the native-born, white middle class. In short, Irish Catholics, but also eastern European Jews and southern Italians, however swarthy their complexions, claimed that their whiteness entitled them to opportunities and opened doors systematically denied to African Americans. Racism trumped class; racism trumped foreignness. Thus, because of their appearance, Koreans were subjected to the same restrictions as the Japanese under the

Gentlemen's Agreement of 1907, and in 1917, Asian Indians were barred along with the Chinese and Japanese. Whiteness, on the other hand, even the whiteness of the most downtrodden, conferred privilege. The eminent African-American scholar W. E. B. DuBois poignantly observed that even poorly paid white workers were "compensated in part by a public and psychological wage." This "surplus wage" to which he referred was their assumption of social superiority over nonwhites in the labor marketplace and their participation, at times, in anti-black violence.

While most European immigrant groups struggled to be as white as native-born Americans, resisting identification with the interests of Chinese, Mexicans, as well as native-born African Americans and blacks from the Caribbean, they soon discovered that white racial identity was not conferred on all newcomers upon arrival. In his 1998 volume *Whiteness of a Different Color,* historian Matthew Frye Jacobson described the contingent quality of European immigrants' whiteness. He demonstrates that from the middle of the nineteenth century through the 1920s, Italians, Irish, eastern European Jews and others were defined as racially different from those of Anglo-Saxon and Teutonic stock. Eugenics, the science of controlled, selective breeding to improve human stock, seemed to lend scientific justification to the demand for immigration restriction. Only after the immigration restriction was legislated in the 1920s did old-stock Americans permit the consolidation of the newer immigrants into the category "Caucasian." Why?

According to Jacobson, "a pattern of Caucasian unity" gradually took the place of the "Anglo-Saxonist exclusivity." Between the mid-1920s and the end of World War II, "'Caucasian' as a 'natural division' of humanity became part of a popular national catechism." The new "scientific" formulation of humanity's hierarchy in both high and low American culture described the subdivisions of mankind as Caucasian, Mongolian, and Negroid. This shift in "scientific" definition of race lumped all Europeans into the Caucasian category. As Jacobson observes, "By the election of 1960 a Celt could become president [John F. Kennedy], and though his religion might have been cause for concern in some quarters, his race never was." Culturally, European immigrants were now included in a "multi-ethnic pan whiteness."

Of course in law, Italians, Irish, eastern European Jews, Greeks, and other Euroethnic groups were regarded as white even before the new racial subdivisions. However, in *White By Law* (1996), legal scholar Ian F. Haney Lopez demonstrates that the subdivisions hardly settled all questions. In naturalization cases, judges turned to legal precedent, congressional intent, common knowledge, and scientific evidence to determine the race and, therefore, the citizenship eligibility of groups such as Armenians, Syrians, Filipinos, Asian Indians, and individuals who were born to parents of different races such as those who were half Japanese and half German. Whatever the color of their skin, Armenians and Syrians were declared Asian and therefore nonwhite by some judges and white by others. Asian Indians were usually considered nonwhite and those of mixed parentage were also usually called nonwhite. Often judges, such as District Judge Smith sitting in the Eastern District of South Carolina, performed legal contortions to avoid such potentially awkward questions as whether Jesus Christ would have been eligible to be an American. Was Jesus white or nonwhite if he had come from the same part of the world as George Dow, the Syrian immigrant standing at the bar of justice, hoping to become a citizen? And what was the relationship of skin tone to inclusion in the Caucasian category? Were both Jesus and Dow Caucasian even though Dow had brown skin? In his opinion, Judge Smith dodged the issue and declared Dow nonwhite. However, a later federal court opinion declared Syrians white and Dow eligible for citizenship. Jesus's eligibility appears to have been left undetermined.

If immigrants hoped that eventually their white identities would be the coin of the realm that would ransom them from society's bottom rung, their immediate economic circumstances required more than a psychological currency. Immigrants battled discriminatory policies and legislation advocated by nativists with whatever weapons they could muster. They turned to politics and pressure groups to counter nativism, fearing that any violence beyond self-defense might meet with even greater brutality or arrests, trials, and deportation. In the anthracite coalfields of Pennsylvania, there was frequent violence over union organization between miners and the ruffians hired by mine owners to squelch union activity during the 1880s. However, most immigrant conflict was initiated by the Irish Catholic Molly Maguires against mine owners, often of Welsh and English background, whom they accused of exploitation. Slavic miners already in the field, perceiving their stay in America to be temporary, usually did not join the Mollies, nor were they invited to do so. Moreover, Irish contentiousness was often exaggerated by anti-unionists who successfully hampered the growth of mine unionism by linking labor organization with terrorism in the public mind.

According to labor historian Melvyn Dubofsky (*Industrialism and the American Worker, 1865–1920,* 1975), scholars cannot agree whether or not the Industrial Workers of the World (IWW), organized in 1905, were "reformers or revolutionaries, political activists or apolitical organizers of the working class, industrial unionists or syndicalists." Although immigrants often shunned unions for fear of losing their jobs as the result of strikes or out of the desire to avoid the expense of union dues, some did move directly onto the front lines of labor conflict. Indeed, many of those who initially joined the IWW, or "Wobblies," were recently arrived, unskilled immigrant laborers. As David Montgomery observes in *The Fall of the House of Labor* (1987), many new arrivals were attracted to the Wobblies by the concept of unionization along industrial, instead of craft lines, while others were drawn to the group by the rhetoric of a class war against capitalism. Moreover, the Wobblies worked actively to promote interethnic cooperation. They organized Caucasian and African-American workers on a nonsegregated basis, especially among southern lumbermen and Philadelphia longshoremen. In eastern cities they designated organizers to speak and translate for workers of particular groups. In Lawrence, Massachusetts, in 1912, the strike committee was structured so that each immigrant group was represented regardless of its size. Though Italians, Poles, and other east Europeans joined the Wobblies to strike against the Pressed Steel Car Company of McKees Rocks, Pennsylvania (1909), and textile mills in Lawrence, Massachusetts (1912), and Paterson, New Jersey (1913), many immigrants left the union after the collapse of the twenty-two-week Paterson strike, and few recent immigrants ever took a leading role in Wobbly disorders. Just as they shunned the violence involving the Molly Maguires, immigrants' fears of losing badly needed jobs or being deported following an arrest deterred many newcomers from sticking with the Wobblies. However, according to historian Rudolph J. Vecoli, the lesson of interethnic cooperation remained as a legacy. During the second Lawrence strike in 1919, the striking workers, 60 percent of whom were immigrant women, enthusiastically sang the "Internationale" and other radical labor songs, each immigrant group singing in its own language but in unison with the others: in spirit, if not in sound, theirs was a song more harmonious than cacophonous.

Until the immigrants became naturalized voters and grew accustomed to regular political participation, they had little clout in national politics. However, at the state and local levels, party bosses perceived the political potential of the new immigrants, just as they had with earlier arrivals. In cities, urban bosses and their machines protected newcomers from nativist hostility, much of which was now directed from state governments. State legislators representing districts with large numbers of native-born voters, who felt beleaguered by an increasing population of alien Catholics and Jews, staunchly sponsored legislation to shape immigrant behavior, such as laws restricting business and recreational activities on the Sabbath. These Sunday "blue laws" in New York were bitterly attacked by Democrats, especially those from Tammany Hall, as anti-immigrant in intent. In his famous discourse on urban politics in 1905, Tammany boss George Washington Plunkitt lashed out at the Republican legislature and governor: "We've got to eat and drink what they tell us to eat and drink, and have got to choose our time for eatin' and drinkin' to suit them. If they don't feel like takin' a glass of beer on Sundays, we must abstain. If they have not got any amusements up in their backwoods, we mustn't have none. We've got to regulate our whole lives to suit them. And then we have to pay their taxes to boot."

Jewish merchants who closed on Saturday and opened on Sunday were especially penalized by Sabbath laws. However, the pushcart peddlers and small shopkeepers on New York's Lower East Side soon learned that they could elude enforcement by "the brass button" (as New York's policemen were known) by paying $5 in protection money to the cop on the beat. Generally the police, many of whom were Irish, were only too pleased to foil Protestant nativism and turn a profit besides.

By the 1920s, new immigrants were beginning to pound on the doors of America's most prestigious universities. Schools such as Columbia, Harvard, Yale, and Princeton responded by trying to install a dead-bolt lock. Wealthy private institutions, protected by influential friends and alumni, were impervious to the efforts of political bosses. Thus, leaders of organizations representing the newcomers had to use the subtler tools of public opinion and private persuasion to help immigrants and their children into the "old boy" network that emanated from major universities and led to positions of affluence and power. Often, however, they were little match for the white Anglo-Saxon Protestant establishment opposing them.

One Harvard University professor expressed the objections of numerous others when he complained that too many students were coming from outside the "element" from which the college had chiefly recruited for 300 years. In response to these complaints, Harvard mounted a restrictive quota system in 1922 that especially affected the increasing number of east European Jews seeking admission. Revised admission questionnaires were designed to flag newcomers by asking "What change, if any, has been made since birth in your name or that of your father?" Louis Marshall of the American Jewish Committee led Jewish leaders in a public attack on Harvard, arguing that such quotas were not only anti-Semitic in intent but that any quotas based on racial or religious criteria were "a calamity to the United States" as well as an elitist violation of a university's broader educational mission. When a special faculty committee appointed to investigate admissions policies reported on April 9, 1923, it recommended that Harvard repudiate earlier changes and retain a policy of "equal opportunity for all, regardless of race or religion" using "no novel process of scrutiny" to screen applicants. However, covert discrimination at Harvard and elsewhere continued, despite public declarations to the contrary.

The immigrants and their supporters could not immediately overcome the powerful and prejudiced doorkeepers of America's elite educational institutions. Fortunately, there were public educational institutions opened to all who could qualify. Great state universities such as the sixty-nine institutions born of the land grants provided by the Morrill Act of 1862 and tuition-free municipal institutions such as the City College of New York educated many millions of newcomers.

Because immigration to the United States was part of a larger transnational process of migration, some immigrants responded to discriminatory policies in the United States by appealing to the governments of their native countries. Foremost among these were the Japanese. Unlike the Chinese, most of whom arrived in poverty, many Japanese came to America with sufficient capital to purchase farmland. Thus, the Japanese became efficient and productive growers in the United States while their homeland was achieving power and prestige in world affairs.

Predictably, the Japanese were viewed by many Americans as ambitious, aggressive, and a little too successful. Old fears of the "Yellow Peril" were stirred up, and racial nativists sounded the alarm. In 1905, the Asiatic Exclusion League was formed in San Francisco and succeeded in persuading the city school board to restrict Japanese pupils to Chinatown schools. The Japanese community responded vigorously and attacked the spineless racism of California politicians. Many Japanese were well educated and articulate. But their own ethnic prejudices caused them to abhor the thought that their children would be sharing classrooms with Chinese children. They petitioned the Japanese government to intervene with American authorities.

In 1906, only ninety-three of San Francisco's 25,000 pupils were Japanese. The Japanese government pointed out the absurdity of segregation to President Theodore Roosevelt. Hoping to avoid further escalation of the incident into an even greater diplomatic issue, Roosevelt pressured the school board into rescinding its directive. In return for Roosevelt's intervention, the Japanese government acceded to the restrictive "Gentlemen's Agreement" of 1907.

Still, discrimination continued. Under the state law of 1913, California's Japanese residents were proscribed from owning land. But when the courts failed to overturn this discriminatory state legislation, the Japanese continued to acquire property by registering it under the names of their American-born children.

The court of law was the logical forum for many of the immigrant's grievances. However, as Lucy Salyer (*Laws Harsh As Tigers, Chinese Immigrants and the Shaping of Modern Immigration Law,* 1995) observes, after 1891 when the federal government assumed full administrative responsibility for the admission of immigrants, "The Supreme Court had no difficulty in acquiescing to the exclusion of the federal courts from immigration decisions." Less than a month after the Act's passage, the federal Circuit Court for the Northern District of California at San Francisco denied a request to review an immigration inspector's decision to exclude from the United States a Japanese woman, Nishimura Ekiu, on the grounds that she was "likely to become a public charge." The Circuit Court said that under the 1891 act it had no right to interfere, and the Supreme Court upheld its decision on the grounds that the Congress was within its rights to deny judicial review of such administrative matters. Justice Horace Gray refused to accept the notion that immigrants seeking admission had recourse to the courts for due process. He wrote, "[For] foreigners who have never been naturalized, nor acquired any domicile or residence within the United States, nor even been admitted into the country pursuant to law . . . the decisions of executive or administrative officers, acting within powers expressly conferred by Congress, *are* due process of law."

As for those immigrants who had gained admission, the courts were often the only protection they had from specific nativist acts. In 1900, a Chinese immigrant, Chick Gin, died of what experts believed to have been bubonic plague, the feared Black Death of the Middle Ages. As word of Chick's death spread, the Chinese were stigmatized as responsible for bringing the plague to San Francisco. Federal authorities with the support of the San Francisco Board of Health quarantined the Chinese and threatened that unless the Chinese population of the city submitted to inoculation with an experimental serum, they would be forbidden to leave San Francisco. The Chinese Six Companies hired the prominent law firm of Reddy, Campbell, and Metson to represent Chinese merchant Wong Wai in a class-action suit. Much to everyone's surprise, Federal Judge William Morrow, a former three-term Republican congressman with a nativist reputation, ruled in favor of Wong Wai, stating that the measures taken, including compulsory inoculation, were "boldly directed against the Asiatic or Mongolian race as a class, without regard to the previous condition, habits, exposure or disease, or residence of the individual" on the unproven assumption that this "race" was more liable to the plague than any other. Morrow found that the racial provision of the order to inoculate clearly violated the equal protection clause of the Fourteenth Amendment. Bubonic plague did appear in San Francisco, but never in a massive outbreak. In 1900, the plague of anti-Asian prejudice was far more widespread.

Usually, immigrants found the legal system ponderous and judges unsympathetic, the procedures unfamiliar and the officials intimidating. In a 1923 study, *The Immigrant's Day in Court,* Kate Holladay Claghorn charged, "The attitude of the immigrant toward the law and the courts, insofar as it is determined by the teaching of the lawyers and runners, will naturally be one of distrust and disrespect. . . . He is taught that bribery and influence are the regular methods of securing favorable decisions, that the extortionate fees he is called upon to pay are necessary to provide the expected bribes, that the immigrant has no chance before the American court without the aid of a lawyer skilled in a special kind of trickery." She advocated legal aid and education for the immigrants in their rights under the American legal system.

The Sacco-Vanzetti case seemed to confirm Claghorn's assessment of the legal system. It demonstrated conclusively that new immigrants confronted a hostility so pervasive that it penetrated the very system of justice that the newcomers were being urged to respect and preserve. Nicola Sacco and Bartolomeo Vanzetti, two Italian immigrant anarchists, were arrested in May 1920 and charged with the robbery and murder of a shoe-company paymaster in South Braintree, Massachusetts. At their trial, the prosecutor was unable to conclusively demonstrate the pair's guilt. Nevertheless, nativist prejudices and a highly charged courtroom atmosphere resulted in a guilty verdict. Judge Webster Thayer of

Worcester, who regarded the accused as "anarchist bastards," sentenced them to death by electrocution in July 1921.

Protests and appeals postponed the execution date for six years. The issue of whether the court was confusing punishing robbery and murder with punishing ideological dissent to protect the nation state was debated transnationally. Intellectuals from around the world, including George Bernard Shaw, H. G. Wells, Albert Einstein, and Anatole France, protested the conviction and the questionable judicial procedures employed to reach it. Governor Alvin T. Fuller of Massachusetts, under heavy political pressure, formed an advisory committee, which recommended that the executions proceed. On August 22, 1927, Sacco and Vanzetti were executed for a crime they may not have committed.

In 1927, some Americans applauded the execution as an appropriate response to the challenge that alien radicals posed to American law. Others regarded Sacco and Vanzetti as martyrs to the excesses of American capitalism. Louis Joughin and Edmund Morgan (*The Legacy of Sacco and Vanzetti,* 1948) wrote, "A feverish society discredited itself in the Sacco-Vanzetti case. Prejudice, chauvinism, hysteria, and malice were endemic to this country in the 1920s." The controversial nature of the case was formally acknowledged by Massachusetts Governor Michael Dukakis, who issued a proclamation on July 19, 1977, stating that Sacco and Vanzetti were not treated justly. A half-century after their execution, a governor of Greek descent repudiated Brahmin injustice to two Italian immigrants.

Newcomers could turn a deaf ear to the harangues of nativist demagogues such as Dennis Kearney, answer in kind the A.P.A.'s threats of violence, counter the political machinations of nativist state legislatures with their votes, seek redress in the courts for denial of due process, and focus public attention on the hypocrisy of discriminatory liberal educators. However, newcomers and those who spoke for them could not halt the public groundswell for restricting immigration. World War I seeded the storm clouds. It sharply altered the relationship of Americans to the rest of the world. No longer did Americans feel isolated and safe, nestled between two great oceans. The world's problems had been handed a pair of water wings, and more than ever Americans felt vulnerable and suspicious. When nativists succeeded in turning that suspicion inward immediately after the war, the immigrants and their advocates were overwhelmed.

IV

Heightened sensitivity to foreigners stirred by World War I propaganda and postwar turmoil lent new authority to the restrictionist movement launched years earlier. But the immigrants, still too new to America, lacked the political and economic muscle to obstruct this drive for restriction.

The foreign born and their American-born children in no way dominated the politics of states such as New York, Massachusetts, Pennsylvania, New Jersey, Illinois, and Ohio, though millions of newcomers lived elbow to elbow in these states' major cities. While immigrants swelled the number of representatives to which those states were entitled, the newcomers were not eligible to vote until naturalization, nor were all of them equally enthusiastic about exercising the franchise once granted. As a result, the native born continued to superintend the congressional and presidential politics of their respective states. According to historian David Burner (*The Politics of Provincialism,* 1968), only the Great Depression of the 1930s kindled intense interest in national politics among the most recent immigrants.

Even those foreign born who were eligible to vote and sufficiently motivated to go to the polls did not vote as a bloc. Voting analysts Samuel Lubell, David Burner, John Allswang, and Allan Lichtman have all explained that, prior to 1932, recently arrived immigrant groups expressed different party preferences in different parts of the United States. In the election of 1920, the immigrant vote split severely over the controversial Wilson Peace Plan. German-American voters were profoundly disillusioned by the actual terms of the Versailles Treaty and felt that President Woodrow Wilson had discarded the spirit of the humane Fourteen Points and desired to punish the German people. Polish voters generally supported Wilson, while Italians and east European Jews joined the anti-British Irish and angry Germans in voting Republican. In rural communities throughout the American Midwest, Scandinavian immigrants joined Germans in their flight from the Democratic Party. According to Allan Lichtman, "During the 1920s, especially in the Midwest and Far West, battles between conservatives and reformers were frequently fought within the dominant party or between third parties and both major parties rather than between the Republicans and their Democratic rivals." In the Southwest, those Mexicans eligible to vote gauged their political preferences according to American behavior toward Mexico between 1910 and 1920 during the Mexican civil war. After the invasion and occupation of Veracruz in 1914 by U.S. Marines, many Mexican newcomers pledged their loyalty to the United States and promised to fight for their adopted country in case of war with Mexico. However, others blamed the tension in El Paso and other places along the border on President Wilson. Mexicans often feared that aggressive political activity might give immigration's opponents an excuse to deport them. Others who wanted to return to Mexico were politically apathetic. By the 1930s it was estimated that fewer than one-fifth of the 1.5 million Mexicans eligible to vote went to the polls. Those who did vote tended to be Democrats. The immigrants were too divided politically to defeat nativism at the polls.

Nor did the immigrants wield sufficient economic power to stymie nativist intentions. Immigrant entrepreneurs were just gaining a foothold in the American economy, and the majority of immigrants were blue collar. Organized labor, which voiced many of the economic grievances of immigrants, favored restriction. The American Federation of Labor and its president, Samuel Gompers, urged drastic reductions in immigration, fearing that a continued influx of unskilled workers from abroad would endanger the position of skilled craftsmen and drive down the wages of all American workers.

It took the anti-alien emotionalism generated by World War I to convert a persistent issue of political debate into a lightning rod for bipartisan support. World War I was a catalyst, not a cause, of restrictionism. To generate enthusiasm for America's war effort, Woodrow Wilson sanctioned a massive propaganda campaign. The Committee on Public Information under George Creel encouraged a voluntary censorship program and employed the newest public relations techniques developed by businessmen to "sell" Americans the war and generate hatred toward the German foe. A staff of public relations experts in Washington and local patriots throughout the country printed pamphlets, arranged speeches, and generally talked up "one hundred percent Americanism." The influence of German culture and ethnicity on American culture and society, once quite strong, was dealt a mortal blow. In the spirit of the moment, sauerkraut was renamed "liberty cabbage" and 75,000 "Four Minute Men" were recruited by Creel's Committee to describe German atrocities to local community and church groups, urging them to buy Liberty Bonds to finance the war effort. Soon, anyone and anything that smacked of foreign culture became suspect, and patriotism often degenerated into an ugly xenophobia that even the Creel Committee did not endorse. German language courses were removed from high school and college curricula. As part of a July 4th celebration, citizens of one Oklahoma town burned German-language books. And, in isolated outbursts of violence, German Americans were beaten and tarred and feathered. In reaction, some families changed their German-sounding last names to avoid embarrassment or to protect their school-age children from harassment by classmates.

In the rural Midwest, where many German immigrants had settled, tensions ran high. According to historian Jon Gjerde, in Lowden, Iowa, a German pastor was forced to leave town within forty-eight hours in late 1918 while others accused of being pro-German were "rounded up, paraded through town, and forced to salute the American flag and make cash contributions to the Red Cross." An Iowa farmer was almost lynched that year when he compared the Kaiser to a local deputy marshall. Most Germans went out of their way to assure their German and non-German neighbors of their patriotism. Those who expressed any criticism of the United States often found themselves at risk, whatever their rank or position. A German Evangelical minister in the Midwest who described the war as "for capitalists only" and Liberty bonds "a great humbug" was convicted of violating the Espionage Act of 1917. His church was burned though the culprits were not caught.

Often confused with the Germans, the Dutch in the Midwest also suffered. In southwestern Minnesota, homes in the Dutch community were painted yellow by vigilantes because their owners had been heard to make statements construed by non-Dutch residents as disloyal.

In the Southwest, World War I heightened efforts to Americanize Mexican immigrants. Prior to the war, California's Commission of Immigration and Housing (CIH), operated by Progressive social reformers, sought to integrate Mexicans into American society while preserving what was positive and enriching about Mexican culture and other immigrant cultures in the state. However, wartime pressures caused the CIH to be dismantled after the war and responsibility for Americanization switched to the state's Department of Education. Immigrant customs and traditions were now seen as impediments to Americanization and discouraged. Historian George J. Sanchez argues that Mexicans were still seen as assimilable compared with Chinese and Japanese living in California in the 1920s.

Most immigrants realized that if they hoped to settle peacefully and live prosperously in the United States they must demonstrate their willingness to be "100% patriotic" and sacrifice for their new homeland. Therefore, many aliens not required to do so volunteered to fight in the armed services. Others worked in war industries and donated money or blood to the American Red Cross. Though many of the new immigrants were from eastern Europe, they cared little about the Austro-Hungarian Empire. Instead, east Europeans such as the Poles, Serbs, and Croatians, hoped for self-determination for their ethnic groups after the war, a priority established by Woodrow Wilson among his Fourteen Points. Unfortunately, many Americans could not distinguish ties of blood and culture from ties of nationalism. Unable and unwilling to recognize the affectionate gratitude felt by most immigrants for the United States, these nativists maintained their suspicious vigil at the base of the flagpole.

During the war, proponents of the literacy test, such as the Immigration Restriction League, took advantage of fears that the

United States would be inundated by unfit immigrants after the war. Though President Wilson had vetoed a bill providing for such tests in 1915, the issue was reintroduced two years later as part of an omnibus bill that sought to tighten anti-radical provisions of the 1903 law and deny admission to the illiterate. In 1916, Democrats and Republicans hesitated to take any action that might forfeit the ethnic vote. However, immediately after the election, the Senate passed the omnibus bill. Wilson vetoed it, but this time immigration opponents overrode the presidential veto in February 1917. Although many more southern and eastern European arrivals were literate compared to their counterparts in the 1890s, there still remained a higher rate of illiteracy in those regions than in western and northern Europe. Thus, the imposition of a literacy test amounted to a de facto quota system.

After the war, a bitterness that so many Americans had been killed or maimed in a conflict triggered by European ineptitude was compounded by the acute fear of communism. The specter of the Russian Revolution, coupled with a postwar economic crisis, set off a major Red Scare. Fresh from battling the enemy abroad, Americans now looked to the subversive enemy within. The most likely culprit was the recent immigrant.

American socialists had been vocal in their enthusiasm for early Bolshevik activities, especially redistribution of private property. Of course, most immigrants were not socialists and had little time for ideological debate of any sort. However, immigrants predominated in the membership of the Socialist Party, so that newcomers, especially in eastern states, became inextricably entwined with political radicalism in the public mind.

After the war, there was an outburst of labor unrest as unions sought to secure their legitimacy as bargaining agents and win long-delayed salary increases for their workers. The steel strike of 1919, textile strikes, and the strike of Boston's police force all lent a chaotic air to the postwar period. This economic turmoil and the remnants of wartime fears of subversion created a highly charged atmosphere. A series of bombings and attempted bombings in the spring of 1919 ignited the mixture. In April a bomb was sent to the mayor of Seattle. Another bomb, mailed to former senator Thomas W. Hardback of Atlanta, blew off the hands of his maid. The Post Office intercepted thirty-four similar parcels addressed to such prominent businessmen as J. P. Morgan and John D. Rockefeller, while newspaper headlines fueled the public imagination. In June, bombs exploded at approximately the same time in eight cities; one even shattering the windows of Attorney General A. Mitchell Palmer's home. Talk of radical conspiracies was rampant.

Attorney General Palmer and his eager young assistant, J. Edgar Hoover, branded the bombings and threats as the work of a radical element they pledged to purge by whatever means necessary. Palmer thought he would find many of these radicals in the immigrant community. According to historian Robert Murray (*Red Scare,* 1955), Palmer did not hesitate to use "insinuation, slander, character assassination, and smear . . . to compel conformity or enforce silence." Frightened middle-class Americans supported Palmer's excesses in the name of patriotism.

At first, agents from the Justice Department proceeded cautiously. Though fifty-four aliens were arrested in connection with a general strike in Seattle early in 1919, only three were actually deported. But strikes and violence in the summer and fall of that year led to more aggressive efforts to expel radical aliens. On November 7, Palmer's agents undertook a countrywide raid against the Union of Russian Workers. Many hundreds of people were seized, though only 246 aliens were ultimately detained and judged to be deportable radicals. Raids against the Communist Party and Communist Labor Parties in January 1919 netted more than 4,000 suspected radicals in thirty-three cities. More raids and more arrests followed, until the campaign reached its zenith in January 1920. Though not all aliens arrested were deported, those taken into custody were often treated harshly, kept in makeshift jails with inadequate food and unsanitary conditions.

The hysteria passed almost as suddenly as it had begun. By early 1920, Americans were tiring of the witch-hunt. They began to realize that the Bolshevik threat to the United States had been greatly exaggerated by Palmer and Hoover. Moreover, the threat that communism posed in Europe appeared to be dwindling. The expulsion of Socialists legally elected to the New York State Legislature in 1920 frightened many Americans, who saw this patriotic hysteria hacking away at the institutions it purported to protect.

A calm settled over the country as the harassment of newcomers subsided and Americans were distracted by a new source of entertainment, the radio, and the loss of an old one, thanks to Prohibition. However, while many citizens retreated into sports and other nonpolitical diversions in pursuit of "normalcy," others, such as members of the Ku Klux Klan and the Immigration Restriction League, continued to lobby for immigration quotas. This time their efforts bore fruit. Restrictionists won a narrow victory in Congress.

V

When postwar immigration rapidly rose to prewar levels, Senator William Paul Dillingham turned to the voluminous report his commission had released in 1911. The Dillingham Commission, a joint Senate-House committee, had published a forty-one volume analysis of every aspect of immigration to the United States. At the time of its release, the report denounced the new immigrants as less fit physically, intellectually, economically, and culturally than earlier American settlers and urged the passage of a literacy test and the consideration of immigration restriction based on nationality.

Senator Dillingham dredged up this idea and in 1920 drafted a bill that limited immigration according to a national quota system. The bill provided an annual quota for each immigrant group equal to 3 percent of the number of foreign-born of that group listed in the federal census of 1910, excepting those Asians barred by previous legislation. Colonies of major nations were treated as separate nations themselves for quota purposes. Thus, colonies in Africa or Asia that belonged to Great Britain or the Netherlands or Spain and had large nonwhite populations would not benefit from the generous quotas to which their mother countries were entitled. The House version of the bill that President Warren G. Harding signed into law in 1921 was scheduled to run for one year, but Congress renewed it twice.

Still, nativists complained that too great a number of Italians, Slavs, east European Jews, and Greeks were eligible for admission. The Immigration Act of 1924, better known as the Johnson-Reed Act, provided for even greater restriction than the earlier legislation. A long act, consisting of thirty-two sections, the Johnson-Reed Act provided for issuance of immigration visas by consular officials abroad. No longer would immigrants arrive who had not been inspected and interrogated by American officials. The Act established national immigration quotas at 2 percent of the 1890 population of aliens of a particular nationality, with a minimum of 100. However, after July 1, 1929, the formula for calculating the annual quota of any nationality was revised and made even more restrictive toward the newer groups. Now the quota for each group must be a number in the same ratio to 150,000 as the existing population of that group already in the U.S. was to the 1920 population of the United States. The minimum quota for a nationality remained pegged at 100, while the total annual quota for all nations covered by the law was limited to 153,714. Immigrants from other nations in the Western Hemisphere were exempt from the quota. And, of course, most Asians were already excluded under earlier laws.

The law served its purpose. It permanently crippled the new immigration. Well over half of the total quota of 153,714 was parceled out to Great Britain, Ireland, Germany, and the Scandinavian countries. While Britain was permitted an annual total of 65,361 migrants, only 5,803 Italians, 6,524 Poles, and 2,784 Russians were eligible for admission each year. Because the Western Hemisphere was not affected by the law, some European immigrants managed to evade the quota by entering via Mexico, Canada, or Latin America; their numbers were submerged in the hundreds of thousands of newcomers to the United States from within the hemisphere annually. No accurate figures are available.

The 1924 Act also delivered the coup de grace to Asian immigrants. It excluded from immigration all aliens ineligible for citizenship. This provision effectively banned Chinese, Japanese, Koreans, and Asian Indians. Some Chinese managed to evade the ban as "paper sons." The 1906 earthquake that devastated San Francisco had destroyed the city's vital statistics. Thousands of Chinese could now fraudulently claim American birth, and therefore, citizenship. Under the law, a child fathered by a U.S. citizen was a U.S. citizen himself no matter where he was born. Therefore, Chinese men who returned to China were able to bring back others (usually men) with them by claiming them as their sons. These "paper sons" were among the 50,000 Chinese to enter the United States between 1900 and 1940. Another group to come in under the wire was the alien wives of Chinese citizens. On May 25, 1925, the Supreme Court ruled that wives of Chinese merchants were still admissible because of treaty obligations. However, the Chinese wives of U.S. citizens could not be admitted because they were not eligible to be citizens, regardless of their husbands' status. In response to the organized efforts of the Chinese American Citizens Alliance, which argued that Chinese merchants should not be entitled to more rights under the immigration laws than nonmerchants, Congress changed the law in 1930. Chinese alien wives of U.S. citizens were admitted, but only if they had been married before May 26, 1924. Still, many Chinese in the United States remained condemned to a life of forced bachelorhood or trans-Pacific marriages. Some escaped celibacy in the arms of prostitutes whose services were in ever-increasing demand. The ban on Chinese citizenship was not fully lifted until 1943; Filipinos and Asian Indians gained eligibility in 1946.

The mass immigration of the late nineteenth and early twentieth century was over. After forty years, nativists finally succeeded in persuading Congress to curb the entry of foreigners into the United States. Ironically, the newcomers, so roundly accused by nativists of subverting American values and exercising undue influence over American institutions, had been unable to marshall sufficient political or economic influence to defeat restriction on the floor of Congress. The anti-alien feelings fed by World War I and its aftermath finally slammed "the golden door" celebrated by Emma Lazarus. Only the illegal route across the Canadian or

Mexican border remained for the most desperate. Statistics are unreliable, but mingled among the French Canadians from the north and the Mexican laborers from the south were people from Europe and Asia who preferred the risks of illegal entry to turning back.

The Johnson-Reed Immigration Act was a boon to Mexican laborers in the robust transnational labor market. Their labor was needed as much as ever by farmers and ranchers in the American Southwest facing seasonal labor demands. The 1917 Immigration Act's literacy test and $8 head tax had temporarily reduced Mexican immigration. However, efforts by the Arizona Council of Defense and others who claimed wartime exigency caused Congress to suspend the literacy test and head tax for Mexicans needed as farm laborers and railroad workers for the duration of the war. After the war, pressure by the railroad, mining, and construction industries, as well as by agriculture, kept the exemptions in force. The 1924 law removed any immediate threat of restriction for Mexicans. The demand for Mexican labor was increased still further by the quotas that limited European immigration. Mexicans came in large numbers until the depression of 1929 began to shrink the labor market, causing tens of thousands to return to Mexico.

For those outside the hemisphere, migration to the United States would now be much harder. Those who had arrived before restriction had been steeled by adversity in their homelands, undeterred by the rhetoric of nativist rabble-rousers, the organized opposition of middle-class critics, or even the occasional violence of their native-born economic competitors. Immigrants vigorously protested exclusionary educational quotas. Their spokesmen and political allies denounced nativism and marshaled the votes of those eligible to go to the polls to battle restrictionist politicians. But such political resistance could be difficult. Many newcomers, though potential voters, were too busy earning their livings to pursue naturalization, remaining legal aliens. In the end, the fight for unrestricted immigration was lost in the face of overwhelming odds. Immigrants who had arrived during the previous forty years were not yet sufficiently ensconced in the bastions of power and influence to do more than delay the coming of restriction in the

1920s. However, the population of the United States as well as those of Canada, Australia, New Zealand, Argentina, Brazil, South Africa, and other host countries had been forever altered. Twenty-three and a half million newcomers had entered the United States alone before restriction. Approximately one-third of them returned, but even some of those remigrated. They came from parts of southern and eastern Europe, Asia, the Caribbean, and Latin America that had seen few if any migrants head for the United States in an earlier era. Those who remained in the United States transformed the cities and the hinterland with their labor, their purchasing power, and their culture and cuisine. Even as they were changed by life in America, the newcomers left an indelible mark on the new home they had chosen.

CHAPTER SIX

Conclusion

Nigerian novelist Chinua Achebe has said that to be human one must have a story. "It's one of the things humans do. Not just to have a story, but to tell a story." The story of the American people is a tale of global movement, of people in motion. From the earliest wanderers who made the journey from Asia on foot, east across the land bridge that is now the Bering Straits, to the most recent arrivals taxiing down the runway at JFK airport in New York or LAX in California, arrivals from other parts of the globe have transplanted themselves in the Americas. In the national narrative of the United States, migration plays an especially central role. Being a "nation of nations," a country of immigrants, a sanctuary for the world's huddled masses is a critical ingredient of the national self-image. Especially dramatic are the recent stories of those who risked their lives to reach American shores. In November 1999, Elian Gonzalez, a six-year-old Cuban boy was rescued from the sea by fishermen. His mother, and nine other people, were drowned when the rickety boat they used to escape Fidel Castro's Cuba capsized. Months later, Elian was returned to Cuba in the custody of his father (the parents were divorced), but not before a national debate erupted over whether or not the United States government was betraying its heritage of sanctuary for the "huddled masses" by returning the youngster to a communist dictatorship. Several years earlier when Cuban baseball pitcher Orlando Hernandez escaped on a raft, he was granted asylum. A lucrative contract from the New York Yankees allowed him to realize the American Dream of fame and fortune almost immediately. Others, such as the undocumented Chinese arrivals, whose ship, the *Golden Venture,* ran aground on Long Beach in 1993, and the undocumented Haitians who nightly sail the choppy waters of the Caribbean toward Florida, hoping to elude the U.S. Coast Guard, often have found political and legal barriers to their emigration as perilous as the seas. The reality of being a host nation for tens of millions of migrants has affected every aspect of the nation's culture, politics, and economics.

Some of the changes that the new immigrants effected in American society were the direct result of mere numbers. As immigrants jostled their way into the labor force, they boosted America's productive capacity even as they broadened the domestic market for manufactured products, swelled the size of the cities, and eventually expanded the eligible electorate. As they joined those native-born Americans moving to towns from the countryside in the same era, immigrants' presence required communities to increase the number and size of churches, schools, hospitals, and prisons. Municipal services from sewage removal to public lighting and playground construction had to be initiated to cope with the congestion. Vast armies of clergy, police, sanitation workers, teachers, and social reformers were recruited to serve immigrant neighborhoods bursting at the seams with people and problems. The size and complexity of government increased, especially at municipal and county levels, as the crush of population propelled government into new roles and redefined old ones. Public servants became stewards of the American way as they frantically tried to force newcomers to adjust themselves to America rather than vice versa.

The contribution of so many varied immigrant cultures to the shape of the American national character is incalculable—if only because that contribution is so elusive. Often the influence of particular groups did not become apparent for a generation or so after arrival. As the immigrants learned English, they left the imprint of their native tongue on local linguistic patterns. In New York, Chicago, and Philadelphia, the English spoken in Polish, Italian, or Jewish enclaves filtered into the speech of nonimmigrant residents and of other ethnic groups. Borrowing vocabulary from their Yiddish-speaking neighbors, even a non-Jew might refer to a compassionate person who assumes responsibility for others as a *mensch*. Similarly, the delicacies of Greece, southern Italy, Mexico, and China found their way onto menus throughout the country. More subtly, but even more important, the new immigrant groups left a legacy of social, moral, and religious values that their descendants have scattered throughout the population. The fierce loyalty of Italians to family, the yearning of east European Jews for scholarship and intellectual inquiry, the Asian emphasis on family and personal honor—all of these cultural imperatives have been woven into the fabric of American values.

At times, cultural differences have promoted the creation of ethnic stereotypes and rivalries damaging to America's social harmony. Ancient antagonisms imported from the Old World have occasionally found their way into national politics, and foreign policy—especially as it relates to the countries of eastern Europe—rouse the slumbering loyalties of second- and third-generation immigrants. Respected scholars have sometimes sharply disagreed over the value of ethnic loyalties. Sociologist Orlando Patterson (*Ethnic Chauvinism: The Reactionary Impulse,* 1977) charged that these loyalties, camouflaged as ethnic pluralism, make a virtue of tribalism and segregation. He and others argue that only a new universalism can counteract the primitive parochialism of those seeking to preserve their Old-World customs in America at the cost of social cohesiveness and justice for the individual. Others disagree. Sociologist Richard Gambino uses the term "creative ethnicity" to describe the predominantly constructive rather than divisive role that new immigrant values contributed to American culture. According to Gambino, the varied heritages of new immigrants have been and can continue to be the inspiration for creative solutions to social problems resulting from life in an affluent, geographically mobile, highly secular society in which individuality, material progress, and change often take precedence over community responsibility, order, and stability. By the end of the twentieth century, multiculturalism celebrated the differences among Americans. Some scholars such as Arthur Schlesinger, Jr., feared the fissures created by overemphasizing ethnic distinctiveness could lead to the disuniting of America. The value of celebrating heterogeneity appears to be an issue that will be debated well into the twenty-first century.

If the mass migration at the turn of the nineteenth century recast American society into an urban industrial nation with a more heterogeneous population than ever before, what did it do to the sojourners? The 23.5 million newcomers who arrived in the United States between 1880 and 1921 were just a portion of the people on the move in that tumultuous era. Demographers suggest that more individuals migrated in that era than in any previous period of recorded human history. The pursuit of great economic opportunity occasioned by the poverty and dislocation born of industrialization, land enclosure, and agricultural change, as well as wars, and persistent patterns of religious and racial discrimination and persecution were powerful "pushes" to those considering migration as a path to better lives. Improvements in transportation and lower costs made migration feasible as well as desirable. Those departing "donor" nations in Latin America, Asia, and especially southern and eastern Europe had many choices. The United States has never had a copyright on the migration story. Argentina, Brazil, Canada, Australia, New Zealand, South Africa, and nations in western Europe were all magnets drawing migrants. However, the United States attracted newcomers both permanent and temporary with strong "pulls." For some it was the pull of plentiful jobs, higher salaries, land ownership, or education. For others it was the freedom to worship God in their way without interference or simply to live without the constant fear of one's neighbors and the government. An ensemble of laws, traditions, and a written constitution enforced by elected officials and interpreted by judicial institutions and processes combined to produce a music sweet to the ears of those who trembled at the sight of a policeman and quaked before rich landowners or a corrupt and cruel nobility.

Social historian Herbert Gutman suggested that the study of dependent American social classes, such as immigrants, must take into consideration how these groups interpreted and dealt with changing economic, social, and political patterns. Gutman looked to French existential philosopher Jean-Paul Sartre, who observed that, "The essential is not what 'one' has done to man, but what man does with what 'one' has done to him." In other words, it is only through examining the choices men and women made, by understanding "how their behavior affected important historical processes," that we can understand the human condition. What do the newcomers tell us of their choices? How did they feel about the chance they were taking, betting on America to better their condition?

Despite the clash between their traditional ways and the demands of industrial America, many new immigrants regarded their decision to emigrate as fortuitous and harbored few regrets. One elderly European Jew wrote a letter to the Yiddish-language *Jewish Daily Forward* in 1956 to discuss the past and reflect on whether the good old days were really that good.

I still remember my home town in Russia, our simple little house lighted at night by a small kerosene lamp, the door thatched with straw nailed down with sackcloth to keep it warm in the winter. I still remember the mud in the streets of the town, so deep it was difficult to get around; our fear of the Gentiles; and who can forget the poverty—the times when there wasn't even a crust of bread?

While immigrant life was hardly easy, the writer recalled, "When we came to New York, I thought we were entering heaven." Now, years later, America seemed even better:

When I think of the modern conveniences we live with now, of the wonderful inventions, achievements in various fields, that we enjoy, and about the opportunities for everyone in this blessed country, I see there's nothing to be nostalgic about.

Another east European Jewish immigrant living in Pittsburgh told an oral historian during the 1970s, "I love my country and the American flag. It gave me everything I ever dreamed of or wanted. I was an American citizen, I made a living, raised my son, gave him an education and saw him successful."

Of course, even immigrants devoted to their new country often still loved their land of birth. Italian immigrant Constantine Panunzio proclaimed in his 1921 memoir, *Soul of an Immigrant,* "I love thee America," but added, "I love thee, Italy, my native land, with that mystic love with which men turn to their native country and as Pilgrims to their shrine." In his 1978 memoir, *An Ethnic at Large,* writer Jerre Mangione, the child of immigrant Sicilian parents, detailed an even greater ambiguity on the part of Italian immigrants than Panunzio suggests. "Among the Italians, more than one million men and women returned to their native land after a brief sojourn. Those who chose to stay, or had no other choice, planted roots in their adopted land by having children, even while enduring the most excruciating hardships. The pain of uprooting themselves and trying to survive in an alien land where they were not made to feel welcome eventually stopped hurting." Of himself, Mangione wrote, "Rarely did I encounter in the American world the sageness and love of life I found among my Sicilian relatives; but theirs was an old and static world which lacked the spirit of enterprise and faith in the future that firmly attached me to that admixture of compatriots known as Americans."

A Bulgarian writer, Stoyan Christowe, evaluated his immigrant experience in a 1929 article, "Half an American." Though he chose to remain in America, even after a return visit to his homeland, Christowe still wondered, "Has the storm in my being lulled now that I have spent two-thirds of my life in a struggle for readjustment and adaptation?" His response was a qualified "yes." Fond of his new country, Christowe still could not feel thoroughly American: "I shall always be the adopted child, not the real son, of a mother that I love more than the one that gave me birth." A Polish immigrant, Valerie Kozaczka Demusz, of Dorchester, Massachusetts, returned to her native land. Enchanted by the improvements, she still remained convinced that her decision to stay in America was the right one, "No, I wouldn't want to live there [in Poland]." For her, America's prosperity had made immigration worthwhile. "But I'm telling you, the people have heaven on earth here, and they don't know it. I don't care—the poorest person lives like a millionaire after what I saw." She chose America over Poland because, "Here are my roots. My children are born here."

Natsu Okuyana Ozawa, a Japanese immigrant, arrived in 1924. Alienated by American racism and discriminatory policies, especially the internment camps into which many Japanese were herded during World War II, she seriously considered returning to Japan. However, following World War II, she began to reassess her yearning for her homeland. "First I thought about going back to Japan, but we had two sons and they are pure citizens, see, so we better stay here. . . . No more always something doing of fright(ening) things or terrible things. I think in many ways very nice the people."

A standard greeting among Chinese immigrants was, "When are you going back to China?" recalls historian Betty Lee Sung. "As a young child, I remembered the adult conversation invariably revolved around going back to China. I gained a deep impression that China must be some sort of fairyland paradise." Years later, however, the conversation changed, according to Sung. "Nowadays, when I go to visit my mother's good friend, I hear no more talk about going back to China. This woman's children are grown and married, living in their own homes near her. Her life, her roots are deeply imbedded in American soil. . . . She barely speaks a word of English, but her mind is now oriented to the thought that she is going to spend the rest of her days in the United States."

To fully understand immigration, one must listen to these personal stories. Ultimately, history is not made by huddled masses, or even by triumphant cavalcades, but by families and individuals, weighing options, making compromises, squaring shoulders, having a joke, and muddling through. Few illustrate with greater clarity than Nicholas Gerros, a Greek, that immigrants were not passive men and women, cowed by historical circumstance (June Namias, ed., *First Generation,* 1978). Gerros arrived from Macedonia as an impoverished youth in 1912. He built a $300,000-a-year garment business and became prominent among Greek Americans of northeastern Massachusetts. Did immigrants have choices? Were there compromises to be made? Certainly, according to Nicholas Gerros:

Don't forget, everything in your life, you decide, nobody else decides, unless they come with a gun at your head and say, "Look decide my way or else." Even then you got a choice either die or do what he says. You see what I mean? But most of the time you're free to decide. Everything else we bring as alibis that's all. They can't stop you from going on your own.

As newcomers would soon learn, the United States was far from perfect. In the United States, those who had been serfs or oppressed peasants in the Old World found themselves competing for opportunity with those who had been slaves on American soil, descendants of the forced migrants of an earlier era. And the newcomers were more often tolerated than welcomed. Still, they kept coming because the American alternative seemed better than what they had left behind. Moreover, millions hoped one day to return to the land of their birth, transformed by the wealth gleaned from the American cornucopia.

The national origins quota system initiated in 1921 and made permanent in 1924 established a legislative levee constricting the migration flow at the shoreline. However, while the Johnson-Reed Immigration Act ended an era, it did not end immigration or the dialogue over immigration's value that was often expressed in struggles over laws and administrative procedures.

During the 1930s, economic depression, especially the shortage of jobs and competition for jobs with native-born workers, further curbed immigration. The number of immigrants declined from 241,700 in 1930 to 23,068 in 1933 and totaled only 528,431 for the entire period, 1931–1940. Half a million people returned to Mexico of their own volition or were deported; almost as many Europeans left America as arrived. In 1930, President Herbert Hoover requested that American consuls abroad use administrative procedures to reduce immigration far below the legal level allowed. The State Department was already using a provision of the

1917 Immigration Act to limit immigration from Mexico. A Mexican considered "likely to become a public charge" was denied a visa. The public charge clause, first included in the 1882 immigration law, was originally aimed at persons lacking the physical or mental abilities necessary for employment. Now "likely to become a public charge" was being interpreted as anyone unlikely to obtain a job in the poor market conditions of the depression.

With public opinion opposed to immigration and President Franklin Roosevelt unwilling to take the political risks attendant on making exceptions for persecuted European minorities, the United States proved a poor sanctuary to those in flight from the Nazis. During the period from 1933 to 1945, only 250,000 Jewish refugees were admitted to the United States, a paltry number, though still the largest accepted by any western nation. Meanwhile, the Third Reich systematically murdered 6 million Jews and millions of others, including Catholics, communists, gypsies, and homosexuals.

After World War II, immigration policy toward those liberated from Nazi concentration camps and others displaced by wartime conditions was ungenerous. The Displaced Persons Acts of 1948 and 1950 admitted only 406,000 Europeans out of an estimated 5 million left homeless by the war. However, there were glimmers of compassion for some whose lives had been altered by the war. War brides, fiancees, and foreign-born children of U.S. servicemen were exempted from visa quotas. Also, the Western Hemisphere remained quota-free, and a robust migration from Mexico and the Caribbean resumed.

With the advent of the Cold War, the United States was re-evaluating its immigration policy in terms of political priorities more than economic or eugenic apprehensions. In 1952, the McCarran-Walter Act niggardly opened the door a crack to allow in some Asians fleeing communism as well as former Nazi scientists and others with exceptional skills who could benefit the United States in its weapons race with the Soviet Union. The law responded to fears that a relaxed quota would flood the United States with Soviet agents disguised as immigrants. A year later, a Congress crusading against communism passed the Refugee Re-

lief Act admitting another 205,000, many of them refugees from
Eastern bloc nations. The postwar laws paved the way for special
legislation to admit Hungarians after the abortive Hungarian upris-
ing of 1956 and Cubans after Fidel Castro's revolution of 1959.

The national origins quota system that began in 1921 was finally ended in 1965. Originally proposed by President John F.
Kennedy, the grandson of Irish immigrants, the 1965 law abandoned national quotas. The Western Hemisphere was allotted
120,00 immigrants annually, though countries in North and South
America were generally permitted to exceed the quota, which
proved an especially helpful safety valve to economically pressed
Mexico. The Eastern Hemisphere had a 170,000 quota with no nation exceeding 20,000 annually. Immediate family members (parents, spouses, minor children) of U.S. citizens were not covered by
the quota restrictions and today approximately 300,000 such relatives enter the United States annually. There were preferences for
relatives of U.S. citizens beyond parents, spouses, and minor children and a priority system based on occupational preferences. In
1976, amendments to the 1965 act redressed statutory inequities
between the hemispheres by extending the preference system and
the 20,000 per country quota to all nations of the Western Hemisphere. In 1978 the separate hemisphere limits were replaced by a
worldwide ceiling of 290,000 legal admissions annually, a limit
reduced to 270,000 during the following decade. However, the admission of more than 50,000 refugees each year actually increased
the total number of arrivals during the 1980s. Political and economic disorder in many parts of the globe compelled American
policymakers to offer sanctuary to an increasing number of refugees.

The distinction between immigrants and refugees, always
somewhat blurred, demanded clarification by the 1970s. In the
middle of that decade, as the United States disengaged itself from
the war in Vietnam, Southeast Asians began arriving in greater
numbers, and the latest wave of immigration was underway. The
Vietnamese emigration has been dwarfed by the ensuing number
of arrivals from South Korea, China, the Philippines, and India.
The Asian immigration yielded a 70-fold increase in the Asian

population of the United States from 1980 to 2000. During the late 1970s and throughout the 1980s, economic stagnation and political instability in Latin America loosed a flood of aliens northward, a trend that continued throughout the remainder of the twentieth century. Some came bearing documents that established their status as legal immigrants, but hundreds of thousands entered illegally without such documents. The end of the Cold War in the early 1990s also brought a renewed migration from eastern Europe as immigrants from countries previously dominated by the Soviets headed west. Like a big, woolly mammoth preserved in a glacier since the great Ice Age, ethnic hatreds suppressed by military and secret police threats during the era of Soviet and Yugoslavian dominance reemerged. Muslims in flight from the murderous "ethnic cleansing" in Bosnia and refugees from the fighting in Kosovo and other zones of ethnic warfare sought refuge in the West.

In a radio broadcast popular American essayist and social commentator Garrison Keillor said that "migration is the great expression of dissent." If he is correct, dissatisfaction was as widespread at the end of the twentieth century as it was at the beginning. Many voted with their feet. Worldwide migration, especially to the United States, soared. Congress passed laws reflecting dilemmas created by people on the move. The plight of Southeast Asians in the late 1970s encouraged passage of the Refugee Act of 1980 to distinguish between immigrants in search of economic opportunity and those in need of sanctuary. The act established a refugee ceiling separate from that of immigrant quotas and a benefits package and cooperative arrangements between the federal government, private agencies, and state governments to assist the newcomers. However, and most significant, the act redefined the term "refugee" to conform with the United Nations definition: "any person who has left his or her country and is unable or unwilling to return because of persecution or a well-founded fear of persecution based on race, religion, nationality, membership in a particular social group, or political opinion." (Refugee Act of 1980, 94 Stat. 102.) Congress imposed an annual ceiling of 50,000 refugees, but left the door open to expand the number, if necessary. Every year the number of refugees has required raising the numerical ceiling.

During the 1980s and 1990s immigration legislation was aimed at curbing undocumented immigration and rationalizing legal immigration to conform to the economic needs of the United States. The 1986 Immigration Reform and Control Act (IRCA) offered amnesty to hundreds of thousands of undocumented immigrants who had violated American law by entering the United States, but had worked hard, started families, and generally had been law-abiding and productive citizens since their arrival. The act also sought to prosecute American businesspeople who encouraged illegal migrants by luring them with jobs, often at very low wages. IRCA was intended to stop such exploitation, though it failed to do so. No effective controls over undocumented immigration had been developed by the end of the century. The immigration law in 1990 increased legal migration by 35 percent. That act and the 1996 legislation sought to eliminate abuses of family reunification provisions of American law and to strengthen that aspect of the law offering occupational preferences to newcomers bringing needed skills or investment capital and thereby benefiting the American economy by their presence.

At the dawn of the twenty-first century the United States was still in the midst of a mass migration. If the annual number of legal immigrants, refugees, and estimated undocumented immigrants are combined, the figure is in excess of 1.25 million per year. The Immigration and Naturalization Service estimated that by the year 2000 there were 5 to 6 million undocumented newcomers swelling the population and straining resources of some states, especially New York, New Jersey, Texas, California, Florida, and Illinois. However, the percentage of foreign born in the American population was only 10 percent as compared to 14 percent in the early 1900s. As in the period from 1880–1921, both the nation and the newcomers were enriched and challenged by the migration.

As transportation becomes ever faster and cheaper, borders prove even more porous. The concerns of Americans over the impact of migrants on the economic security, public health, and cultural vitality of the United States continue to come and go in re-

sponse to the ebb and flow of economic and political circumstances, echoing the apprehensions of a century ago. So, too, do
the migrants' fears of economic exploitation and loss of their children to American culture. Indeed, permanent immigration and the
desire for integration into a new society may be less appealing to
migrants than it was a century ago. Some highly skilled workers
who might have emigrated to the United States a century ago now
remain overseas and send the product of their labor to American
contractors via computer modem. The globalization of this elec-
tronic labor market creates fresh havoc for American labor unions
as they try to protect the wages of American workers from this foreign competition entering the marketplace via cyberspace. In response, labor unions seek cooperation with their brother and sister
organizations beyond American borders. There is increasing
awareness of the exploitation of child and prisoner labor among
America's trading partners.

The globalization of culture redefines what kinds of music, literature, cuisine, and art individuals can access. Especially apt for
migration in the new millennium, then, is the two-part African
prayer that Nigerian novelist Chinua Achebe recited in an address
at American University in Washington: "May the guest not kill the
host by his visit. . . . And when he departs may he not go with a
broken back." The peopling of the United States remains an ongoing saga, sometimes comedy, sometimes tragedy. It is a transnational tale, affecting those in donor societies losing population,
often the most talented in the population, no less than it affects
those native-born Americans who are the newcomers' hosts. However much migration recasts the fates of nations and communities
and economic systems, it most affects those bold men and women
who choose to journey far from home in search of better lives. It
was true at the end of the nineteenth century and remains true in
the first decade of the twenty-first.

BIBLIOGRAPHICAL ESSAY

The notion of the United States as a "nation of nations" has become standard fare in history classrooms throughout the country. Today, the challenge is to gradually abandon as outmoded the immigration paradigm focusing upon immigration as a dimension of nation-building, and to start seeing immigration in the broader dimension of transnational migration patterns. This is a significant change in a short period; indeed, until the 1960s immigration was largely absent as even a chapter in the national history of the United States.

Several historiographical essays have appeared that offer insightful updates of immigration history as it has been recast. These include John J. Bukowczyk and Nora Faires, "Immigration History in the United States, 1865–1900: A Selective Critical Appraisal," *Canadian Ethnic Studies* 33 (1991): 1–23; and Jon Gjerde, "New Growth on Old Vines—The State of the Field: The Social History of Ethnicity and Immigration in the United States," *Journal of American Ethnic History* 18 (Summer, 1999): 40–65. In an earlier historiographical essay by Rudolph J. Vecoli, "Ethnicity: A Neglected Dimension of American History" in Herbert Bass, ed., *The State of American History* (Chicago, 1970), the author observed the long neglect of immigration by American historians, an indifference that lasted until the late 1960s. He blamed the lacuna on American historians' failure to write national history in the context of the "enormous diversity of race, culture, and religion that has characterized the American people." Until the 1960s, most American academicians believed that the vitality of the country's capitalist economy and its republican institutions quickly converted Europe's "wretched refuse" into a new people. In fact, historians of the 1950s who preferred a consensus model to a conflict model of American history argued that dwelling on Americans' diverse ethnic origins could be destructive and divisive.

If American historians resisted the notion of an ethnically diverse United States, this was consistent with their own homogeneity. Before 1920, most historians were old-stock white Anglo-Saxon Protestants, unsympathetic to immigrants and at times even given to a mild nativism in their scholarship. By the 1920s and 1930s, the children of the northern and western European immigrants were writing the history of their own groups, scarcely noticing those from southern and eastern Europe, Latin America, and Asia. Study of these people was left to sociologists and social reformers. At the University of Chicago, social scientists of the so-called "Chicago school," such as Robert Park, Louis Wirth, and collaborators William I. Thomas and Florian Znaniecki studied these groups. So, too, did sociologist Peter Roberts (*The New Immigrants: A Study of the Industrial and Social Life of Southeastern Europeans in America,* New York, 1912). Roberts drew upon his scholarly observations to support his advocacy of rapid integration of the newcomers. He told his readers, "I believe in the immigrant. He has in him the making of an American, provided a sympathetic hand guides him and smooths the path which leads to assimilation."

The great American historian Frederick Jackson Turner had observed early-twentieth-century immigration firsthand. In 1901, he wrote a series of newspaper articles that were filled with the stereotypes and clichés of the era. He found Italians "quick witted and supple in morals," and Jews "thrifty to disgracefulness, while their ability to drive a bargain amounts to genius." Nevertheless, Turner was aware of the need for more scholarly treatment of immigration. Even as he hailed the western frontier as a beneficent force for homogenization, Turner believed that the diversity of stocks "with their different habits, morals and religious doctrines and ideals . . . led to cross-fertilization and the evolution of a profoundly modified society."

Of Turner's students, only Marcus Lee Hansen made a lasting contribution to the study of immigration. The son of Scandinavian parents, Hansen recognized that the peopling of America began in Europe and that it was as important to understand why some left and others stayed as to know why America was so attractive. His seminal essay, "The History of American Immigration as a Field for Research," *American Historical Review,* 32 (1926–27): 500–518, called for the systematic collection and examination of "raw materials" on every aspect of immigrant life.

Not until Oscar Handlin's *The Uprooted* (Boston, 1951), did anyone focus on turn-of-the-century immigrants and their personal encounters with America. Grounded in the social disorganization model developed at the Chicago school, Handlin's almost poetic description of European peasants seeking better lives in the New World has been praised for its imagery, but criticized for its inaccuracies. Among the first critics was Rudolph J. Vecoli in "Contadini in Chicago: A Critique of *"The Uprooted,"* *Journal of American History,* 51 (December 1964). Citing the experiences of the Italians who settled in Chicago, Vecoli persuasively refuted Handlin's profile, noting in particular that Handlin failed to distinguish among immigrants of different groups who were motivated to migrate by different pushes and pulls. Other critics suggested the need for greater specificity in defining the complex causes of European emigration in the late-nineteenth and early-twentieth centuries as well as the need to focus on non-European groups.

A decade after Handlin, Maldwyn Allen Jones published a valuable, comprehensive survey, *American Immigration* (Chicago, 1960). While recognizing that different groups arrived at different times, he denied the significance of these differences, abandoning the traditional distinction between old and new immigrants. Jones, a Briton, stressed the continuity of the larger social process of international migration. Another English scholar, Philip Taylor (*The Distant Magnet: European Emigration to the U.S.A.,* New York, 1971), also emphasized the similarities rather than the distinctions between the experiences of successive immigrant groups. The subtitle of his book, "European Emigration to the U.S.A.," accurately conveys the author's focus on the journey rather than the arrival and settlement. The title also conveys a Eurocentrism that neglected the significant presence of Asians, Latin Americans, and migrants from the Caribbean. By emphasizing broad social forces that generated transoceanic migration, both Jones and Taylor miss the distinctive quality of the experiences of each group and the major changes in American society from the 1840s and 1850s, when the Irish and Germans were most numerous among the newcomers, to the end of the nineteenth century when southern and eastern Europeans, Asians, and Latin Americans dominated the flow. Two overviews corrected such flaws: Thomas Archdeacon's *Becoming American: An Ethnic History* (New York, 1983) and the very useful synthesis by Roger Daniels, *Coming to America: A History of Immigration and Ethnicity in American Life* (New York, 1990).

What should be the working agenda of serious scholars of international migration? In a brilliant 1960 essay, Frank Thistle–thwaite turned historians away from a view of immigration as "American fever" and began placing it in a larger international context, calling for studies of different groups and the local conditions that caused them to consider migration as an option. See "Migration from Europe Overseas in the Nineteenth and Twentieth Centuries" in Rudolph J. Vecoli and Suzanne M. Sinke, eds., *A Century of European Migrations* (Urbana, IL, 1991), reprinted from Xie Congres International des Sciences Historiques, *Rapports,* Uppsala, 1960, 5:32–60.

Thistlethwaite's essay foreshadowed transnationalism in its perspective and has kept migration historians busy for the past forty years. Since the first edition of *Huddled Masses* appeared in

1982, there has been an ever larger explosion of books and articles on migration, generally, and especially on the 1880s–1920s migration, in particular. This second edition continues to be informed by the notion that immigrants must be studied as distinct individuals as well as group members, a perspective offered by Herbert Gutman in a provocative essay on the study of American "dependent" social classes. Gutman argues that immigrants—as well as slaves, poor free blacks, and union and nonunion workers—must be understood in terms of how effectively they dealt with large social forces, making deliberate choices among perceived options. Though the options might be limited, the migrant never was reduced to being merely a passive victim. See Herbert Gutman, "Labor History and the 'Sartre Question'," *Humanities* 1 (September/ October, 1980). However, that perspective has been modified by John Bodnar, in his influential synthesis, *The Transplanted, A History of Immigrants in Urban America* (Bloomington, IN, 1985). Bodnar places the decisions made by migrants in the context of family and community life in their home countries and links these decisions to larger forces such as the labor requirements of developing industrial capitalism and urban growth. Whatever decisions immigrants to the United States made, the options were limited by forces beyond them.

During the past two decades, historians and social scientists, many themselves descendants of immigrants who arrived in the United States earlier in the twentieth century, increased our knowledge of migration well beyond what it was when the first edition of *Huddled Masses* arrived in bookstores. What follows are works that continue to shape my understanding of migration to the United States in the period 1880 to 1921, as well as newer volumes that aided me as I rethought my own work. Because of limitations of space, the list hardly exhausts the fine work done in the past twenty years.

Central to the revision of an older immigration paradigm is the notion of *transnationalism*. The term *transnationalism* was first used by writer and critic Randolph Bourne in a July, 1916, *Atlantic Monthly* article to describe the cultural pluralism that migration patterns seemed to be causing to spread beyond national boundaries. For Bourne, transnationalism constituted an optimistic vision of a new American possibility. Today, the term transnationalism is used to convey how migrations often proceed fluidly, swirling in response to broader economic and political forces rather than simply back and forth between two nation states. The transnational model suggests that migrants do not substitute the human networks, activities, and patterns of life of their adopted society for those of the country they have departed. Instead, transnational migrants often maintain some combination of the social, political, and cultural networks, activities, and patterns that span borders and nations, neither in donor or host societies, but in both simultaneously. Scholars often see transnationalism as the product of new labor markets and faster, more efficient modes of transportation and communication. Much recent work on transnationalism has been done by sociologists and cultural anthropologists. Several important works include: Linda Basch, Nina Glick Schiller, and Cristina Szanton Blanton, *Nations Unbound, Transnational Projects, Postcolonial Predicaments, and Deterritorialized Nation-States* (Amsterdam, 1994); and edited by the same three scholars, *Towards A Transnational Perspective on Migration, Race Class, Ethnicity and Nationalism Reconsidered* (New York, 1992). Historians have embraced the new conceptualizations as evidenced by the fine essays in Virginia Yans-McLaughlin, ed., *Immigration Reconsidered: History, Sociology, and Politics* (New York, 1990); and in an essay by Donna R. Gabaccia, "Is Everywhere Nowhere? Nomads, Nations, and the Immigrant Paradigm of United States History," in the *Journal of American History* 86 (December, 1999), p. 1115–1134.

The term *diaspora* is also frequently employed as a way to describe the dispersal of a population across a broad area, while maintaining a positive and continuing relationship between migrants and the countries and communities from which they have come. A useful discussion of diasporas is sociologist Robin Cohen's *Global Diasporas, An Introduction* (Seattle, 1997).

Most of the studies undertaken by scholars continue to focus on the experience of particular national groups that emigrated and settled in specific cities, rural communities, or regions of the United States. Indeed, during the past quarter century the preference for in-depth local studies has led scholars to paint on narrower, not broader canvasses. However, individual groups are often part of multiple narratives. Thus the historiography of Italian agrarians or Chinese agrarians, respectively, must be included in the historiography of each particular ethnic group, but also in the historiography of American agricultural history.

On the Italians, there are several classics: Robert Foerster's *Italian Emigration of Our Times* (Cambridge, MA, 1919, reprinted 1968) and John H. Mariano's *The Italian Contribution to American Democracy* (Boston, 1924, reprinted 1975). The latter is especially rich in its portrayal of Italian housing, education, occupations, and social welfare. Still engaging is sociologist Richard Gambino's *Blood of My Blood* (New York, 1975), a rich anecdotal account of three generations of southern Italians. Important and accessible works on the Italians include John Briggs's *An Italian Passage: Immigrants to Three American Cities, 1890–1930* (New Haven, CT, 1978), a systematic study of Italian immigrant life in three midsized cities: Utica and Rochester, New York, and Kansas City, Missouri; and Virginia Yans-McLaughlin's *Family and Community: Italian Immigrants in Buffalo, 1880–1930* (Ithaca, NY, 1977), a fine study of family and community relationships. Dino Cinel's *From Italy to San Francisco, The Immigrant Experience* (Stanford, CA, 1982) examines a 2,000-family sample of Italians who migrated to San Francisco from the 1850s to the 1930s, while Donna Gabaccia explores the Italian experience in New York City in *From Sicily to Elizabeth Street, Housing and Social Change Among Italian Immigrants, 1880–1930* (Albany, NY, 1984); and Micaela Di Leonardo, *The Varieties of Ethnic Experience: Kinship, Class, and Gender Among California Italian-Americans* (Ithaca, NY, 1984) offers a nuanced firsthand account of gender roles and class differences among California Indians. Anthropologist Robert Orsi plumbed the power of Catholicism in the Italian immigrant community in *The Madonna of 115th Street, Faith and Community in Italian Harlem, 1880–1950* (New Haven, CT,

1985). Andrew Rolle's *The Immigrant Upraised: Italian Adventurers and Colonists in An Expanding America* (Norman, OK, 1968) a study of Italians who settled in rural America, provides a nonurban perspective neglected by most other studies.

No group's literature has expanded more than that on east European Jews. Moses Rischin's *The Promised City: New York's Jews, 1870–1914* (Cambridge, MA, 1962), Ronald Sanders, *The Downtown Jews* (New York, 1969), Arthur S. Goren's *New York Jews and the Quest for Community: The Kehillah Experiment: 1908–1922* (New York, 1970), and Irving Howe's *World of Our Fathers, The Journey of the East European Jews to America and the Life They Found and Made* (New York, 1976) remain useful explorations of the New York Jewish immigrant experience. The latter, especially, captures the rich texture of the teeming, steamy streets of the Lower East Side, as does journalist Hutchins Hapgood's 1902 classic, *The Spirit of the Ghetto* (New York, reprinted 1965). Ande Manners, in *Poor Cousins* (New York, 1972), provides a broader picture of the conflict between the German and Russian Jews. A recent synthesis is Gerald Sorin's *A Time For Building: The Third Migration, 1880–1920* (Baltimore, 1992). The experience of the immigrants' children in New York is explored in Deborah Dash Moore's *At Home in America, Second Generation New York Jews* (New York, 1981). The need for histories of Jewish communities in other cities and smaller towns is fulfilled by Marc Lee Raphael's *Jews and Judaism in a Midwestern Community: Columbus, Ohio, 1840–1875* (Columbus, OH, 1979); Judith E. Smith's fine comparative study, *Family Connections: A History of Italian and Jewish Immigrant Lives in Providence Rhode Island, 1900–1940* (Albany, 1985); and Deborah Dash Moore's *To the Golden Cities, Pursuing the American Dream in Miami and L.A.* (Cambridge, MA, 1994); as well as by the essays in Moses Rischin and John Livingston, eds., *Jews of the American West* (Detroit, 1991). Perhaps the finest addition to the study of small-town Jewry is that of sociologist Ewa Morawska, *Insecure Prosperity, Small-Town Jews in Industrial America, 1890–1940* (Princeton, NJ, 1996). Much more attention has been paid to the immigrant experience of Jewish women. Two useful works are Susan A. Glenn's *Daughters of the Shtetl, Life and Labor in the Immigrant*

Generation (Ithaca, NY, 1990) and Ruth Jacknow Markowitz's *My Daughter, the Teacher* (New Brunswick, NJ, 1993). Some of the freshest work is being done on the social patterns of Jewish immigrant life, such as Andrew Heinze's work on consumerism, *Adapting to Abundance, Jewish Immigrants, Mass Consumption, and the Search for American Identity* (New York, 1990); and Daniel Soyer's *Jewish Immigrant Associations and American Identity in New York, 1880–1939* (Cambridge, MA, 1997). Also useful is Jenna Weisman Joselit's *The Wonders of America, Reinventing Jewish Culture, 1880–1950* (New York, 1994). On anti-Semitism see Leonard Dinnerstein, *Anti-Semitism in America* (New York, 1994) and Frederic Cople Jaher, *A Scapegoat in the New Wilderness: The Origins and Rise of Anti-Semitism in America* (Cambridge, MA, 1994). Still useful are essays in David A. Gerber, ed., *Anti-Semitism in American History* (Urbana, IL, 1986).

Other immigrant groups are also receiving fresh scholarly attention. Two old but still useful volumes on the Poles are Paul Fox, *The Poles in America* (New York, 1922, reprinted 1970), and W. I. Thomas and F. Znaniecki, *The Polish Peasant in Europe and America,* 2 volumes (New York, 1958). The best volumes on Polish institutions in America are Joseph Wytrawal, *America's Polish Heritage: A Social History of the Poles in America* (Detroit, 1961), and *The Poles in America* (Minneapolis, MN, 1969). An excellent overview in Helen Znaniecki Lopata, *Polish Americans: Status and Competition in an Ethnic Community* (Englewood Cliffs, NJ, 1976). For the Polish transition from alien to American, see Victor R. Greene's *For God and Country: The Rise of Polish and Lithuanian Ethnic Consciousness in America, 1860–1910* (Madison, WI, 1975). Three excellent additions to this literature are Joseph John Parot, *Polish Catholics in Chicago, 1850–1920* (DeKalb, IL, 1981); John J. Bukowczyk, *And My Children Did Not Know Me, A History of the Polish-Americans* (Bloomington, IN, 1987); and Dominic Pacyga, *Polish Immigrants and Industrial Chicago: Workers on the South Side, 1880–1922* (Columbus, OH, 1991).

There have also been studies of other central and eastern European groups. The best of these are Emily Balch, *Our Slavic Fellow Citizens* (New York, 1910, reprinted 1969); Wasyl Halich,

Ukrainians in the United States (Chicago, 1937, reprinted 1970); Emil Lengyel, *Americans From Hungary* (Philadelphia, 1948, reprinted 1975); George J. Prpic, *Croatian Immigrants in America* (New York, 1971); and Jerome Davis, *The Russian Immigrant* (New York, 1922, reprinted 1969). A very fine interdisciplinary study of these groups is historical sociologist Ewa Morawska's volume, *For Bread With Butter, Life-Worlds of East Central Europeans in Johnstown, Pennsylvania, 1890–1940* (New York, 1985). A study emphasizing the central role of religious institutions in the Slovak community is June Granatir Alexander, *The Immigrant Church and Community: Pittsburgh's Slovak Catholics and Lutherans, 1880–1915* (Pittsburgh, 1987).

On Mediterranean immigrants, the undisputed authority on Greeks is Theodore Saloutos, *The Greeks in the United States* (Cambridge, MA, 1963). A more concise but thorough and useful volume is Charles C. Moskos, Jr.'s *Greek Americans: Struggle and Success* (Englewood Cliffs, NJ, 1980). Armenians are treated in Aram Yeretizian, *A History of Armenian Immigration to America with Special Reference to Los Angeles* (San Francisco, 1974); and in Robert Mirah, *Torn Between Two Lands: Armenians in America, 1890 to World War I* (Cambridge, MA, 1983). A personal memoir, Michael J. Arlen's *Passage to Ararat* (New York, 1975), is a poignant account of the Armenian experience and the issue of integration. On the Arabs, see Habib Ibrahim Katibah, *Arab-Speaking Americans* (New York, 1946), Barbara Aswad, *Arabic Speaking Communities in American Cities* (New York, 1974), and Alixa Naff's *Becoming American: The Early Arab Immigrant Experience* (Carbondale, IL, 1985). There is still a great need for further studies of the Arab immigrant experience in the period 1880–1921.

Literature on the Asian immigrant experience has grown steadily. Among the works covering several groups are Roger Daniels, *Asian America: Chinese and Japanese in the United States Since 1850* (Seattle, 1988); Ronald Takaki, *Strangers From a Different Shore: A History of Asian Americans* (Boston, 1989); and Sucheng Chan, *Asian Americans: An Interpretive History (Boston, 1991).* For an early-twentieth-century perspective on the

Chinese, see Mary B. Coolidge, *Chinese Immigration* (New York, 1909, reprinted, 1969). An excellent overview of the Chinese experience is Shih-Shan Henry Tsai, *The Chinese Experience in America* (Bloomington, IN, 1986). Still useful are Jack Tchen's *The Chinese in America* (New York, 1980) and Betty Lee Sung's *Mountain of Gold* (New York, 1967). The Chinese rural experience is dealt with masterfully in Sucheng Chan's *The Bitter-Sweet Soil, The Chinese in California Agriculture, 1860–1910* (Berkeley, CA, 1986). On Chinese entrepreneurship, see Paul C.P. Siu, (edited by John Kuo Wei Tchen) *The Chinese Laundryman: A Study of Social Isolation* (New York, 1987; orig. 1953). Chinese women are the subject of Judy Yung's excellent volume, *Unbound Feet, A Social History of Chinese Women in San Francisco* (Berkeley, CA, 1995), and George Anthony Peffer, *If They Don't Bring Their Women Here, Chinese Female Immigration Before Exclusion* (Urbana, IL, 1999). The exclusion of the Chinese has been the subject of two fine volumes. Lucy E. Salyer's *Laws Harsh As Tigers, Chinese Immigrants and the Shaping of Modern Immigration Law* (Chapel Hill, NC, 1995) argues that the Chinese struggle over exclusion established fundamental principles that affected other groups by recasting the contours of modern immigration law. Andrew Gyory's *Closing the Gate: Race, Politics and the Chinese Exclusion Act* (Chapel Hill, NC, 1998) suggests that Chinese exclusion was a convenient surrogate for a host of divisive problems caused by industrialization, for which politicians had no ready solutions.

On the Japanese, Yamato Ichihashi's volume written in response to the critics of Japanese immigration is still important, *Japanese in the United States* (Stanford, CA, 1932, reprinted 1969). Other works combining historical and sociological approaches include Harry Kitano, *Japanese Americans: The Evolution of a Subculture* (Englewood Cliffs, NJ, 1969) and William Petersen, *Japanese Americans: Oppression and Success* (New York, 1971). Bill Hosokawa's *Nisei, The Quiet Americans* (New York, 1969) remains a good overview of the experience of American-born children of Japanese immigrants. On the economics of the Japanese immigrant community, see Edna Bonacich and John

Modell, *The Economic Basis of Ethnic Solidarity: Small Business in the Japanese-American Community* (Berkeley, CA, 1980). Excellent recent work on several generations of Japanese-Americans include, Yuji Ichioka's *The Issei, The World of the First Generation of Japanese Immigrants, 1885–1924* (New York, 1988); Eileen H. Tamura's *Americanization, Acculturation and Ethnic Identity: The Nisei Generation in Hawaii* (Urbana, IL, 1994); Brian Masaru Hayashi, *"For the Sake of Our Japanese Brethren": Assimilation, Nationalism, and Protestantism Among the Japanese of Los Angeles, 1895–1942* (Stanford, CA, 1995), Jere Takahashi, *Nisei/Sansei: Shifting Japanese American Identities and Politics* (Philadelphia, 1997); and David K. Yoo, *Growing Up Nisei, Race, Generation, and Culture among Japanese Americans of California, 1924–1949* (Champaign, IL, 2000).

Studies of Canadian migration include Marcus Lee Hansen, *The Mingling of the Canadian and American Peoples* (New Haven, CT, 1940, reprinted 1970); Maurice Violette, *The Franco Americans* (New York, 1976); and Gerald J. Brault, *The French-Canadian Heritage in New England* (Hanover, NH, 1986); and for a fine comparative study see Bruno Ramirez, *On the Move: French Canadian and Italian Migrants in the North Atlantic Economy, 1860–1914* (Toronto, 1991).

The size of the legal and undocumented migration from Mexico and the growth in the influence of Latino culture in the United States has spurred scholarship on all Latino groups, but especially on the Mexicans. Several older but still useful volumes are Manuel Gamio, *Mexican Immigration and the United States* (Chicago, 1930, reprinted 1969) and *The Mexican Immigrant: His Life Story* (Chicago, 1931, reprinted 1969). Less scholarly, but always readable is Carey McWilliams, *North from Mexico: The Spanish People in the United States* (Philadelphia, 1948). The best of the new work in the past twenty years includes: Albert Camarillo, *Chicanos in a Changing Society, From Mexican Pueblos to American Barrios in Santa Barbara and Southern California, 1848–1930* (Cambridge, MA, 1979); Mario T. Garcia, *Desert Immigrants, The Mexicans of El Paso, 1880–1920* (New Haven, CT, 1981); and *Mexican Americans, Leadership, Ideology, &*

Identity, 1830–1960 (New Haven, CT, 1989); Ricardo Romo, *East Los Angeles, History of a Barrio* (Austin, TX, 1983); Vicki L. Ruiz, *Cannery Women, Cannery Lives: Mexican Women, Unionization, and the California Food Processing Industry, 1930–1950* (Albuquerque, NM, 1987); David Montejano, *Anglos and Mexicans in the Making of Texas, 1836–1986* (Austin, TX, 1987); Rodolfo Acuna, *Occupied America, A History of Chicanos*, Third Edition (New York, 1988); George J. Sanchez, *Becoming Mexican American: Ethnicity, Culture and Identity in Chicano Los Angeles, 1900–1945* (New York, 1993); Oscar J. Martinez, *Border People: Life and Society in the U.S.-Mexico Borderlands* (Tucson, AZ, 1994); Pierrette Hondagneu-Sotelo, *Gendered Transitions: Mexican Experiences of Immigration* (Berkeley, CA, 1994); Camille Guerin-Gonzalez, *Mexican Workers & American Dreams, Immigration, Repatriation, and California Farm Labor, 1900–1939* (New Brunswick, NJ, 1996); and Neil Foley's superb volume on race and ethnicity in Texas, *The White Scourge: Mexicans, Blacks, and Poor Whites in Texas Cotton Culture* (Berkeley, CA, 1998).

Caribbean immigrants are treated in D.L. Hendricks, *The Dominican Diaspora: From the Dominican Republic to New York City* (New York, 1974), Michael S. Laguerre, *American Odyssey, Haitians in New York City* (Ithaca, NY, 1984), Ransford W. Palmer, *In Search of a Better Life: Perspectives on Migration from the Caribbean* (New York, 1990); Eugenia Georges, *The Making of a Transnational Community: Migration, Development, and Cultural Change in the Dominican Republic* (New York, 1990); Irma Watkins-Owens, *Blood Relations: Caribbean Immigrants and the Harlem Community, 1900–1930* (Bloomington, IN, 1996); and Mary C. Waters, *Black Identities, West Indian Immigrant Dreams and American Realities* (Cambridge, MA, 1999).

The only major group of African immigrants emigrating to the United States were the Cape Verdeans. Their fascinating history is recounted in Marilyn Halter, *Between Race and Ethnicity, Cape Verdean American Immigrants, 1860–1965* (Urbana, IL, 1993).

Although the focus of migration to the United States shifted from northern and western Europe to other parts of the globe at the turn of the last century, the European migration hardly ceased. Im-

portant works on European groups include: on the Irish, Hasia
Diner, *Erin's Daughters in America: Immigrant Women in the
Nineteenth Century* (Baltimore, 1983); and Kerby Miller, *Emigrants and Exiles: Ireland and the Irish Exodus to North America*
(New York, 1985). On the Germans see Hartmut Keil and John B.
Jentz, eds., *German Workers in Industrial Chicago, 1850–1910: A
Comparative Perspective* (DeKalb, IL, 1983); and Frederick C.
Luebke's three volumes, *Immigrants and Politics, The Germans of
Nebraska, 1880–1900* (Lincoln, 1969), *Bonds of Loyalty, German
Americans and World War I* (DeKalb, IL, 1974), and *Germans in
the New World, Essays in the History of Immigration* (Urbana, IL,
1990). On the Swedes, see Philip J. Anderson and Dag Blanck,
eds., *Swedish-American Life in Chicago: Cultural and Urban Aspects of an Immigrant People, 1850–1930* (Urbana, IL, 1992).
Two volumes by Jon Gjerde that focus on the settlement of northern and western European immigrants in the middle west are *From
Peasants To Farmers, The Migration From Balestrand, Norway, To
the Upper Middle West* (New York, 1985) and *The Minds of the
West, Ethnocultural Evolution in the Rural Middle West, 1830–
1917* (Chapel Hill, NC, 1997). The role of immigrants in settling
the West is in Walter K. Nugent, *Into the West: The Story of Its
People* (New York, 1999).

All U.S. government statistics on the dimensions of the late-
nineteenth/early-twentieth century migration to this country are
suspect because of inconsistent, even haphazard collection procedures. As reliable as any are those compiled in Walter F. Wilcox,
ed., *International Migrations*, 2 volumes (New York, 1929). Return migration is especially difficult to accurately document. The
best overview is Mark Wyman, *Round-Trip to America, The Immigrants Return to Europe, 1880–1930* (Ithaca, NY, 1993). Italian
return migration and repatriation is treated in Betty Boyd Caroli,
Italian Repatriation from the United States, 1900–1914 (Staten Island, NY, 1973), and Dino Cinel, *The National Integration of Italian Return Migration, 1870–1929* (New York, 1991).

The immigrant's entry into the socioeconomic structure of the
United States has become a topic in the larger historiographical
debate over mobility. Though it does not deal with late-nineteenth-

century migration, every student of socioeconomic mobility must begin with Stephan Thernstrom's *Poverty and Progress: Social Mobility in a Nineteenth Century City* (Cambridge, MA, 1964), which rescued the methodology of the social historian from speculation and impressionism. In this book, as in subsequent works by other historians, mobility is defined occupationally. Thernstrom's second volume traces both new immigrants and the native born in Boston over several generations, *The Other Bostonians: Poverty and Progress in the American Metropolis, 1880–1970* (Cambridge, MA, 1969). Taking their cue from Thernstrom, scholars of the new immigration have applied social scientific methods to the exploration of occupational mobility. Humbert Nelli studied a single group in one city in *Italians in Chicago, 1880–1930: A Study of Ethnic Mobility* (New York, 1970). Others have compared different new immigrant groups residing in the same locale: Josef Barton, *Peasants and Strangers: Italians, Rumanians, and Slovaks in an American City, 1890–1950* (Cambridge, MA, 1975); and Thomas Kessner, *The Golden Door: Italian and Jewish Immigrant Mobility in New York City, 1880–1915* (New York, 1977). James A. Henretta contended that some new immigrants placed higher priority on noneconomic values such as close family ties and community involvement rather than on economic success. See Henretta's penetrating critique, "The Study of Social Mobility: Ideological Assumptions and Conceptual Bias," *Labor History* 18 (Spring 1977), 165–178.

Much remains to be known about how immigrants selected their homes and jobs and pursued the "good life" in America. Edward P. Hutchinson, *Immigrants and Their Children, 1850–1950* (New York, 1956, new edition, 1976) traces the migration and occupational patterns of European ethnic populations across the United States over several generations. A study of the Polish community in Philadelphia by Caroline Golab, *Immigrant Destinations* (Philadelphia, 1977), persuasively demonstrates that industrial opportunities, more than any other variable, account for newcomers' migration patterns within the United States. More recently, Olivier Zunz has shown how industrialization often erased intraethnic channels for upward mobility. One shoe factory could eliminate the entrepreneurial opportunity for dozens of would-be self-employed cobblers in ethnic enclaves throughout a city. See Zunz's *The Changing Face of Inequality: Urbanization, Industrial Development, and Immigrants in Detroit, 1880–1920* (Chicago, 1982). Historical studies comparing entrepreneurial activity of different groups are still sparse. An excellent comparative study of Asian immigrants and American blacks is by sociologist Ivan H. Light, *Ethnic Enterprise in America: Business and Welfare Among the Chinese, Japanese and Blacks* (Berkeley, CA, 1972). He argues that voluntary associations were critical in enabling newcomers to amass capital for investment and to sustain infant ethnic enterprises. See also John Bodnar, Roger Simon, and Michael P. Weber, *Lives of Their Own: Blacks, Italians, and Poles in Pittsburgh, 1900–1960* (Urbana, IL, 1982).

Much of the literature on immigrants focuses on cities and industrial life. However, many newcomers made their lives in rural America. Some were farmers. Others owned businesses that served agrarian communities. Many of these studies are cited above with their respective groups. They include Sucheng Chan's volume on Chinese farmers in California, Jon Gjerde's books on Scandinavian and German immigrants in the Midwest, David Montejano's volume on the Mexicans in Texas, Camille Guerin-Gonzales's book on Mexican California farm laborers, and Eileen Tamura's study of the Japanese in Hawaii, among many others that deal with rural as well as urban immigrant life and labor.

Over the past quarter-century, historians have paid particular attention to the immigrant's place in working class life and the role of the immigrant in the evolution of the American labor movement. There is no better place to begin an understanding of the American working class than with the insightful essays of Herbert G. Gutman. See his *Work, Culture and Society in Industrializing America* (New York, 1977) and the posthumously published collection edited by Ira Berlin, *Power & Culture, Essays on the American Working Class* (New York, 1987).

Immigrant workers served as catalysts in the growth of the labor movement. The classic histories of the labor movement are John R. Commons et al., *History of Labor in the United States,* 4 volumes (New York, 1918–1935); and Selig Perlman's *A Theory of the Labor Movement* (New York, 1928). Essential new volumes include David Montgomery's *Workers' Control in America: Studies in the History of Work, Technology, and Labor Struggles* (New York, 1979) and his later tour de force, *The Fall of the House of Labor: The Workplace, the State and American Labor Activism, 1865–1925* (New York, 1987). See also: James R. Green, *The World of the Worker: Labor in Twentieth Century America* (New York, 1980); Melvyn Dubofsky, *Industrialism and the American Worker, 1865–1920,* Third Edition, (Wheeling, IL, 1996); David Brody, *Workers in Industrial America: Essays in Twentieth Century Struggle,* Second Edition, (New York, 1993); and Daniel Nelson, *Farm and Factory: Workers in the Midwest, 1880–1990* (Bloomington, IN, 1995). Also see the fine essays in Melvyn Dubofsky, *Hard Work, The Making of Labor History* (Urbana, IL, 2000).

Most useful in specifying the influence of each immigrant group upon the labor movement were: Melech Epstein, *Jewish Labor in the United States, 1882–1952,* 2 volumes (New York, 1950–1953); Edwin Fenton, *Immigrants and Unions, A Case Study: Italians and American Labor* (New York, 1975); Victor Greene, *The Slavic Community on Strike: Immigrant Labor in Pennsylvania Anthracite* (South Bend, IN, 1968); and Gerald Rosenblum, *Immigrant Workers: Their Impact on American Labor Radicalism* (New York, 1973). The latter two discuss the old-world experiences and fears at the root of immigrants' initial hesitation to be militant or even to join unions. Especially important in understanding linkages of class, unionism, ethnicity, and politics is Gary Gerstle's study of European immigrants and French-Canadian Catholics in the Independent Textile Union of Woonsocket, Rhode Island, *Working-class Americanism, The Politics of Labor in a Textile City, 1914–1960* (New York, 1989). Also crucial is David Emmons, *The Butte Irish: Class and Ethnicity in an American Mining Town, 1875–1925* (Urbana, IL, 1989). Working-class life is brilliantly treated in Lizabeth Cohen's *Making a New Deal, Industrial Workers in Chicago, 1919–1939* (New York, 1990). There has been an increasing effort to view labor markets, labor

244 BIBLIOGRAPHICAL ESSAY

brokers, and the role of the state in controlling integration in a transnational perspective. Two important articles are Gunther Peck's "Reinventing Free Labor: Immigrant Padrones and Contract Laborers in North America, 1885–1925," *The Journal of American History* 83 (December 1996): 848–871, and Catherine Collomp's comparative essay, "Immigrants, Labor Markets, and the State, a Comparative Approach: France and the United States, 1880–1930," *The Journal of American History* 86 (June 1999): 41–66. Much room for research remains in the field of immigration's influence on the American labor movement and the internal dynamics of ethnic labor organization. A modern history of the eastern European Jewish and Italian labor movements in the United States would be welcome additions.

Early unionization with the Knights of Labor is covered by Leon Fink, *Workingmen's Democracy: The Knights of Labor and American Politics* (Urbana, IL, 1983). The radical Industrial Workers of the World are treated in several works, including Patrick Renshaw's *The Wobblies: The Story of Syndicalism in the United States* (Garden City, NY, 1967); Melvyn Dubofsky's *We Shall Be All: A History of the Industrial Workers of the World* (Chicago, 1969); Joseph R. Conlin, *Bread and Roses Too: Studies of the Wobblies* (Westport, CT, 1969); and edited by Conlin, *At the Point of Production: The Local History of the I.W.W.* (Westport, CT, 1981). On the role of anarchists in labor protest, see Paul Avrich's *The Haymarket Tragedy* (Princeton, NJ, 1984).

In the immigrant family, women as well as men worked. Still impressive is Leslie Woodstock Tentler's *Wage-Earning Women: Industrial Work and Family Life in the United States, 1900–1930* (New York, 1979). Tentler places immigrant women and the immigrant family in the larger context of industrial America, a difficult but crucial task. Equally important is Alice Kessler-Harris, *Out to Work: A History of Wage-Earning Women in the United States* (New York, 1982). Homework played an important role in the life of many urban immigrant women. See Eileen Boris's excellent study, *Home to Work, Motherhood and the Politics of Industrial Homework in the United States* (New York, 1994). Since the first edition of *Huddled Masses* there has been an increasing number of books written about working immigrant women and their lives. Among the older works still useful are Caroline Manning, *The Immigrant Woman and Her Job* (Washington, DC, 1930, reprinted 1970); Elizabeth Beadsley Butler, *Woman and Her Trades: Pittsburgh, 1907–1908* (New York, 1909, reprinted 1969); Louise Odencrantz, *Italian Women in Industry* (New York, 1919); Bessie Pekotsky, *The Slavic Immigrant Woman* (Cincinnati, OH, 1925, reprinted 1971); and Grace Abbott, *The Immigrant and the Community* (New York, 1917, reprinted 1971). More recently, scholarship in this field has been stimulated by the explosion in women's history and gender studies. These include the fine overview by Donna R. Gabaccia, *From the Other Side: Women, Gender, and Immigrant Life in the U.S., 1820–1990* (Bloomington, IN, 1994), and the volume she edited, *Seeking Common Ground, Multidisciplinary Studies of Immigrant Women in the United States* (Westport, CT, 1992). Elizabeth Ewen, *Immigrant Women in the Land of Dollars, Life and Culture on the Lower East Side, 1890–1925* (New York, 1985) describes how women immigrants were frequently the victims of American capitalism. However, a volume better grounded in Yiddish language sources is Paula E. Hyman, *Gender and Assimilation in Modern Jewish History: The Roles and Representations of Women* (Seattle, 1995). An earlier volume is Cecyle S. Needle, *America's Immigrant Women* (Boston, 1975). A volume on Jewish and Italian working women is Kathie Friedman-Kasaba, *Memories of Migration, Gender, Ethnicity, and Work in the Lives of Jewish and Italian Women in New York, 1870–1924* (Albany, NY, 1996). On Italian women see Miriam Cohen, *Workshop to Office, Two Generations of Italian Women in New York City, 1900–1950* (Ithaca, NY, 1992) and on eastern European Jews, see Susan A. Glenn, *Daughters of the Shtetl* and Jacknow Markowitz's *My Daughter, the Teacher,* both cited above. Also cited above are Vicki Ruiz's *Cannery Women, Cannery Lives,* on Mexican women; and Judy Yung's *Unbound Feet,* on Chinese women. For a perspective on an industry that employed women as well as men, see Patricia A. Cooper, *Once a Cigar Maker: Men, Women, and*

Work Culture in American Factories, 1900–1919 (Urbana, IL, 1987). *Immigrant Women* (Philadelphia, 1981), a documentary study edited by Maxine Schwartz Seller, is a valuable anthology of memoirs, diaries, oral histories, and fiction to which scholars can turn.

What did workers do when they were not on the job? The best volume on this question is still Roy Rosenzweig's *Eight Hours For What We Will: Workers and Leisure in an Industrial City, 1870–1920* (New York, 1983). See also Perry R. Duis, *The Saloon: Public Drinking in Chicago and Boston, 1880–1920* (Urbana, IL, 1983). On women immigrants and leisure, see Kathy Peiss, *Cheap Amusements: Working Women and Leisure in Turn-of-the-Century New York* (Philadelphia, 1986).

There is much work to be done on the cultural dimension of the immigration experience. An important exploration of music in the immigrant community is Victor Greene's *A Passion for Polka, Old-Time Ethnic Music in America* (Berkeley, CA, 1992). On cuisine see Donna R. Gabaccia, *We Are What We Eat, Ethnic Food and the Making of Americans* (Cambridge, MA, 1998). On the relationship of ethnicity and consumerism see Marilyn Halter, *Shopping for Identity: The Marketing of Ethnicity* (New York, 2000).

Many scholars now prefer the term incorporation to "assimilation" as the best way to characterize the process of transformation from alien to American. *Whiteness* studies explore how race often sets the parameters of that shift. The broader history of *whiteness as a defining concept* is explored in Alexander Saxton, *The Rise and Fall of the White Republic, Class Politics and Mass Culture in Nineteenth-Century America* (New York, 1990), and Theodore W. Allen, *The Invention of the White Race, Volume One, Racial Oppression and Social Control* (New York, 1994). The role of race in class formation is the subject of David Roedigger's masterful *The Wages of Whiteness, Race and the Making of the American Working Class* (New York, 1991). Noel Ignatiev describes the role of whiteness in the integration of antebellum Irish immigrants in *How the Irish Became White* (New York, 1995). European immigrants' "whiteness" is the subject of Matthew Frye Jacobson's *Whiteness of a Different Color, European Immigrants and the Al-*

chemy of Race (Cambridge, MA, 1998). The specific case of the Jews and their changing identification in the American mind is the focus of Karen Brodkin's *How Jews Became White Folks & What That Says About Race in America* (New Brunswick, NJ, 1998).

In this book, the three vehicles of incorporation of immigrants into American society discussed are: schools, social reform, and politics. The debate among historians and educators over the role of the public school in the immigrant community waxed hot during recent decades. New Left scholars such as Colin Greer, *The Great School Legend: A Revisionist Interpretation of American Public Education* (New York, 1972) have argued that schools were weapons of social control used by the American establishment to control the poor, including immigrants, and to inhibit their progress, thereby preserving the existing class structure. I have found such arguments unpersuasive, though there can be little doubt that schools have fostered incorporation and that individual immigrant groups had very different educational experiences, often a function of differing cultural values and expectations. Diane Ravitch describes the conflict-ridden field of public education in *The Great School Wars: New York City, 1805–1973: A History of the Public Schools as Battlefields of Social Change* (New York, 1974). Also useful is Selma Cantor Berrol, *Immigrants at School: New York City, 1898–1914* (New York, 1978). Volumes on individual immigrant groups include Leonard Covello, *The Social Background of the Italo-American School Child* (Totowa, NJ, 1967); Stephan F. Brumberg, *Going to America, Going to School: The Jewish Immigrant Public School Encounter in Turn-of-the-Century New York City* (New York, 1986); and the essays in Bernard J. Weiss, ed. *American Education and the European Immigrant: 1840 and 1940* (Urbana, IL, 1982). While much is often made over the success of Jewish children compared to those of other groups, there is still no major comparative historical study to prove or deny this idea. The best volume to date on the role of the school is Joel Perlmann's study of Providence, Rhode Island, *Ethnic Differences: Schooling and Social Structure Among the Irish, Italians, Jews & Blacks in An American City* (Cambridge, MA, 1988).

Volumes still useful for exploring the role of education in the Americanization process are: Edward Hartmann, *The Movement to Americanize the Immigrant* (New York, 1948); Lawrence A. Cremin, *The Transformation of the School: Progressiveness in American Education, 1876–1957* (New York, 1961); David Tyack, *The One Best System: A History of American Urban Education* (Cambridge, MA, 1974); Gerd Korman, *Industrialization, Immigrants, and Americanizers: Two Views From Milwaukee, 1866–1921* (Madison, WI, 1967); and Robert Carlson, *The Quest for Conformity: Americanization Through Education* (New York, 1975). On Catholic parochial schools, see James W. Sanders, *The Education of an Urban Minority: Catholics in Chicago, 1883–1965* (New York, 1977). An essential volume on the immigrants' efforts to preserve their own language is Joshua Fishman and Vladimir Nahirny, *Language Loyalty in the United States* (The Hague, Netherlands, 1966). A valuable collection of essays on language is Werner Sollors, ed., *Multilingual America: Transnationalism, Ethnicity, and the Languages of American Literature* (New York, 1998).

Social problems confronting newcomers, especially those encountered in urban areas, have been the subject of several classic sociological studies, including William Foote Whyte, *Street Corner Society: The Social Structure of an Italian Slum* (Chicago, 1943) and Herbert Gans, *The Urban Villagers: Group and Class Life of Italian Americans* (Glencoe, IL, 1962). Organized crime is thoughtfully treated by Humbert Nelli, *The Business of Crime: Italians and Syndicate Crime in the United States* (New York, 1976). In *Chinese Subculture and Criminality, Non-traditional Crime Groups in America* (Westport, CT, 1990), criminologist Ko-Lin Chin deals with tongs, street gangs, and ethnicity in America's Chinatowns. Jewish gangsters have become a topic of interest to scholars. See Jenna Weissman Joselit, *Our Gang: Jewish Crime and the New York Jewish Community, 1900–1940* (Bloomington, IN, 1983); and Albert Fried, *The Rise and Fall of the Jewish Gangster in America* (New York, 1993). The problems of immigrants dealing with a strange and awesome legal system are studied by Kate Claghorn, *The Immigrant's Day in Court* (New York, 1923, reprinted 1969).

Progressive reformers and politicians addressed themselves to immigration, but also to problems of agricultural and industrial development and those environmental and social problems that bedeviled urban and rural America, respectively. Still highly regarded is Robert Wiebe's overview, *The Search For Order, 1877–1920* (New York, 1967). Also useful are Nell Irvin Painter's *Standing at Armageddon: The United States, 1877–1919* (New York, 1987), Morton Keller's *Affairs of State, Public Life in Late Nineteenth Century America* (Cambridge, MA, 1977), and Alan Dawley's *Social Responsibility and the Liberal State* (Cambridge, MA, 1991).

Assistance was rendered to the immigrants by native-born reformers, the newcomers' own churches and associations, and the local apparatus of American political parties. The richest, boldest study of reform is Daniel T. Rodgers, *Atlantic Crossings, Social Politics in a Progressive Age* (Cambridge, MA, 1998), which places progressive reform into a truly transnational perspective as it describes international reform networks that spanned the Atlantic in the late-nineteenth and early-twentieth centuries. Much fine work has been done on the urban social settlements that served immigrants. Allen F. Davis finds settlement workers less paternalistic than many Progressive reformers in *Spearheads for Reform: The Social Settlements and the Progressive Movement, 1890–1914* (New York, 1967). A critical view of settlement workers can be found in John F. McClymer, *War and Welfare: Social Engineering in America, 1880–1925* (Westport, CT, 1980). A crisp, hard-hitting critique of reformers can also be found in Paul McBride, *Culture Clash: Immigrants and Reformers, 1880–1920* (San Francisco, 1975). Paul Boyer's *Urban Masses and Moral Order in America, 1820–1920* (Cambridge, MA, 1978) effectively places Progressive reform into the broader historical context of efforts to tame the cities. The sympathetic, but often condescending attitudes of reformers toward immigrants can be detected firsthand in Jacob Riis, *How the Other Half Lives* (New York, 1890, reprinted many times) as well as Riis's earlier volume, *The Battle with the Slums* (New York, 1902, reprinted 1969); John Spargo, *The Bitter Cry of the Children* (New York, 1908, reprinted 1969); Lillian Wald, *The House on Henry Street* (New York, 1915, reprinted 1969); Jane

Addams, *Twenty Years at Hull House* (New York, 1910, reprinted 1961); and Robert Hunter, *Poverty* (New York, 1904). There is an increasingly voluminous literature on specific settlement houses, including Allen F. Davis, *American Heroine, The Life and Legend of Jane Addams* (New York, 1973). See also Mary Lynn McCree Bryan and Allen F. Davis, eds., *100 Years at Hull House* (Bloomington, IN, 1990; orig. 1969); Rivka Shpak Lissak, *Pluralism and Progressives: Hull House and the New Immigrants, 1890–1919* (Chicago, 1989); and Beatrice Siegel, *Lillian Wald of Henry Street* (New York, 1983). An especially fine biography of a Progressive reformer is Kathryn Kish Sklar's *Florence Kelley and the Nation's Work: The Rise of Women's Political Culture, 1830–1900* (New Haven, CT, 1995).

Volumes that effectively treat the immigrants' voluntary associations are still needed. Several on the eastern European Jews are Daniel Soyer's *Jewish Immigrant Associations and American Identity* cited above; Hyman Bogen's *The Luckiest Orphans, A History of the Hebrew Orphan Asylum of New York* (Champaign, IL, 1992); and Shelley Tenenbaum's *A Credit to Their Community, Jewish Loan Societies in the United States, 1880–1945* (Detroit 1993). In *Dispersing the Ghetto, The Relocation of Jewish Immigrants across America* (Ithaca, NY, 1998), Jack Glazier tells the fascinating story of how the German Jews who founded the Industrial Removal Office sought to redistribute the high concentration of eastern European Jews concentrated in east coast cities to the nation's interior. Ethnic cooperation between Italians, Spaniards, and Cubans is treated in Gary R. Mormino and George E. Pozzetta, *The Immigrant World of Ybor City, Italians and Their Latin Neighbors in Tampa, 1885–1985* (Urbana, IL, 1987). The best overview of the role of fraternal societies in supplying social services is David T. Beito, *From Mutual Aid to the Welfare State, Fraternal Societies and Social Services, 1890–1967* (Chapel Hill, NC, 2000).

Protestant efforts to reach newcomers are outlined in Carroll Smith-Rosenberg, *Religion and the Rise of the American City: The New York City Mission Movement, 1812–1870* (Ithaca, NY, 1971). The Protestant missions, already operating by the time new immigrants arrived in the 1880s, served as challenges to Catholic and

Jewish clergymen. See Aaron Abell, *American Catholicism and Social Action: A Search for Social Justice, 1865–1900* (Garden City, NY, 1960). See also the excellent essays on the Poles, Slovaks, east European Jews, Czechs, and Armenians in Randall M. Miller and Thomas D. Mazrik, eds., *Immigrants and Religion in Urban America* (Philadelphia, 1977). Some scholars contend that the Catholic Church paid less attention to the new immigrants than it had to the Irish in an earlier era. A very persuasive case for this is made in Richard M. Linkh, *American Catholicism and European Immigrants, 1900–1924* (Staten Island, NY, 1975).

The finest single volume on urban government in the era is Jon C. Teaford's optimistic study, *The Unheralded Triumph: City Government in America, 1870–1900* (Baltimore, 1983). On the urban political machine and its relationship to change, see John D. Buenker, *Urban Liberalism and Progressive Reform* (New York, 1973). See also Kenneth Finegold, *Experts and Politicians: Reform Challenges to Machine Politics in New York, Cleveland and Chicago* (Princeton, NJ, 1995). Urban political machines that sought to barter assistance for the votes of the newcomers have been the focus of a literature too extensive to cite here. The greatest insight into the urban political machine can be found in the words of Tammany boss G. W. Plunkitt as recorded by William L. Riordan and edited by Arthur Mann, *Plunkitt of Tammany Hall* (New York, 1963). Journalist Oliver E. Allen's *The Tiger, The Rise and Fall of Tammany Hall* (New York, 1993) presents a comprehensive history of the renowned New York City political machine. The most erudite theoretical discussion of how the machine functioned can be found in Robert K. Merton's *Social Theory and Social Structure* (Glencoe, IL, 1957). Several fine historical treatments of bosses are Seymour Mandelbaum's *Boss Tweed's New York* (New York, 1965) and Alex Gottfried's *Boss Cermak of Chicago: A Study of Political Leadership* (Seattle, 1962). Evidence uncovered by Leo Hershkowitz suggests that Boss Tweed may not have been quite the thief he is reputed to have been. See his *Tweed's New York: Another Look* (Garden City, 1977). John M. Allswang's *Bosses, Machines, and Urban Voters*, revised ed. (Baltimore, 1997), offers a balanced perspective. Allswang neither presents the bosses as devils nor the reformers as unwitting dupes.

The most exciting new work on Progressive politics and the immigrants is James J. Connolly's *The Triumph of Ethnic Progressivism, Urban Political Culture in Boston, 1900–1925* (Cambridge, MA, 1998). Connolly demonstrates how Mayor James Curley and others used Progressive tactics to tame ethnic rivalries that threatened their power. The best contemporary critique of machine politics is Lincoln Steffens, *The Shame of the Cities* (New York, 1904). J. Joseph Huthmacher attacks the notion that the new immigrants were merely manipulated by politicians and suggests that ethnic communities were actually the source of reform in *Senator Robert F. Wagner and the Rise of Urban Liberalism* (New York, 1968). There have been voting studies of immigrant communities such as Arthur Goren, "A Portrait of Ethnic Politics: The Socialists and the 1908 and 1910 Congressional Elections on the East Side," *Publication of the American Jewish Historical Society* 50 (March 1961), 202–238. Other studies include Edward R. Kantrowicz, *Polish-American Politics in Chicago, 1888–1940* (Chicago, 1975); Thomas Henderson, *Tammany Hall and the New Immigrants: The Progressive Years* (New York, 1976); and the essays in Angela T. Pienkos, ed., *Ethnic Politics in Urban America: The Polish Experience in Four Cities* (Chicago, 1978). An engaging study of the eastern European Jews and the radicalism that underlay their political consciousness is Gerald Sorin's *The Prophetic Minority, American Jewish Immigrant Radicals, 1880–1920* (Bloomington, IN, 1985). A political history of eastern European Jewish immigrants who were not radicals—that is, the majority—has yet to be written.

Two volumes that explore the role of leadership in immigrant communities are Victor Greene, *American Immigrant Leaders, 1800–1910, Marginality and Identity* (Baltimore, 1987), and John Higham, ed., *Ethnic Leadership in America* (Baltimore, 1978).

Many political scientists and ethnocultural political historians regard the immigrant vote as a variable of increasing significance in national politics in the twentieth century. See Samuel Lubell's *The Future of American Politics* (New York, 1951); John Allswang, *A House for All People: Chicago's Ethnic Groups and Their Politics, 1890–1936* (Lexington, KY, 1971); Thomas J. Pavlak, *Ethnic Identification and Political Behavior* (San Francisco, 1976); and Allan J. Lichtman, *Prejudice and the Old Politics: The Presidential Election of 1928* (Chapel Hill, NC, 1979). Impressive new work on the political agendas of ethnic groups and how they were shaped by events abroad, and especially by nationalist ideologies, is Matthew Frye Jacobson's *Special Sorrows, The Diasporic Imagination of Irish, Polish, and Jewish Immigrants in the United States* (Cambridge, MA, 1995). Louis Gerson treats the impact of ethnic communities on foreign policy after 1900 in *The Hyphenate in Recent American Politics and Diplomacy* (Lawrence, KS, 1964). The close relationship between racial perspectives that underlay American expansionism and attitudes toward immigrants is explored in Matthew Frye Jacobson's *Barbarian Virtues, The United States Encounters Foreign Peoples at Home and Abroad, 1876–1917* (New York, 2000).

There has been rich debate on the subject of incorporation. The finest single volume on the role of ethnicity in the making of an American civic culture is Lawrence H. Fuchs, *The American Kaleidoscope, Race, Ethnicity, and the Civic Culture* (Hanover, NH, 1990). Especially valuable is a forum that appeared in *The Journal of American Ethnic History* 12 (Fall 1992): 3–63, featuring an article by Kathleen Neils Conzen, David A. Gerber, Ewa Morawska, George Pozzetta, and Rudolph J. Vecoli, "The Invention of Ethnicity: A Perspective for the U.S.A." Ewa Morowska seeks to retain assimilation as a useful conceptualization by rejecting the outdated notion of one people fully absorbing another in her fine article, "The Sociology and Historiography of Immigration" in *Immigration Reconsidered,* ed., McLaughlin, p. 254–292. See also Russell A. Kazal, "Revisiting Assimilation: The Rise, Fall, and Reappraisal of a Concept in American Ethnic History," *American Historical Review* 100 (April 1995): 437–471. On the role of the nation in an age of mass migration, see the essays by Gary Gerstle, David A. Hollinger, and Donna R. Gabaccia in the forum on "People in Motion, Nation in Question: The Case of Twentieth Century America" in *The Journal of American History* 84 (September 1997). A special issue of *The Journal of American History* 86 (September 1999), was devoted to "Rethinking History and the Nation-State: Mexico and the United States as a Case Study." Still a very important work is Milton M. Gordon, *Assimi-*

lation in American Life: The Role of Race, Religion and National Origins (New York, 1964). The classic defense of cultural pluralism is Horace M. Kallen, *Culture and Democracy in the United States* (New York, 1924). Will Herberg's triple melting-pot model in *Protestant, Catholic, and Jew* (New York, 1955, reprinted 1960) remains a provocative theory but fails to take into consideration how those not part of the Judeo-Christian religious tradition became incorporated into American society. The "pluralist integration" or "salad bowl" model described by John Higham in *Send These to Me: Jews and Other Immigrants in Urban America* (New Brunswick, NJ, 1955) remains a much discussed approach to understanding the making of the American people. Two recent volumes of importance are Richard D. Alba, *Ethnic Identity: The Transformation of White America* (New Haven, CT, 1990) and Mary C. Waters, *Ethnic Options: Choosing Identities in America* (Berkeley, CA, 1990).

Nativism and less ideological forms of anti-immigrant prejudice have generated a rich and diverse literature. The classic historical work on nativism in the period after the Civil War remains John Higham, *Strangers in the Land: Patterns of American Nativism, 1860–1925* (New Brunswick, NJ, 1955). The popularity that nativist writers enjoyed at the turn of the century makes it useful to consult their writings to understand their arguments about the impact of immigration on American society. See Edward Alsworth Ross, *The Old World in the New* (New York, 1914); Madison Grant, *The Passing of the Great Race* (New York, 1916); and Lothrop Stoddard, *The Rising Tide of Color* (New York, 1920). The classic nativist assault on Roman Catholicism in the post–Civil War period is Rev. Josiah Strong, *Our Country, Its Possible Future and Its Present Crisis* (New York, 1885). Nativist assertions of the biological inferiority of immigrants did not go unanswered. See Franz Boas, *Changes in Bodily Form of Descendants of Immigrants in Reports of the Immigration Commission* (61 Cong., 2 Sess., Senate Document No. 208, Washington, DC, 1911) and *Race and Democratic Society* (New York, 1945).

New arrivals were often accused of being the carriers of infectious disease. The medicalization of nativism has been explored by Alan M. Kraut, *Silent Travelers, Germs, Genes, and the "Immi-*

grant Menace" (New York, 1994), and Howard Markel, *Quarantine!, East European Jewish Immigrants and the New York City Epidemics of 1892* (Baltimore, 1997).

Some volumes that examine acts of anti-immigrant violence and institutional nativism and anti-Semitism include Leonard Dinnerstein, *The Leo Frank Case* (New York, 1968); Marcia Graham Synott, *The Half-Opened Door: Discrimination and Admissions at Harvard, Yale and Princeton, 1900–1970* (Westport, CT, 1979); Dan Oren, *Joining the Club, A History of Jews and Yale* (New Haven, CT, 1986), Robert K. Murray, *Red Scare: A Study in National Hysteria, 1919–1920* (Minneapolis, MN, 1955); Donald Kinzer, *An Episode in Anti-Catholicism: The American Protective Association* (Seattle, 1964); and Stuart Creighton Miller, *The Unwelcome Immigrant: The American Image of the Chinese, 1785–1882* (Berkeley, CA, 1969). Material on the Ku Klux Klan abounds, but the best volumes on anti-immigrant activities are Kenneth T. Jackson, *The Ku Klux Klan in the City, 1915–1930* (New York, 1967), and Leonard J. Moore, *Citizen Klansmen, The Ku Klux Klan in Indiana, 1921–1928* (Chapel Hill, NC, 1991). The best volume on the cultural milieu in which the Sacco-Vanzetti case occurred is Edmund M. Morgan and Louis Joughin, *The Legacy of Sacco and Vanzetti* (New York, 1948, reprinted 1977). Herbert B. Ehrmann's *The Case That Will Not Die: Commonwealth vs. Sacco and Vanzetti* (Boston, 1969) sets forth the legal issues most lucidly. The best volume on the anarchist politics of Sacco and Vanzetti is Paul Avrich, *Sacco and Vanzetti, The Anarchist Background* (Princeton, NJ, 1991).

The relationship among immigrant groups is still a fertile area for research. A useful volume that addresses intergroup tensions is Ronald H. Bayor, *Neighbors in Conflict: The Irish, Germans, Jews, and Italians of New York City, 1919–1941* (Baltimore, 1978); and for cooperation, see George Pozetta and Gary Mormino's *The World of Ybor City*, and Neil Foley's *The White Scourge* mentioned above.

The debate over the value of ethnic loyalties, the legacy of immigration, is the subject of some provocative volumes, including Michael Novak, *The Rise of the Unmeltable Ethnics* (New York, 1971); Orlando Patterson, *Ethnic Chauvinism: the Reactionary*

Impulse (New York, 1977); Howard F. Stein and Robert F. Hill, *The Ethnic Imperative* (Philadelphia, 1977); and Stephen Steinberg, *The Ethnic Myth: Race, Ethnicity and Class in America* (New York, 1981). More recently, the debate has been reinvigorated by the debate over multiculturalism. A compassionate, conciliatory approach is set forth by David A. Hollinger, who believes that the solution to cultural divisiveness is to construct a "postethnic perspective" which favors "voluntary over involuntary affiliations, balances an appreciation for communities of descent with a determination to make room for new communities, and promotes solidarities of wide scope that incorporate people with different ethnic and racial backgrounds." See Hollinger, *Postethnic America, Beyond Multiculturalism* (New York, 1995). A more dyspeptic view is Arthur M. Schlesinger, Jr.'s *The Disuniting of America, Reflections on a Multicultural Society* (New York, 1991), and a resigned, but no less skeptical perspective on multiculturalism is Nathan Glazer's *We Are All Multiculturalists Now* (Cambridge, MA, 1997).

The basic policies and legislation on American immigration that affected the immigrants arriving between 1880 and 1921 are set forth succinctly and clearly in Marion T. Bennett, *American Immigration Policies: A History* (Washington, DC, 1963), and Robert A. Divine, *American Immigration Policy, 1924–1952* (New Haven, CT, 1957, reprinted 1972). A valuable documentary history is Michael LeMay and Elliot Robert Barkan's *U.S. Immigration and Naturalization Laws and Issues* (Westport, CT, 1999). On the role of ethnicity in shaping American foreign policy, see Alexander DeConde, *Ethnicity, Race, and American Foreign Policy, A History* (Boston, 1992). An especially incisive perspective on how racial constructs have been inscribed in American law is Ian F. Haney Lopez, *White By Law, The Legal Construction of Race* (New York, 1996). On the impact of legislation in shaping an ethnic community, see Bill Ong Hing, *Making and Remaking Asian America Through Immigration Policy, 1850–1990* (Stanford, CA, 1993). For a historiographical update in this area, see Erika Lee, "Immigrants and Immigration Law: A State of the Field Assessment," *Journal of American Ethnic History* 18 (Summer 1999): 85–114).

Immigrants tell their own stories best. The most informative accounts of the newcomers' motives, objectives, and reflections cited throughout the text come from immigrant memoirs such as: Louis Adamic, *Laughing in the Jungle* (New York, 1932), the odyssey of a Yugoslavian lad; *From Plotzk to Boston* (Boston, 1899) and *The Promised Land* (Boston, 1912) by Mary Antin, a Russian Jew who became a writer in America; *The Soul of an Immigrant* (New York, 1921) by Italian minister and social worker Constantine Panunzio; *From Immigrant to Inventor* by Serbian physicist Michael Pupin (New York, 1922); *Rosa, The Life of an Italian Immigrant* by Marie Hal Ets (Minneapolis, MN, 1970; reissued, Madison, WI, 1999); and *Bread Upon the Waters* (New York, 1944), by Rose Pesotta, the Russian Jew who served four times as the I.L.G.W.U.'s vice president. Jewish immigrants tell of their problems in their letters to the *Jewish Daily Forward*'s editor Abraham Cahan in Isaac Metzker, ed., *A Bintel Brief* (New York, 1971). *The Education of Abraham Cahan* (Philadelphia, 1969), the autobiography of a journalist and immigrant advocate, is a valuable source. Irving Howe and Kenneth Libo have made available many of the valuable documents they cited in *World of Our Fathers* in *How We Lived: A Documentary History of Immigrant Jews in America, 1880–1930* (New York, 1979). A rich trove of memories about growing up the American-born child of Sicilian immigrant parents is Jerre Mangione, *An Ethnic at Large: A Memoir of America in the Thirties and Forties* (New York, 1978). A fine collection of documents and essays is Jon Gjerde, ed., *Major Problems in American Immigration and Ethnic History* (Boston, 1998).

Since the late 1970s, the emphasis on ethnicity and the rediscovery of one's roots has yielded valuable oral histories. Volumes of testimony I found especially useful in 1982 were: *By Myself I'm a Book: An Oral History of the Immigrant Jewish Experience* prepared by the Pittsburgh Section of the National Council of Jewish Women (Waltham, MA, 1972); June Namias's fine compilation of oral histories, *First Generation* (Boston, 1978); Joan Morrison and Charlotte Fox Zabusky, *American Mosaic: The Immigrant Experience in the Words of Those Who Lived It* (New York, 1980); and Tamara Hareven and Randolph Lagenbach, *Amoskeag, Life and*

Work in an American Factory City (New York, 1978). More recent volumes include a collection of some of the interviews conducted for the reopening of Ellis Island as an immigration museum and archive. See Peter Morton Coan, *Ellis Island Interviews, In Their Own Words* (New York, 1997). Other volumes of immigrant testimony are Theresa S. Malkiel, *The Diary of a Shirtwaist Striker* (orig. 1910; Ithaca, NY, 1990); Marilyn P. Davis, *Mexican Voices, American Dreams, An Oral History of Mexican Immigrants to the United States* (New York, 1990); Solveig Zempel, *In Their Own Words, Letters from Norwegian Immigrants* (Minneapolis, 1991); Thomas Dublin, ed., *Immigrant Voices, New Lives in America, 1773–1986* (Urbana, IL, 1993); Bruce M. Stave and John F. Sutherland, eds., with Aldo Salerno, *From the Old Country, An Oral History of European Migration to America* (Hanover, NH, 1994); J. Sanford Rikoon, ed., *Rachel Calof's Story, Jewish Homesteader on the Northern Plains* (Bloomington, IN, 1995), and Robert A. Rockaway, *Words of the Uprooted, Jewish Immigrants in Early Twentieth-Century America* (Ithaca, NY, 1998). Workers' voices are heard in Mary Blewitt, *The Lost Generation: Work and Life in the Textile Mills of Lowell, Massachusetts, 1910–1960* (Amherst, MA, 1990). Immigrant radicals from many countries present their recollections in Paul Avrich's *Anarchist Voices: An Oral History of Anarchism in America* (Princeton, NJ, 1995). Many more such works are needed, especially for Asian, Latin American, and Caribbean groups.

The relationship of American restrictionism in the 1920s and refugee policy in the 1930s is explained in Richard Breitman and Alan M. Kraut, *American Refugee Policy and European Jewry, 1933–1945* (Bloomington, IN, 1987). For an overview of immigration since the 1920s, see Elliott Robert Barkan, *And Still They Come, Immigrants and American Society 1920 to the 1990s* (Wheeling, IL, 1996), and also for the period after World War II, see David M. Reimers, *Still the Golden Door, The Third World Comes to America*, Second Edition (New York, 1992). On contemporay nativism, see Reimers, *Unwelcome Strangers, American Identity and the Turn Against Immigration* (New York, 1998).

INDEX

The Huddled Masses: The Immigrant in American Society, 1880–1921,
Second Edition
Developmental editor: Andrew J. Davidson
Copy editor and Production editor: Lucy Herz
Proofreader: Claudia Siler
Indexer: Melissa Kirkpatrick
Printer: McNaughton & Gunn, Inc.